T0287974

THE WORLD OF ULYSSES S. GRANT

SERIES EDITORS

John F. Marszalek & Timothy B. Smith

The IMPULSE *of* VICTORY

ULYSSES S. GRANT AT CHATTANOOGA

DAVID A. POWELL

Southern Illinois University Press
Carbondale

Southern Illinois University Press
www.siupress.com

23 22 21 20   4 3 2 1

Jacket illustration: "Battle of Chattanooga" / Thulstrup; chromolitho-
graph facsimile print (Boston: Prang & Co., 1880). Library of Congress Prints and Photographs Division, Washington, D.C.; reprod.
no. LC-DIG-pga-04032.

Library of Congress Cataloging-in-Publication Data
Names: Powell, David A. (David Alan), 1961– author.
Title: The impulse of victory : Ulysses S. Grant at Chattanooga /
David A. Powell.
Other titles: World of Ulysses S. Grant.
Description: Carbondale : Southern Illinois University Press, [2020]
| Series: The world of Ulysses S. Grant | Includes bibliographical
references and index.
Identifiers: LCCN 2020003537 (print) | LCCN 2020003538 (ebook)
| ISBN 9780809338016 (cloth) | ISBN 9780809338023 (ebook)
Subjects: LCSH: Grant, Ulysses S. (Ulysses Simpson), 1822–1885.
| Chattanooga, Battle of, Chattanooga, Tenn., 1863.
Classification: LCC E475.97 .P695 2020 (print) | LCC E475.97 (ebook)
| DDC 973.7/359—dc23
LC record available at https://lccn.loc.gov/2020003537
LC ebook record available at https://lccn.loc.gov/2020003538

To the eternally helpful National Park staff
of the Chickamauga-Chattanooga National Military Park,
for all the support and information provided over the years.
Thank you all.

CONTENTS

ILLUSTRATIONS

Sherman's attack on Missionary Ridge

100th Indiana at Missionary Ridge

32nd Indiana at Missionary Ridge

Captured Confederate artillery

Grant on Lookout Mountain

ACKNOWLEDGMENTS

*E*very successful book project requires the help of many people, and *The Impulse of Victory* is no exception. First and foremost, my thanks go to my ever-so-patient wife, Anne, who always supports my writing. My many trips away, either for research, giving talks and tours, or just to walk the ground one more time took up numerous weekends. Her forbearance while I am away renders my work possible, and I could not accomplish nearly as much without her support.

I would also like to thank Timothy B. Smith and John F. Marszelek for the opportunity to work with them on this project. It is inspiring to work with such accomplished scholars, whose work I deeply respect.

Further, I must extend my thanks to Southern Illinois University Press, executive editor Sylvia Frank Rodrigue, and editorial assistant Jennifer Egan, who have labored to turn my manuscript into such a fine publication. Thanks go equally to Theodore Savas and the staff at Savas Beatie, who have published a number of my books, who have taught me much about the business of publishing, and who have graciously granted permission to use a number of maps that first appeared in *Battle above the Clouds* and *All Hell Can't Stop Them*. Thanks also to the man who drafted them, Hal Jesperson. His clear graphical presentation makes the maps a joy to include.

The indefatigable Jim Ogden of the National Park Service, historian of the Chickamauga-Chattanooga National Military Park, has proven once again to be an indispensable fount of information and suggestion when it comes to understanding the battles for Chattanooga in 1863. This work is vastly better for his insights.

I also must thank the legion of archivists and librarians who have helped me locate obscure resources or guided my research in literally dozens of repositories. They are too numerous to mention by name, but their work on a daily basis preserves the primary sources without which no historical work can really succeed. I am indebted to them all.

I also want to take note of a small group of good friends, with whom I share battlefield adventures and numerous historical trips. Among them, Pat McCormick, Andy Papen, Brad Butkovich, Scott Felsen, Sam Simons, and Darryl Smith have all accompanied me on explorations of the Chattanooga battlefields, making those trips enjoyable as well as productive. Thanks to you all.

Dogs hold a special place in my heart. One noble bloodhound, Killian, was always my research partner, slumbering at my feet as I worked. He is greatly missed. But a second hound, Cletus, has assumed his important duties, much to my great delight. Thank you, pups, past and present.

THE IMPULSE OF VICTORY

PROLOGUE

$\mathscr{O}$n Tuesday morning, September 22, 1863, Maj. Gen. Ulysses S. Grant opened a packet of dispatches accumulated and passed downriver from Memphis over the previous week. One of them proved anything but routine:

> Washington City, September 15, [1863]—5 P.M.
> Maj. Gen. Stephen A. Hurlbut,
>
> > *Memphis:*
>
> All the troops that can possibly be spared in Western Tennessee and on the Mississippi River should be sent without delay to assist General Rosecrans on the Tennessee River. Urge Sherman to act with all possible promptness. If you have boats, send them down to bring up his troops. Information just received indicates that a part of Lee's army has been sent [from Virginia] to reinforce Bragg.
>
> > H. W. Halleck
> > *General-in-Chief*

Hurlbut, who commanded the District of West Tennessee in Grant's department, received this ominous communique on September 18, immediately forwarding it downriver. Its arrival at Grant's headquarters four days later upset Union plans across the entire western theater and threw the general's command into disarray.[1]

At the time, Grant commanded the Department of the Tennessee as well as the army of the same name. His authority embraced a broad swath of territory: those parts of Kentucky and Tennessee west of the Tennessee River; the strategically important city of Cairo, Illinois, at the confluence of the Ohio and Mississippi Rivers; and northern Mississippi were all within his sphere of operations. Over the course of the previous spring and summer, Grant had waged a tenacious, months-long campaign to capture the Rebel stronghold of Vicksburg. Portentously, that citadel fell to Union arms on July 4—Independence Day.

1

At its peak Grant's military strength numbered more than 100,000 troops, not counting the overwhelming Union naval presence on the Mississippi River. But after Vicksburg's fall—and with it the surrender of a Confederate army of almost 30,000 men—his forces lapsed into inactivity. Large numbers of men had dispersed to garrisons throughout that newly won geography, while Federal commanders elsewhere, sensing now-idle resources, sought support for their own operations. In Arkansas, Maj. Gen. Frederick Steele had just captured Little Rock and requested reinforcements to forge ahead into the southwestern part of that state. In East Tennessee Maj. Gen. Ambrose Burnside pressed for the return of the IX Corps, loaned out to Grant that spring to aid in Vicksburg's capture. Personally, Grant next favored a move against Mobile, Alabama, on the Gulf coast, envisioning a joint effort using troops drawn from his own forces and those of Maj. Gen. Nathaniel P. Banks, who commanded the Department of the Gulf from his headquarters in New Orleans. Grant and Banks met at Vicksburg on August 1 to discuss just such a move.[2]

In Washington Federal authorities had additional concerns. Pres. Abraham Lincoln and Secretary of War Edwin M. Stanton were pressing for a westward movement: "I see," wrote Lincoln, "that you incline quite strongly towards an expedition against Mobile. This would appear tempting to me also, were it not that in view of recent events in Mexico, I am greatly impressed with the importance of re-establishing the national authority in Western Texas, as soon as possible." Though Lincoln insisted, "I am not making an order," there could be little doubt of what the administration expected.[3]

Those recent Mexican events included the occupation of Mexico City by French troops that June and the subsequent declaration of a French-dominated "Second Mexican Empire" barely a month later. Archduke Maximillian of Austria was installed on the throne. Maximillian was essentially a puppet: French emperor Napoleon III, supported by the governments of Britain and Spain, intended to exploit the distraction in US foreign policy caused by the Civil War to regain an influential foothold in the New World, lost when his illustrious great-uncle, Napoleon I, sold off the Louisiana Purchase in 1803. Maximillian's investiture was a clear challenge to the Monroe Doctrine, the longstanding US policy of excluding European influence in what Washington regarded as the American sphere of influence. Admittedly, there was little the Federal government could do about French meddling south of the Rio Grande amid the current crisis. However, reasoned Lincoln, if Grant and Banks cooperated in efforts to clear Confederate forces from northern Louisiana and the Texas coast, a large Union army operating in Texas might give the European interlopers pause.

Grant journeyed to New Orleans on September 2 to discuss details of the proposed effort. His meeting with Banks produced the beginnings of a plan, with Grant agreeing to supply 20,000 men, including the entire XIII Corps, to support a move up the Red River toward Alexandria and Shreveport. From there, East Texas was within easy reach.

That trip also produced one of the more controversial moments of Grant's wartime career. Ever since he resigned his commission in the prewar army in 1854, rumors of excessive drinking had dogged him. The Battle of Shiloh did nothing to silence the whispers. This visit to New Orleans provided fresh grist for the rumor mill when Grant's horse—an unruly steed loaned to him by Banks, not his own usual mount—bolted at a train whistle and fell on him. The general, usually a superb horseman, suffered a serious injury that would keep him bedridden for weeks. Accusations of drunkenness now followed anew. Grant and many of his defenders would later insist that alcohol had nothing to do with the incident, but several credible witnesses differed, at least in private correspondence.[4]

Grant was laid up in New Orleans for a fortnight. He departed the Crescent City to return to Vicksburg on September 14, though he was still abed and forced to dictate rather than write all his correspondence. Fortunately, everything seemed calm. For the next eight days, he busied himself with administrative duties. There were matters of recruiting more blacks into the army (a policy Grant favored) and questions of reconstruction. Even as the war still raged, the Lincoln administration was thinking about how best to return the Confederate states to the Union and solicited opinions on the matter. While Grant was away, his senior corps commander, Maj. Gen. William T. Sherman—Grant's most trusted subordinate—penned a lengthy missive advocating harsh measures toward the returning Rebels. Upon reading it, Grant offered a different opinion, believing that the once-blazing flames of secession were now guttering in Louisiana and Mississippi, likely to be extinguished altogether if "Rebels from other states" could be kept away. During this time, there was little hint of the drama unfolding between the opposing armies commanded by Maj. Gen. William S. Rosecrans and Gen. Braxton Bragg.

Those items became moot with the arrival of Halleck's September 15 dispatch, seven days in transit. The primary reason for that delay was low water in the rivers. The only reliable telegraphic connection to Grant's department headquarters terminated at Cairo, some six hundred river-boat miles upstream. From there, all dispatches had to be transcribed and shipped down to Memphis or Vicksburg. Thanks to a drought that began in the fall of 1862 and persisted up through September, all the western rivers were low, exposing snags and sandbars by the hundreds. Any boat navigating those waters proceeded cautiously yet still met with numerous difficulties. Groundings were frequent, and travel was slow. To compound the delay, according to General Hurlbut's adjutant in Memphis, whoever aboard the "Steamer Minnehaha" was in charge of these particular dis-patches, despite being "marked 'Important Govt dispatches to be delivered immediately,'" failed to deliver them promptly. At Vicksburg Grant was effectively isolated from the rest of the Federal war machine, and thus in the dark about how things were progressing elsewhere.[5]

All of which meant that even as he was reading his dispatches on Sep-tember 22, the department commander had no idea that Rosecrans's peril was far more immediate than even what Halleck's now-outdated com-munique conveyed. On September 18 Bragg's Army of Tennessee, now flush with Rebel reinforcements from Virginia and elsewhere, attacked. The ensuing Battle of Chickamauga continued throughout September 19 and 20. The result was a serious Union defeat. Rosecrans, two corps commanders, and one-third of his army were routed off the battlefield, riding hard for the city of Chattanooga a dozen miles to the rear. Only Maj. Gen. George H. Thomas's determined stand saved the army from greater disaster; even so, Thomas was forced to fall back at nightfall. By the twenty-second, Rosecrans and his Army of the Cumberland were almost encircled in Chattanooga, besieged by Bragg. From far-off Washington, D.C., the situation appeared to be Vicksburg in reverse.

Grant knew none of these most recent developments when he responded to Halleck's September 15 directive, but he nonetheless wasted no time. He ordered two divisions—one of them already on boats and preparing to join Steele in Arkansas—to head up the Mississippi to Memphis. Banks and Steele would have to do without.

Over the next three days, two more badly delayed dispatches reached Grant, both again sent by Halleck, dated September 13 and 14. While neither bore news of the recent disaster at Chickamauga, they provided amplification concerning the intended move along the Tennessee River to support Rosecrans, prompting Grant to inform Sherman that "despatches [sic] from Genl Halleck of Date the thirteenth inst show that the forces from here are to move via Corinth & Tuscumbia to Cooperate with Rosecranz—You will therefore hold two 2 of the remaining Divisions of your corps in readiness to move to this place for embarkation to Memphis on receipt of notice that transportation is provided. You will go in command."[6]

In the last days of September, prior to gaining a full understanding of circumstances at Chattanooga, both Sherman and Grant still favored a move against Mobile as the better way to help Rosecrans, instead of sending troops across northern Alabama. On the twenty-fifth Grant renewed his pitch for a move against Mobile, reasoning that the city might fall easily to "a comparatively small force. At least a demonstration in that direction would either result in the abandonment of the city or force the enemy to weaken Bragg's army to hold it."[7]

Curiously, it would take several more days, and a communication with the enemy via a flag of truce, to fully enlighten Grant of Rosecrans's plight. Although rumors had started filtering down the river, details were sparse. On September 27 Hurlbut wrote calmingly that "the extreme urgency of the case has passed. An accumulation of force from east and west was suddenly thrown upon Rosecrans to destroy his army; thence intended to strike with like effect . . . on Burnside. General Thomas, by his heroic resistance, has saved the Army of the Cumberland from actual destruction and the enemy are too severely crippled to pursue the advantage gained." In fact, Hurlbut concluded, "Rosecrans should be reinforced to enable him to profit by the reflux of this tide." Two days later Halleck was even more opaque, wiring, "the enemy seems to have concentrated upon General Rosecrans all his available forces from every direction." More ominously, he also warned that "should Bragg move by Rome into Northern Alabama to turn Rosecrans' right, your [Grant's] forces on that line may require all your assistance." Collectively, these dispatches seemed to suggest that the immediate crisis was past, though a strategic threat to Tennessee still had to be considered.[8]

Grant's best source of information turned out to be—of all people— General Joseph E. Johnston, Confederate commander in Mississippi. On September 25 Grant sent Col. George N. Coolbaugh under a flag of truce to Johnston's headquarters in Meridian, Mississippi, where the general was happy to share news and details of the Confederate victory. When Cool-baugh returned on the thirtieth, he informed Grant that, per Johnston: "Rosecrans still occupies Chattanooga—Longstreet, Lookout Mountain 12 miles south. . . . Burnside was coming up, but with what force not known. Our loss was fifty-four pieces of artillery and from 15,000 to 20,000 men killed, wounded, missing. Rebels' loss about the same." Johnston also provided other tidbits, including the rumor that Maj. Gen. Joseph Wheeler's Confederate cavalry was operating against Rosecrans's supply line, a detail that proved accurate, if slightly premature. Grant's season of inactivity was at an end.[9]

1

"SOME WESTERN GENERAL OF HIGH RANK"

$\mathcal{S}$ecretary of War Stanton was a frustrated man. Snappish and short-tempered at the best of times, by the beginning of October 1863, he seemed to be constantly fuming over the state of affairs in Tennessee. The army, apparently ensnarled in the usual red tape of bureaucracy, seemed to be moving as if in quicksand in response to the unfolding crisis at Chattanooga.

From Washington, D.C., it appeared that Major General Rosecrans had two likely sources of succor. One was Grant's army, sitting idle in Mississippi. The other was in East Tennessee, where Major General Burnside commanded close to 20,000 troops. With Burnside's headquarters in Knoxville a mere 110 miles from Chattanooga, his force seemed the obvious choice to render immediate support. Orders to that effect were not long in going out.

Back on September 9, when Rosecrans's army first occupied Chattanooga, Burnside was in contact with the Army of the Cumberland and soon discovered via Maj. Gen. Thomas L. Crittenden (commanding the XXI Corps in Rosecrans's army) that the Confederates were retreating deep into Georgia. Only a cavalry screen was needed to connect his force with Rosecrans at that time. Halleck then ordered Burnside to guard the mountain passes along the North Carolina border and to watch for a Confederate advance out of southwestern Virginia. The latter threat seemed increasingly likely; some reports placed as many as 15,000 Confederate troops under Maj. Gen. Samuel Jones at Jonesborough, Tennessee, one hundred miles northeast of Knoxville near the Virginia line. Accordingly, Burnside increasingly massed his available forces in that direction and away from Chattanooga.[1]

Much like the orders to Grant, by mid-September Halleck was sending multiple directives to Burnside, asking him to be prepared to support Rosecrans should the latter need help, especially once the extent of the Confederate reinforcements became apparent. Significantly, Halleck did not issue a direct order instructing Burnside to reinforce Chattanooga;

he was waiting to see what would happen next. This was unfortunate, for like Grant, Burnside also suffered from the lack of a direct telegraphic link with Washington. His line of communications ran overland from Knoxville via the Cumberland Gap, then to Crab Orchard, Kentucky, where it finally reached a telegraphic connection with the North. This resulted in a time lag of forty-eight to seventy-two hours between sending and receiving messages, which left Burnside reacting to stale intelligence days out of date.

Still, Burnside complied as best he could, positioning roughly 11,000 men near Loudon, Tennessee, perhaps a third of the distance between Chattanooga and Knoxville. He also continued his operations against Jonesborough, well to his north, where additional scouting reports placed the Rebel presence there at closer to 6,000 troops, fortunately a more manageable figure given Burnside's stretched resources. The general also intended to shift the returning IX Corps troops toward Chattanooga as soon as they reached him.

Then came Chickamauga. Unlike his fellow Federal commanders, Rosecrans did possess a nearly direct wire link with the North. He exchanged messages with Washington in as little as twelve to twenty-four hours, much faster than could either Burnside or Grant. Lincoln knew on September 18 that battle was about to be joined and that Bragg was heavily reinforced. Suddenly, affairs in North Georgia took a critical turn. When Burnside's travel-lagged dispatches arrived in the capital, they reached the administration amid this unfolding crisis, triggering Lincoln's frustration. Burnside's September 17 wire, for example, responding to Halleck's communiques of September 13 and 14, only reached the seat of government at 10:40 A.M. on September 19. By then, Rosecrans was fully engaged in a great battle, with Lincoln, Stanton, and Halleck all hanging on every click of the key. Thus, when Burnside promised that "orders to go below [to Chattanooga] will be obeyed as soon as possible," the president erupted with a rare public profanity when the general then added, "I go to Greenville tonight. Dispositions for attacking the enemy at Jonesborough made." Lincoln thundered in frustration, "Damn Jonesborough!"[2]

Worse was to come. By late evening on September 20, the first disastrous messages from both Charles A. Dana—the former newspaperman turned assistant secretary of war sent by Stanton to be his personal representative to Rosecrans—and the general himself reached Washington. Dana's wire, sent at 4:00 P.M., delivered a bombshell: "Chickamauga," he wrote, "is as fatal a name in our history as Bull Run." At 5:00 P.M. Rosecrans's own dispatch was hardly more promising: "We have met with a serious disaster; extent not yet ascertained. Enemy overwhelmed us, drove our right, pierced our center, and scattered troops." Both dispatches were in Lincoln's hands that same night.[3]

At 12:35 A.M. on September 21, just hours after the news of Chickamauga first reached Washington, the president wired reassurance to Rosecrans: "Be of good cheer," he urged. "We have unabated confidence in you and in your soldiers and officers. . . . [S]ave your army by taking strong positions until Burnside joins you, when I hope you can turn the tide." At 2:00 A.M. Lincoln ordered Burnside to "go to Rosecrans with your force without a moment's delay." At 11:00 A.M. the president amplified his intentions: "If you are to do any good to Rosecrans it will not do to waste time with Jonesborough." By way of further rebuke, he added: "It is already too late to do the most good that might have been done, but I hope it will still do some good. Please do not lose a moment." To his secretary John Hay, the president fumed that Burnside, "instead of obeying orders . . . and going to R[osecrans] has gone up on a foolish affair to Jonesboro to capture a party of guerrillas."[4]

But how quickly could Burnside comply? As it turned out, not very. Burnside received Lincoln's peremptory order only on September 24, when he returned to his Knoxville headquarters to discover a mountain of unwelcome news. It also left the general in a quandary: Was he to abandon all the gains in East Tennessee and march at once with all his forces to Chattanooga, or should he leave troops sufficient to hold East Tennessee and move only with those he could spare? Halleck's orders suggested the former, but Lincoln's stinging reproof seemed to suggest the latter.

Over the next week there followed a series of exchanges that highlighted both the emotional nature and the ambiguity of the government's response to the crisis. On September 30 Burnside finally resorted to outlining three different plans to try and help Rosecrans, seeking guidance on which the administration preferred. "The first," as summarized by historian William Marvel, "required the complete abandonment of East Tennessee and a complete junction of Burnside's twenty thousand men with Rosecrans. . . . The second option entailed slinking south . . . from Loudon and attacking Bragg's right wing with about fifteen thousand [men], leaving the other five thousand to face Jones. The final alternative called for a combined force of cavalry and infantry, twelve thousand strong, which would . . . circle south of Bragg's right flank, cutting [his] railroad connection from

Dalton to Atlanta . . . , [and eventually] living off the land in a march to the sea." Interestingly, Burnside favored the third alternative, which was by far the most ambitious.[5]

By the time Burnside made his proposals, communications with both Rosecrans in Chattanooga and Halleck in Washington were greatly improved; his newest dispatch was received a mere nine hours after being transmitted. Things were also much calmer in Chattanooga, from where Rosecrans wired that, while he was besieged, he was in no immediate danger of losing the city. On the morning of October 1, Halleck informed Burnside that since "Rosecrans has now telegraphed . . . that it is not necessary to join him at Chattanooga, . . . only move down to such a position that you can go to his assistance, if he should require it" at some later time. For the moment at least, East Tennessee would not be abandoned.[6]

The Washington authorities were certainly frustrated by Burnside's apparent balkiness, but several members of Lincoln's cabinet also thought that the crisis brought out the worst in Halleck. Writing in his diary on September 26, Secretary of the Navy Gideon Welles scoffed: "General Halleck has earnestly and constantly smoked cigars and rubbed his elbows, while the Rebels have been vigorously concentrating their forces to overwhelm Rosecrans. We all, except General Halleck, know that Longstreet with 20,000 men has gone from Lee's army somewhere. The information does not seem to have reached Halleck. . . . H[alleck] has never seemed to realize the importance of that position [Chattanooga]—nor, I am sorry to say, of any other." On the twenty-ninth Welles recorded similar sentiments from Secretary of the Treasury Salmon P. Chase, who "expressed great disgust towards Halleck: says Halleck has done nothing while the Rebels were concentrating. . . . Halleck, he said, was good for nothing, and everybody knew it but the President."[7]

But no cabinet officer was angrier than Stanton. Nor was the secretary of war one to wait patiently while the generals sorted things out. He thought that if Gen. Robert E. Lee could send troops from his Army of Northern Virginia to Bragg, then Maj. Gen. George G. Meade, commander of the Army of the Potomac, could do the same for Rosecrans. On September 23, once it became clear that neither Grant nor Burnside were going to be able to respond quickly, Stanton took the highly unusual step of summoning a cabinet meeting. Lincoln was "considerably disturbed" by the request, since never before had Stanton "ever sent for him." Was this a harbinger of some new crisis?[8]

Despite the president's gloomy expectations, when he reached the War Department offices, he found reassurance. First, Stanton produced a "dispatch from Rosecrans [probably Dana's of that morning] stating that he could hold Chattanooga against double his number: [the city] could not be taken until after a great battle: his stampede evidently over." The second order of business was reinforcements. Burnside, thought Halleck, could get 20,000 men to Chattanooga within ten days, "if uninterrupted," and 12,000 in just over a week. Grant's forces might take ten days to arrive as well, further estimated "Old Brains," assuming the orders sent to Mississippi arrived in a timely fashion; Halleck was still awaiting confirmation on that detail. As these reports were being digested, Stanton flummoxed everyone by presenting a scheme to send 30,000 men—two corps—from the Army of the Potomac to reinforce Rosecrans immediately, suggesting they could arrive at Bridgeport with five days.[9]

Stanton's pronouncement was greeted skeptically, not the least by Lincoln. Halleck glumly opined that it would take closer to forty days than five to transfer the troops from the East. Much discussion ensued. Most doubted the feat could be done. Stanton, however, had an ace in the hole, with the superintendent of military railroads, Col. Daniel C. McCallum. Just prior to calling the meeting, Stanton asked McCallum and his staff to put together an estimate of how long such a project would take to complete. Now the secretary summoned McCallum, who asserted to the gathered officials that "the transfer can be begun and fully completed within seven days." Stanton was ebullient, the others astounded. "'Good! I told you so,' shouted Stanton. Then, scowling at Halleck, he added: 'Forty days! Forty days indeed, when the life of the nation is at stake!' The triumphant secretary turned to McCallum and said, 'go ahead, begin now.'"[10]

The man tapped to lead this force was Maj. Gen. Joseph Hooker, who had commanded the Army of the Potomac until June 28, 1863. On that date he resigned, nominally over the use of troops at Harpers Ferry, and was replaced by Meade three days before the Battle of Gettysburg. While Hooker likely only offered up his resignation in a miscalculated game of brinksmanship with the administration in quest of a freer operational hand, it was immediately accepted by Lincoln and Stanton, who lacked confidence in the general after his defeat at Chancellorsville. That resignation idled him at a critical moment in the contest, and he was eager to get back into the war.[11]

The decision to send Hooker to lead this new expedition, however, was part and parcel of another troubling issue: who would command all these assembled forces once they arrived in Rosecrans's department? Burnside ranked the Army of the Cumberland commander, but should the two men join forces, he would be operating outside his own department and within the geographic confines of Rosecrans's authority. Hooker was the man who replaced Burnside at the helm of the Army of the Potomac after the Fredericksburg debacle the previous winter. And while Sherman was junior to all three generals, he belonged to Grant's Army of the Tennessee and brought with him a major portion of that force.

Then there was the matter of Rosecrans's competence. The general could be a difficult subordinate, and Stanton was an exceedingly difficult superior. Their relationship took a bad turn early in the war, while Rosecrans headed up the Department of West Virginia. Though Rosecrans was in many ways an excellent soldier, a solid strategist, and perhaps the army's most effective organizer and logistician, he was tone deaf to politics, internal or otherwise. He tended to lecture his superiors on things that seemed obvious, overstepping his bounds on a regular basis. In 1862, while in West Virginia, Rosecrans watched from afar as Maj. Gen. Thomas J. "Stonewall" Jackson demolished one Federal force after another in the Shenandoah Valley. "Rosecrans urged the administration to put the fragmented Federal forces in the region under a single command: His." That suggestion proved counterproductive. "Within a few days," as historian Frank Varney has noted, Rosecrans "received a letter from Gen. George Hartsuff, informing him that 'Secretary Stanton has taken a dislike to you, due to your suggestions.'"[12]

Shortly thereafter, Rosecrans was sent west to serve under Grant. Rosecrans commanded the district encompassing Corinth, Mississippi, in the fall of 1862, fighting two battles during that time, Iuka in September and Corinth in October. At Iuka he commanded one element of a two-pronged advance under Grant's overall authority, which through delay and miscommunication turned into an engagement where Rosecrans's column did all the fighting while the other force, under Maj. Gen. E. O. C. Ord (and accompanied by Grant), missed the engagement entirely. Mutual recriminations followed, cut short first by the battle at Corinth two weeks later, then by Rosecrans's transfer to Kentucky to replace Maj. Gen. Don Carlos Buell in command of what would become the Army of the Cumberland. Grant became further incensed when articles highly critical of him appeared in northern newspapers, apparently originating from Rosecrans's headquarters. The upshot of Rosecrans's time in Mississippi was that he and Grant did not part harmoniously. Should the two men serve together again, friction seemed inevitable.[13]

For Stanton, the final straw proved to be Rosecrans's controversial actions at Chickamauga. On September 20, in the wake of a Confederate breakthrough, Rosecrans, along with Major Generals Crittenden and Alexander McCook, ended his day in Chattanooga, a dozen miles from the battlefield. Only Major Generals Thomas and Gordon Granger remained on the field, fighting until the close of day. Their stand saved the Army of the Cumberland from a larger disaster but only further highlighted the absence of the army commander. Assistant Secretary Dana's September 23 telegram itemized the reasons for the disaster and highlighted McCook's failures in particular, but Stanton would hear none of it: "I know the reasons well enough," he snapped. "Rosecrans ran away from his fighting men and did not stop for thirteen miles. . . . No, they need not shuffle it off on McCook, he is not much of a soldier . . . but he is not accountable for this business. He and Crittenden made pretty good time away from the fight to Chattanooga, but Rosecrans beat them both."[14]

If Stanton feared that his assistant was trying to absolve Rosecrans, however, those fears were groundless. As September waned and gave way to October, Dana maintained a daily telegraphic correspondence with Washington, painting an increasingly alarming portrait of the man in charge of the Army of the Cumberland.

A former New York newspaperman, Dana took up a job offer from Stanton in the summer of 1862. Initially appointed to investigate unresolved claims on behalf of the Quartermaster's Department, Dana performed well, and Stanton kept him in mind for other things. In March 1863 he asked Dana to accept a position as assistant secretary of war and undertake a mission to the western armies. His "ostensible function," explained Stanton, "will be that of special commissioner . . . to investigate the pay service of the Western armies, but your real duty will be to report to me every day what you see." The former journalist agreed.[15]

Dana was, in effect, Stanton's spy. Armed with letters of authority, a secret code that only he knew, and a War Department draft for one thousand dollars, he traveled first to Grant's headquarters, having become well acquainted with the general thanks to his quartermaster's work, and spent the spring and summer of 1863 with the Army of the Tennessee. Dana observed the entire Vicksburg Campaign, enjoying complete access to Grant and his senior officers, and maintained a steady stream of positive reports flowing back to Washington. He did not confine himself to mere military observations, however, but kept Stanton informed of army gossip and, perhaps most importantly, offered up his own opinions on the character and ability of the men he observed. Stanton was delighted with the results.

With Vicksburg captured and Grant's army idled, Dana next traveled to the Army of the Cumberland. His first meeting with Rosecrans was not nearly as auspicious and set the tone for things to come. Dana reached Chattanooga on September 11, 1863, one day after it was occupied by the Federals. Reaching army headquarters, he was taken somewhat aback when, after reading Stanton's letter of introduction, Rosecrans "burst out in angry abuse of the Government. He had not been sustained, he said. His requests had been ignored, his plans thwarted. Both Stanton and Halleck had done all they could, he declared, to prevent his success."[16]

Dana's description of that outburst may or may not have been wholly accurate, but it was in keeping with grievances Rosecrans had been airing directly to Washington—as well as to anyone else who would listen. Despite any suspicions the general harbored against the War Department, however, he did not stint in cooperating with Dana, who was granted full access to planning and with whom Rosecrans freely shared his thoughts as the campaign unfolded. This frankness shocked some in Rosecrans's entourage, official and otherwise. Journalist Henry Villard, who visited the army in October, observed that "Dana had intimate intercourse, day and night, with General Rosecrans, and he enjoyed his personal hospitality, sitting at the same table, and sleeping in the same building. . . . [Dana's] reports," he thought, "proved that he deliberately drew the General into confidential communications, the substance of which he used against him, and that [Dana] held talks with [other] general officers regarding Rosecrans which were nothing less than insubordination." Less delicately, General Granger later dismissed Dana as "a loathsome pimp" who deliberately undermined Rosecrans's standing with the War Department.[17]

Fully reproduced in the *Official Records,* Dana's dispatches up to September 20 paint a detailed picture of the day-to-day military situation as seen from the Army of the Cumberland's headquarters; their tone is optimistic and even enthusiastic. That fatal Sunday, however, represented a turning point. After Chickamauga, Dana felt Rosecrans had to go. His reports took on a darker tone. Dana implied that the general lacked energy and could not decide what to do. For example, on September 27 he informed Stanton that "the defects of [Rosecrans's] character complicate the difficulty" concerning what to do about Generals McCook and Crittenden. "He abounds in friendliness and approbativeness, and is greatly lacking in firmness and steadiness of will." Worse yet, the soldiers had lost confidence in him so "that they do not now cheer him until they are ordered to do so." Dana also offered a solution: "If it be decided to change the chief commander," he wrote, "I would take the liberty of suggesting that some Western general of high rank and great prestige, like Grant, for instance, would be preferable."[18]

On October 6 Dana secretly warned Stanton that Rosecrans intended to "elaborately show that the blame of his failure . . . rest[s] on the Administration; that is, on the Secretary of War and General-in-Chief, who did not foresee that Bragg would be reinforced." By October 12 Dana ratcheted up the personal animosity, assailing the army commander for being "sometimes as obstinate and inaccessible to reason as at others he is irresolute, vacillating, and inconclusive. . . . He has inventive fertility and knowledge, but he has no strength of will and no concentration of purpose. . . . [H]e is a feeble commander."[19]

Dana's latest round of character assassination came amid a time of renewed concern—this time for the army's supply situation. By September 25 the Army of the Cumberland was very nearly isolated in Chattanooga. The Nashville & Chattanooga Railroad now terminated at Bridgeport, since the Confederates had destroyed the line's bridge over the Tennessee at that point. Rosecrans had already planned for that contingency, but it would be months before a new bridge could be constructed; it would be of no use, however until the Confederates could be driven out of Lookout Valley. The only route left open for Federal use ran over Walden's Ridge on the north side of the Tennessee and then down through Sequatchie Valley to Bridgeport, a torturous mountain road—barely more than a path—that was insufficient to keep the army in food and fodder even in the best weather. Heavy autumn rains reduced supplies to a trickle, and the looming winter promised worse to come. If a better supply line could not be opened soon, the Army of the Cumberland would have to retreat, abandoning its wagons and artillery as well.[20]

By mid-October those supply difficulties increased, and so too did Dana's attacks. On October 16 he reported that "nothing can prevent the retreat of the army from [Chattanooga] within a fortnight . . . except the opening of the river. . . . General Rosecrans seems to be insensible to the impending danger, and dawdles with trifles. . . . I never saw anything which seemed so lamentable and hopeless." By the eighteenth Dana's agitprop reached a crescendo: "The practical incapacity of the general commanding is astonishing, and it often seems difficult to believe him of sound mind. His imbecility appears to be contagious, and it is difficult for anyone to get anything done."[21]

The assistant secretary's increasingly hysterical dispatches certainly fostered further alarm in Washington. Even President Lincoln now despaired. He fretted to John Hay that Rosecrans seemed "confused and stunned, like a duck hit on the head." The general's days in command now seemed numbered. Stanton's mind was certainly made up. As early as September 30, Stanton informed Dana that with Hooker on the way, "all that the Army of the Cumberland can need will be a competent commander."[22]

On October 15 Secretary Stanton ordered Col. Anson Stager, head of the U.S. Military Telegraph Department, to arrange for a special train. The secretary departed Washington the next day, Stager joining him along the way. They reached Indianapolis on the seventeenth.

Grant arrived at Cairo on the morning of the sixteenth, summoned there by Stanton on October 3, a dispatch not placed in the general's hand until October 10—low water on the Mississippi was still playing hob with message traffic. "I was still very lame, but started without delay," recalled Grant. He reached Columbus, Kentucky, late on the fifteenth, where he acknowledged receipt of Stanton's earlier communique, and then traveled on to Cairo. Upon reaching the Illinois town, a location he knew well from the days of 1861, he informed one subordinate: "I am here by order of the Gen. in Chief to receive orders. What they will be I don[']t know." For the time being, Grant remained in the dark, for all he found was an additional communique "directing me to proceed immediately to the Galt House, Louisville, where I would meet with an officer of the War Department with my instructions."[23]

Grant's rail route to Louisville also took him through Indianapolis, where he arrived sometime in the afternoon of October 17. Stanton had waited for the general's train. While on the platform, the secretary met with Indiana's powerful Republican governor, Oliver P. Morton, who was stunned to learn that "relieving General Rosecrans . . . [was] the object of [Stanton's] trip." Though Rosecrans was a Democrat, he was also very popular with the rank and file of the Army of the Cumberland, many thousands of whom were Morton's constituents; the governor himself "had great admiration" for the general. Stanton further astounded Morton by telling him that Rosecrans had wired Lincoln on October 3, claiming that it "was useless to talk of putting down the rebellion and recommending an armistice with a view of agreeing on terms of peace."[24]

Had that been true, Morton would certainly have reason to be taken aback. But in relating this tale, Stanton did Rosecrans a great injustice: the general's original dispatch said nothing of the kind. Instead, he suggested to Lincoln that the Federal government should offer a general amnesty to any Rebel deserters. While Lincoln agreed in concept, he also realized how such an offer would be perceived as weak in the wake of a defeat like Chickamauga and politely rebuffed the idea as untimely. Besides, it far overstepped Rosecrans's authority. Stanton took umbrage at this new example of the general's temerity and misrepresented it to Morton (and probably others) to further justify removing Rosecrans from command.[25]

Grant's train was just pulling out of Indianapolis when "a messenger came running up to stop it, saying the Secretary of War was coming into the Station and wanted to see me." This was the first face-to-face meeting between the North's most victorious field commander and the secretary. Boarding Grant's car, Stanton accompanied the general to Louisville. As was his wont, Stanton wasted little time in small talk. In his memoirs Grant recalled that "soon after we started the Secretary handed me two orders, saying that I might take my choice of them. The two were identical in all but one particular. Both created the 'Military Division of the Mississippi,' (giving me command) composed of the Departments of the Ohio, the Cumberland, and the Tennessee." In one, Rosecrans was left in command, while in the other, Rosecrans was replaced by Thomas. "I accepted the latter."[26]

The nature of this choice raises some interesting questions. Was Grant really given a completely free hand in the selection? Stanton's communications with Dana demonstrate that he was determined to replace Rosecrans since at least September 27, certainly by the thirtieth. He had also just informed Governor Morton that Rosecrans was out before leaving Indianapolis—and before meeting with Grant.

Relieving Rosecrans was a controversial step. Even after Chickamauga Rosecrans was still well regarded within the army and by many midwesterners, and as a popular War Democrat, he was a potential candidate for president in the 1864 elections. If the administration removed him, it could be viewed as a case of political intrigue rather than of military necessity. But if Grant issued the order, making the matter a military decision, the political dimension would be muted. Grant clearly understood all this, whether or not the secretary spelled it out in that private rail car. For his part, Stanton almost certainly knew that Grant had no intention of retaining Rosecrans and would immediately take the second choice offered.

It was a safe bet for both men. When Stanton informed Halleck of Grant's acceptance, the secretary added that Grant "consider[ed] it indispensable that Rosecrans should be relieved because he would not obey orders." This last was a direct reference to the Iuka controversy in 1862. As John Rawlins, Grant's chief of staff, later explained, his boss "could not in justice to himself and the cause of his country think again of commanding General Rosecrans, after his experience with him in the fall and summer of 1862." Rosecrans, said Rawlins, had not only deviated "from the plan and entire order of battle" but also displayed "a general spirit of insubordination towards General Grant," all while "profess[ing] towards him the highest regards both as a Man and Officer."[27]

Further evidence of Grant's animosity can be found in the diary of John Hay and from Rosecrans's former chief of staff, Brig. Gen. James A. Garfield. Hay's diary entry for November 2 recorded a conversation in which Lincoln stated "that it was because of Grant's opposition that Rosecrans is not in command of the Army of the Cumberland. . . . Grant was to determine the question for himself. [Grant] said at once that he preferred Rosecrans should be relieved—that he (R.) never would obey orders." Garfield, writing to Rosecrans after a conversation with Sen. Benjamin F. Wade of Ohio, a powerful force among the Radical Republicans in Congress, stated that Wade was of the opinion that Lincoln intended to retain Rosecrans, with "Grant . . . in command of the whole, BUT [and here Garfield supplied the emphasis] GRANT MADE IT A CONDITION OF ACCEPTING . . . THAT [ROSECRANS] BE REMOVED."[28]

By the time that Stanton and Grant's train pulled into Louisville on the cold, drizzly evening of October 17, Rosecrans was out of a job, though that fact would remain under wraps until the order was officially published. The timing of that publication would a matter of some discretion. Both men spent the following day conferring, hashing out details concerning the sweeping authority of Grant's new position, and then Grant and his wife, Julia, went to visit relatives in Louisville. While they were away from the hotel, Stanton received Dana's latest bit of hysteria, sent at 11:00 A.M.

that morning: "If the effort which Rosecrans intends to make to open the river should be futile, the immediate retreat of this army will follow."[29]

Unable to locate Grant in the hotel, Stanton paced impatiently in his dressing gown until the general returned, whereupon both men decided to immediately issue the orders establishing the Military Division of the Mississippi and relieving Rosecrans. The orders went out under Grant's signature.[30]

The directive reached the army's headquarters on the afternoon of October 19 while Rosecrans was out—ironically, inspecting potential bridge sites over the Tennessee River in preparation for implementing his plan to break the siege. Major General Granger was the ranking officer present; he examined the orders and then quietly set them on the commanding general's desk. Upon his return at dusk, Rosecrans read them, sent an acknowledgement, and then informed his staff that he would depart the army quietly at 5:00 A.M. the next morning. Thomas offered to resign in protest, but Rosecrans cut him off: "George, we are in the face of the enemy. No one but you can safely take my place now."[31]

At 11:30 P.M. on October 19, Grant wired his first communication to the new army commander, Major General Thomas: "Hold Chattanooga at all hazards. I will be there as soon as possible. Please inform me how long your present supplies will last and the prospects for keeping them up." Rosecrans and Thomas found the telegram insulting, implying that they needed to be ordered to remain in Chattanooga, a suggestion, wrote Rosecrans, which both men thought "only ignorance or malice could have inspired." Thomas immediately replied—with great precision—that the Army of the Cumberland had "two hundred four thousand four hundred sixty-two (204,462) rations in storehouses," with another 90,000 due to "arrive tomorrow. . . . I will hold the town till we starve."[32]

Rosecrans departed Chattanooga at 5:00 A.M. on the twentieth. Grant and his staff departed for Nashville that same morning, spending the night in Tennessee's capital city, where they met with Gov. Andrew Johnson and other officials. They did not travel past Nashville at this time, Grant noted, because it was unsafe to do so after dark, a suggestion that Rebel activity was still a serious concern through Middle Tennessee and across the Cumberland Plateau. Grant also met Assistant Secretary Dana, who arrived at 10:00 P.M. on his way to Louisville by order of Stanton. Grant intercepted him. "'I am going to interfere with your journey, Mr. Dana.

. . . I have gotten the Secretary's permission to take you back with me to Chattanooga.' . . . So of course," recalled Dana, "I went."[33]

The augmented party left on the morning of October 21 for Stevenson and Bridgeport, from where Grant would have to leave the comfort of the rails and travel by horseback over the same disastrous mountain road that was proving so inadequate to keep the Army of the Cumberland from starvation's door. Grant's train reached Stevenson "after dark." There he found Rosecrans, who had just arrived from Chattanooga. Rosecrans "came into my car and we had a brief interview," recalled Grant, "in which he described very clearly the situation at Chattanooga, and made some excellent suggestions as to what should be done. My only wonder was that he had not carried them out."[34]

Stevenson was not all that much of a place, "a poor town with some half-dozen miserable houses" and an "accumulation of supplies for Rosecrans's army." While waiting for Rosecrans, word circulated among the troops there that Grant had arrived. "When it was known he was on the train," recollected Sgt. Rice Bull of the 123rd New York, "men grouped around his car and began to cheer. After a little time he came out on the platform leaning on two crutches. . . . He wore an army slouch hat with bronze cord around it, quite a long military coat, unbuttoned, no sword or belt, and there was nothing to indicate his rank. His appearance would have attracted no attention had he not been General Grant. When the boys called for a speech he bowed and said nothing."[35]

Grant also encountered two other generals: Hooker and Oliver O. Howard. Major General Howard had traveled to Stevenson from Bridgeport with Rosecrans. "There I met Gen. Grant," noted Howard in a letter home, "who had telegraphed that he would be at this place that night." First, Howard stopped in to have a word with his commanding officer, Hooker. In an address delivered twenty-five years later, he recalled the moment. "During the interview [Hooker] told me that Grant was on the train coming south from Nashville. Hooker had made preparations to receive the general and have him conducted to his own quarters [since] Grant was at that time very lame. . . . Hooker sent a spring wagon and an officer of his staff to the depot, but for some reason he did not go himself."[36]

This proved to be a mistake on Hooker's part. At about that time, Howard also went to the depot to catch a train back to Bridgeport, ten miles east, the site of his own XI Corps headquarters. He found Grant while there and went to pay his respects before leaving the station. Howard expected a man of "very large size and rough appearance," but instead he found Grant "not larger than [Maj. Gen. George B.] McClellan, at the time very thin in flesh and pale in complexion, and noticeably self-contained and retiring." Soon after Hooker's staff officer arrived, conveying that general's invitation, which Howard expected Grant to accept. The reply, noted the corps commander, "astonished me." Grant took offense at Hooker's failure to appear in person and, "with some emphasis," said, "if General Hooker wishes to see me he will find me on this train."[37]

Dutifully Hooker soon appeared, but Grant declined the invitation to spend the night. Howard, no fan of Hooker's since the defeat at Chancellorsville created ill-will between them, approved of the gamesmanship. Grant, he noted, "never left the necessity for gaining a proper ascendency over subordinate generals, where it was likely to be questioned, to a second interview."[38]

In his memoir James H. Wilson, then a lieutenant colonel on Grant's staff, recalled the same incident, though somewhat differently. "Word came from Hooker that he was not well and would like Grant to call on him at his quarters. They had been brother officers and boon companions years before on the Columbia, but had not met since the outbreak of the war. It was at once evident that Hooker was 'trying it on' with Grant and naturally both Rawlins and I were struck by the message." Wilson also remembered the rebuff coming from the ever-vigilant Rawlins, not from Grant: "Without waiting for Grant to reply, Rawlins said at once and in a tone that could not be misunderstood: 'General Grant himself is not very well and will not leave his car tonight. He expects General Hooker and all other generals who have business with him to call at once. . . . This," Wilson gloated, "settled it promptly and unmistakably for Hooker as well as for everybody else."[39]

Wilson's account was published nearly fifty years after the fact and differs from Howard's in some interesting details, but in each officer's recollection, the disdain for Hooker is hard to miss. Grant is usually viewed as a man disinterested in ceremony, a soldiers' general who made little fuss over military niceties. And yet here he very clearly made a point of forcing Hooker to come to him, a point on which his biographers have been sympathetic. In his *Memoirs* even Grant took umbrage at examples of excessive pride, noting that "the worst excuse a soldier can make for declining service is that he once ranked the commander he is ordered to report to." In Grant's defense, as historian Brooks Simpson has pointed out, "military courtesy demanded that subordinates called on their commander, not the other way around." And yet this was not a formal call at an established military post; Grant was passing through, he had no established quarters or lodging, and Hooker was offering the comfortable hospitality of his own facilities. Hooker's historical reputation has been largely negative, of course, creating a tendency to put him in the worst possible light. But Wilson and Howard, who were the only witnesses to have recorded this encounter, were also far from objective. The incident suggests that Grant could be as sensitive to the niceties of rank and position as any other old-army man.[40]

With Hooker put in his place, Grant traveled the remaining ten miles to Bridgeport to spend the night at Howard's modest headquarters, a simple canvas wall tent. There was a moment of humor—at least on Grant's part—when he spied "a liquor flask" in his host's quarters. Howard, a noted Methodist and army-renowned teetotaler, flushed with embarrassment and hastened to explain: "'that flask is not mine. . . . It was left here by an officer to be returned to Chattanooga; I never drink.' 'Neither do I,' was [Grant's] prompt reply."[41]

Early on October 22 Grant departed for Chattanooga, even though he was still so incapacitated that Rawlins had to lift him into the saddle. Ahead lay nearly fifty miles of the worst road imaginable, including "mud, knee-deep in places, . . . from washouts on the mountainsides." The route was also "strewn with the *debris* of broken wagons and the carcasses of thousands of starved mules and horses." Grant and the main party made it only halfway to Chattanooga on the twenty-second, spending the night in an unnamed "hamlet" twenty to twenty-five miles beyond Bridgeport, somewhere on Walden's Ridge. Wilson and Dana did not stop, though, breaking away from the party at Jasper and pressing on to reach Chattanooga around midnight. Grant would arrive the next evening.[42]

2
"WET, DIRTY, AND WELL"

$\mathcal{G}$rant and his party rode into Chattanooga on the evening of October 23. Their trip had not been easy. Chief of Staff Rawlins later professed that "if . . . he did not see it with his own eyes, [he] would not believe it possible" that the road was traversable. They also journeyed through "pelting rains and cold mountain winds." Along the way they encountered pitiful groups of Unionist refugees struggling over those same highlands headed for Bridgeport, their wretchedness moving Rawlins to write: "I have seen much of human misery . . . [in] this war, . . . but never before in so distressing a form." In what could have been a fresh disaster, as Grant's party entered the besieged town, Surg. Edward Kittoe noted, "the Generals horse fell flat on his side but luckily did not hurt the General at all."[1]

Once remounted, Grant made for Thomas's headquarters at 316 Walnut Street, a "1-story frame house" owned by English tanner and leather merchant Thomas Richardson. It must have been a comfortable dwelling. It was popular with generals, having served the same function for Confederates John C. Breckinridge, Joseph E. Johnston, and John Hunt Morgan before Rosecrans established his headquarters there on September 10.[2]

Despite the historic nature of this meeting between Thomas and Grant, there are only two detailed descriptions of the event, both written long after the war and recorded by relatively junior officers, Lieutenant Colonel Wilson and Capt. Horace Porter. Porter was a West Point classmate of Wilson's, currently serving as an ordnance officer with the Army of the Cumberland. When Wilson and Assistant Secretary Dana stumbled into town late the previous night, they found their way to Porter's quarters and bunked with him. There is also one shorter account, this one left by Maj. Gen. Joseph J. Reynolds in an interview also recorded years after the fact. Reynolds, who was both a personal friend of Grant's and the Army of the Cumberland's chief of staff under Thomas, was uniquely situated to comment on the encounter.

Wilson's and Porter's versions, outwardly similar, are nonetheless very different in tone. Wilson described a cold reception, verging on openly hostile. "Getting back to headquarters," he wrote, "I found Grant at one side of the fireplace, steaming from the heat over a small puddle which had run from his sodden clothing. Thomas was on the other side, neither saying a word, but both looking glum and ill at ease. . . . [L]earning from Rawlins that nothing had yet been offered for their comfort, and knowing that Grant would not condescend to ask for . . . hospitality," Wilson jumped right in. "General Thomas, General Grant is wet and tired and ought to have some dry clothes, particularly a pair of socks and a pair of slippers. He is hungry besides, and needs something to eat. Can't your officers attend to these matters for him?" This interjection, claimed Wilson, broke the ice, and soon "everything possible was done and apparently in the most cheerful manner."[3]

Wilson's account has been widely repeated, suggesting as it did an undercurrent of disrespect, even contempt, directed toward Grant by Thomas and his staff. Historian Brooks Simpson wrote that Thomas "received his new commander rather coolly," a charge that echoed Bruce Catton's observation that the reception was "somewhat chilly." Grant's most recent biographer, Ron Chernow, elevated the condition to "frosty." Other writers have largely followed suit.[4]

How accurate was Wilson's recall? Certainly, Rosecrans's staff (and indeed most of the men in the Army of the Cumberland) resented their general's relief and were angry at the way their outgoing commander had been treated. Just a few days before, when Brig. Gen. James A. Garfield departed Chattanooga to journey back to Washington, D.C., to take a House seat in Congress, Thomas took him aside to insist: "You know the injustice of all these attacks on Rosecrans. Make it your first business to set these matters right." But did Thomas lay the blame for those attacks, and the injustice done, at Grant's feet?[5]

Regardless, the evidence that Grant was met with thinly veiled disdain is sparse. Grant makes no mention of any such discourtesy in his memoirs. Nor did other observers who, if not all in the room that night, were certainly around headquarters at the time. Contemporary retellings of the reception take no note of any such tension. In his October 25 dispatch, Dana merely recorded that "Grant arrived . . . wet, dirty, and well." Wilson's diary—in sharp contrast to his memoir—matched Dana's wording precisely. The next day both Grant and Surgeon Kittoe wrote to Julia Grant, with neither man mentioning any friction. Grant merely informed his wife, "I stood [the trip] very well however but was very much fatigued." Kittoe echoed this, writing that the general "stood the journey very well and does not seem at all the worse or even fatigued. . . . [H]e is in fine spirits."[6]

Then there is Porter's description. Porter recalled that he had been "summoned to headquarters" about "an hour after nightfall." Entering the room, "in an armchair facing the fireplace was seated a general officer, slight in figure . . . whose face bore an expression of weariness. He was carelessly dressed . . . and held a lighted cigar in his mouth." Thomas introduced the officer as "General Grant." The new arrival had already eaten "a light supper immediately after his arrival." As Porter watched, "a member of General Thomas's staff quietly called that officer's attention to the fact that the distinguished guest's clothes were pretty wet and his boots were thoroughly soaked . . . and intimated that colds were usually no respecter of persons." Thomas, noted Porter, had been so focused on "arranging for a conference of officers, that he had entirely overlooked his guest's travel-stained condition." Upon that condition being called to his attention, immediately the big Virginian "begged" Grant to take the chance "to step into a bedroom and change his clothes." His guest "thanked him politely, but positively declined to make any additions to his personal comfort, except to light a fresh cigar."[7]

Porter would go on to serve under Grant in Virginia for the duration of the war and later as his personal secretary in the White House. He became a firm friend. In his memoirs Porter wrote glowingly of his time with Grant. Despite his service under both Rosecrans and Thomas, and his attachment to the latter commander, he was hardly a Grant detractor. Porter's account of this first meeting, published in 1897, appeared fifteen years prior to Wilson's version. It lacks the undercurrent of tension and resentment present in the latter. Porter did not find a "glum silence"; instead, things were bustling with activity. Further, far from lacking refreshment, Grant had already eaten a "light supper." Also, Porter recalled that it was one of Thomas's own staff officers who called his general's attention to Grant's need for dry apparel, not Lieutenant Colonel Wilson. Grant politely declined this offer, suggesting that the new arrival could not have been too wet or uncomfortable.

Finally, there is Reynolds's account. Reynolds offered few details of this meeting but did comment on the tone: "I saw [Grant] when he came into Thomas headquarters in Chattanooga. He was covered with mud and wet through. There was no feeling between Grant and Thomas. Thomas was slow to do things for [Grant] but did not intend to be inhospitable." He also recalled that "Thomas said to me this: 'Tell Grant to have no hesitancy about giving me orders. I will be ready to obey his every wish.' I don't believe," added Reynolds, "there was any feeling in the matter."[8]

Reynolds's version supports Porter's less-charged recollection of the incident. Yet despite the lack of corroboration, Wilson's account has largely prevailed.

Notwithstanding his exhausting journey, Grant wasted no time. The rest of the evening was taken up with reports and assessments of the military situation. Thomas and Brig. Gen. William F. "Baldy" Smith detailed the Army of the Cumberland's current circumstances and dispositions as well as the positions of the Confederates. Grant listened intently and, when they were done, "began to fire off whole volleys of questions at the officers present." Porter was deeply impressed: "He made a profound impression upon every one by the quickness of his perception." Thomas had already reported on the army's rations in that earlier telegram. Now Grant also asked Porter about how much ammunition was on hand. "Barely enough here to fight one day's battle," the captain replied, "but an ample supply has been accumulated at Bridgeport." It was a telling inquiry. Grant was already looking ahead to his next offensive move.[9]

The main issue of the moment, however, was rations. The army could not survive the winter if forced to rely solely on the track (it could hardly be called a road) over Walden's Ridge for sustenance. The worse the weather grew, fewer supplies would trickle in while more animals would perish in the attempt. The army's horses were already starving; all local feed and fodder was badly depleted. In another month no animals would be left in Chattanooga to haul artillery, ammunition, or rations.

The 1863 town of Chattanooga sat on the south bank of the Tennessee, nestled in a bend of the river that formed the city's northern and western boundaries. A couple of miles below Chattanooga, the river bends again as it butts up against the brow of Lookout Mountain, turning to flow northward for a stretch, and forming the peninsula known as Moccasin Bend. Another series of curves take the river westward through the Tennessee River gorge for a dozen miles until it swings generally southwest into Alabama, flowing past Bridgeport and Stevenson. The Tennessee River was navigable along this stretch in 1863 but not all the way to the Ohio River; Muscle Shoals in northern Alabama divided the river into upper and lower reaches, preventing boats from steaming the entire length of the watercourse. More immediately, a series of rapids between Bridgeport and Chattanooga created additional navigation challenges, now of lesser concern due to the higher water; the incessant rains of the past few weeks had at least helped with that problem. The river made Chattanooga a vital strategic point, because here was the only water-level passage through the south end of the Appalachian Mountains for hundreds of miles.[10]

The area was a travel route long before Europeans came, one known as the Middle Cherokee Trading Path. The U.S. government negotiated a federal right-of-way with the Cherokee Nation in 1803, connecting Tennessee with Georgia, which lasted until the Cherokees themselves were removed in the 1830s. Railroads came to Chattanooga in the late 1850s, following that same terrain access. By 1861 Chattanooga connected three important sets of tracks: the Nashville & Chattanooga Railroad; the East Tennessee, which ran northeast to Knoxville and on into Virginia; and the Western & Atlantic Railroad, which headed south to Atlanta. The Memphis & Charleston also tied into this hub, connecting with the Nashville & Chattanooga at Stevenson.[11]

In 1861 Chattanooga numbered about 2,500 residents. By 1863 most of those civilians were gone, having refugeed south. Some Unionists remained, but Chattanooga was now very much an army town, becoming more of one over the next year. By the time Grant arrived, it was also a heavily fortified camp. The Confederates began that work, with the Army of the Cumberland massively improving on the existing defenses in September and October. Now a line of trenches and forts ran in an arc from bank to bank, completely enclosing the town from the south, defended by 40,000 troops. Any direct Confederate assault here would clearly be suicidal—if Federal ammunition held out.

Two other important features further complicated the terrain picture: Lookout Mountain and Missionary Ridge. Rising nearly 2,400 feet above sea level (and 1,700 feet above Chattanooga's 676-foot elevation), Lookout Mountain (geographically a part of the Cumberland Plateau) runs on a southwest angle from Moccasin Bend deep into Alabama. Its palisades— cliff-like rock walls forming the last third of the mountain's slope—are pierced by gaps only in a few places, severely limiting access up, over, and across the mountain. Lookout Creek drains into the Tennessee west of the mountain, creating Lookout Valley, while Chattanooga Creek flows to the Tennessee between Lookout Mountain and Missionary Ridge. Missionary

Ridge runs parallel to Lookout Mountain about three miles to the east but is not nearly as long. It terminates in a series of lower hills a few miles into northern Georgia. The ridge is also not as high, rising to only about 900 feet above sea level, but near the city its slopes are extremely steep.

When Grant arrived, the Confederates controlled both Lookout Mountain and Missionary Ridge and occupied the south bank of the Tennessee River in Lookout Valley. This allowed Bragg's army to seal off the roads that followed both the northern and southern riverbanks and the rail line as well as to interdict boat traffic on the river itself.

The Confederate ability to project combat power into Lookout Valley, however, was far from unfettered. This inadequacy had multiple reasons, a shortage of transport and the lack of infrastructure being chief among them. The Army of Tennessee was severely hampered by both the limited capacity of the Western & Atlantic Railroad and a severe lack of supply wagons. Thanks to an influx of reinforcements just before Chickamauga, Bragg's forces doubled in manpower within the space of six weeks, swelling from fewer than 40,000 men to more than 70,000 troops; but in the urgency of the moment, most of those commands were forced to leave their transport and draft animals behind. This translated to crippled mobility, as Bragg did not have the wagons to haul food any significant distance from his railhead.[12]

To compound that problem, the Western & Atlantic was having difficulties in delivering sufficient food for the newly expanded Rebel army, meaning that those additional wagons and draft animals could not be shipped in without further reducing rations to the men. Moving the extra transport overland was, for most of those arrivals, not a practical solution: Lt. Gen. James Longstreet's corps from the Army of Northern Virginia, for example, traveled 900 miles via rail to arrive in North Georgia. Their supply wagons, much of their artillery, and many of their animals would spend the winter of 1863–64 in Richmond, awaiting their return.

In addition to those constraints, the other serious limit to projecting combat power into Lookout Valley was the limited road network. There were only two good pathways over the mountain: the Wauhatchie Pike, which crossed the northern shoulder of Lookout between its palisades and the Tennessee River, and a second road that descended the west face of the mountain in a place called Johnson's Crook, twenty-four miles to the south. The Wauhatchie Pike would have served Confederate needs nicely but for one problem: It was completely exposed to artillery fire from a range of hills on Moccasin Bend, where ten Union cannon were planted specifically to interdict that traffic. The artillerymen did their job well.[13]

Any Rebels crossing the over the north face of Lookout had to run this gauntlet of fire. Pvt. E. H. Acker of Hampton's Legion, a South Carolina unit serving in Brig. Gen. Micah Jenkins's brigade of Longstreet's command, regularly transited that road during the month of October while engaged in picket duty. He remembered that "often in going and returning we would be shelled from what the boys called the Moccasin Battery." Sgt. Samuel Sprott of the 40th Alabama was stationed on the mountain in November. "Owing to the fact that the Northern part of the mountain was exposed to a raking fire from a Federal battery," recalled Sprott, "the movement of troops had to take place under cover of darkness, and one can well imagine the difficulties of attending such a movement."[14]

Of course, those difficulties were even worse for a convoy of slow-moving, road-bound supply wagons. As a result, the Rebels were rarely able to sustain more than a brigade—about 2,000 troops—in Lookout Valley for any length of time. This force was sufficient to prevent Union wagon trains from coming up from Bridgeport while the soldiers sniped at other Federal convoys trying to use the road along the north bank of the Tennessee. This fire proved so effective that they closed that road completely due to slaughtered mules, but the Rebels were not strong enough to prevent a major Federal command from seizing the valley if it tried. Additional Confederate forces would be required to prevent that from happening, but they could not linger indefinitely in the area without slowly starving to death. This Rebel dilemma would prove to be the key to reopening an effective Union supply line into Chattanooga.[15]

The plan for reestablishing the flow of supplies would in later years become a point of contention among some of the Federal officers. "Baldy" Smith claimed that he, not Rosecrans, had devised the operation to save the Army of the Cumberland. Smith arrived in Chattanooga on September 30, transferred from Virginia to replace Rosecrans's outgoing chief engineer, James St. Clair Morton. An 1845 graduate of West Point, Smith did very well early in the war, rising to command of the Army of the Potomac's VI Corps by the time of the Battle of Fredericksburg in December 1862.[16]

But Smith, a friend of the recently deposed McClellan, could not stay out of politics. Along with Maj. Gen. William B. Franklin, he penned a controversial letter to Lincoln in early 1863, trying to get Burnside ousted as commander of the Army of the Potomac. Instead, Smith was himself relieved of command, and his pending promotion to major general passed out of the Senate without action. By March 1863 he was "off the active list," benched for what appeared to be the war's duration, and "viewed by" Stanton and Halleck "as a devoted adherent of General McClellan." Smith saw limited service organizing Pennsylvania and New York militia during the Gettysburg Campaign, but after that emergency concluded, he was again sidelined until Rosecrans needed a replacement for Morton.[17]

Smith would later try and take sole credit for devising the plan that would result in establishing the "Cracker Line." Others in the Army of the Cumberland disputed this, crediting General Rosecrans with the concept, but there is no question that Smith, as chief engineer, had a hand in the details.

That plan involved several intricate elements, each one vital; orchestrating them would require careful timing. First, there was the matter of boats. One of the needs Rosecrans anticipated prior to commencing his campaign was for vessels to haul supplies from Bridgeport to Chattanooga until the rail bridge across the Tennessee could be rebuilt. Accordingly, he ordered engines and other needed machinery shipped to Bridgeport, where a boat builder named Turner, from Lake Erie, would craft several "flat-bottomed, light-draught river steamers." The first of those vessels, reported Quartermaster General Montgomery Meigs, "was ready for service" by September 27, with another "nearing completion." But according to Capt. William Le Duc, chief quartermaster of the XI Corps and assigned to oversee that construction, the next boat was not finished until October 23, the same day Grant entered Chattanooga, and launched on the twenty-fourth.[18]

The next component involved Hooker's column, which was intended to clear Lookout Valley of Rebels. Crossing at Bridgeport, his troops were to march via Shellmound and the settlement of Whiteside, through Running Water Creek gorge, and into Lookout Valley. From there they would move north, clearing the valley of Confederates. The steamboats could then safely navigate between Bridgeport and Kelley's Ferry, where supplies could be offloaded and hauled by wagon through Cummings Gap in Raccoon Mountain to Chattanooga.

The third element was the most complicated aspect of them all: a nighttime amphibious assault across the Tennessee at Brown's Ferry, to be conducted by Brig. Gen. William B. Hazen's brigade in newly constructed pontoon boats. These vessels were built across from Chattanooga on the north bank of the Tennessee, where a sawmill and an impromptu boatyard had been constructed along North Chickamauga Creek. Hazen's men were to board the pontoons in the creek, shove out into the river, and then float downstream for a dozen miles to the intended bridge site at Brown's Ferry. There they would land, seize a range of hills on the south bank, dig in, and wait for a second brigade to be ferried across the river in the pontoons. After the site was secure, engineers would assemble those boats into a pontoon bridge to bring over reinforcements and then to serve as the supply route into Chattanooga from Kelley's Ferry. Once Hooker's column and Hazen's forces were in contact and the Brown's Ferry bridge emplaced, the Union hold on Lookout Valley would be secure.[19]

As noted, timing was critical. If Hooker moved before Hazen's assault force was ready, or if Hazen's troops failed to secure a lodgment, Hooker's

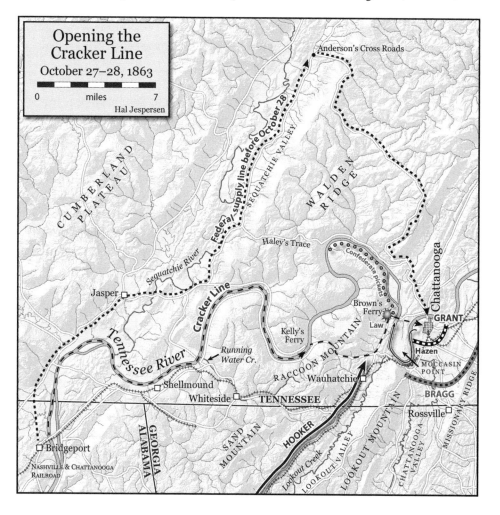

men might be left unsupported to deal with an overwhelming force of Confederates. (The Federals were unaware of just how much Rebel supply difficulties were impeding General Bragg's siege effort.) If the effort was only partially successful, or if the route was only held open for a short time before a Rebel counterattack retook the valley, the steamboats had to be ready to surge supplies into Chattanooga through whatever narrow window existed. All the plan's pieces had to work together to achieve success, always a difficult proposition in war.

This was the plan Dana referred to in his alarmist telegram of October 18 and that Rosecrans outlined to Grant on the evening of October 21; the "excellent suggestions" that left Grant wondering why the outgoing commander "had not carried them out." This postwar statement by Grant is curious, for at the time the delay was easily explained—not everything was ready to go before late October—and he should have been fully briefed on those details then.[20]

Even though Brigadier General Meigs reported one boat ready as early as September 27, he also noted that the water level in the Tennessee was too low for it to operate. It would take October's heavy rains to raise the river, and they still needed more time to finish additional river transports. One other problem, however, complicated the equation: Hooker's reinforcing column was not yet ready to move.

Stanton's intended troop transfer began well enough. A member of the 136th New York in the XI Corps wrote: "Our journey from manassas junction to Bridgeport Ala. was begun Sept. 25th and terminated Sept. 30. We came all the way by rail, stopping only to change cars and precure [sic] rations." That timeframe was well within Stanton's and Colonel McCallum's anticipated transit time, but their calculations did not factor in any Rebel interference. On the day the 136th New York reached Bridgeport, Maj. Gen. Joseph Wheeler and 5,000 Rebel horsemen crossed to the north bank of the Tennessee River upstream from Chattanooga at Cottonport, Tennessee. Wheeler's mission was to cripple the existing Union supply line.[21]

After a notable success on October 2—destroying a large Union supply train at Anderson's crossroads in the Sequatchie Valley, estimated by Wheeler at "between 800 and 1,500 wagons"—the Rebels rode deep into Middle Tennessee, striking next at McMinnville. The Union garrison there surrendered on the fourth, allowing Wheeler's men the chance to move west to cut the Nashville and Chattanooga Railroad. Between the fourth and the sixth, the Rebel horsemen struck at bridges and track between

Murfreesboro and the town of Wartrace, disrupting the railroad along a twenty-five-mile stretch.[22]

The Federals responded strongly. The Army of the Cumberland's cavalry began an immediate pursuit, while elements of Hooker's force either halted in place or even reversed course to strengthen existing rail garrisons. On the morning of October 4, Lt. Russell M. Tuttle of the 107th New York found himself "way down in Alabama" at Stevenson, writing a letter to a friend, when orders came to "embark again, and we were taken back over the mountain to Decherd." There, Tuttle recorded, the regiment "laid out a new camp and settled down to the strange conviction that the 12th Corp is to guard the railroad instead of going to the front." That plan was also soon overtaken by events.[23]

On October 6 General Hooker ordered his chief of staff, Maj. Gen. Daniel E. Butterfield, to move back up the rail line from Bridgeport to "Decherd [Tennessee], and assume command of the XII Corps and of all the troops in that district," with further instructions to reopen communications with Murfreesboro. Lieutenant Tuttle found himself "waiting around for Forrest's guerrillas," who, he noted, were "at work on the railroad. At near midnight, through darkness, and driving rain and dust we embarked on the cars, *en route* for the enemy. Cars awfully crowded, no comfort, no sleep."[24]

The next day Union cavalry caught up to Wheeler, took his men by surprise, and inflicted a stinging defeat on the Rebels just outside the small village of Farmington. The Federals suffered about 100 casualties while reporting that the Confederates lost at least "86 dead, . . . 270 prisoners," and an unrecorded number of wounded. This blow was sufficiently damaging to send Wheeler south to recross the Tennessee River at Muscle Shoals. Though the rails were soon repaired, Wheeler's intervention delayed the tail end of Hooker's force for about a week, all told, and left elements of his command permanently scattered on garrison duty between Nashville and Stevenson.[25]

One other factor complicated Hooker's logistics. Just as the Confederates had left their supply wagons behind in rushing reinforcements to Bragg, the XI and XII Corps had left behind important mobility assets when moving west—their mules were "turned in to the depot quartermaster at Alexandria." Captain LeDuc protested this "most unnecessary blunder . . . in vain. Our disciplined, well broken mules were taken from us," to be replaced at Nashville. But "the corral there was supplied with broken down and young, unbroken mules—colts." They proved wholly unsatisfactory, and, as LeDuc noted, "many of them died" on the way to Bridgeport. To the captain's growing frustration, when at last some of his "good serviceable mules were finally shipped out to Nashville" as replacements, the quartermasters there retained them "to work in the city."[26]

Many of those wagons and teams were still toiling their way to the front in late October, forcing the Federals to compromise. On the twenty-third, noting that one division of the XII Corps would remain in Middle Tennessee on rail-guard duties, General Thomas ordered Hooker to adapt and use the XI Corps wagons to support elements of both corps, if available. If not, he added, "prepare to use flats and barges, which can be protected from the shore." Fortunately for the move, Hooker reported at 6:10 P.M. the next day, October 24, that "the rear (100 wagons) of the train furnished the Eleventh Corps, leaving Nashville on the 12th instant, arrived here [Stevenson] today." At last, a day after Grant reached Chattanooga, all the pieces of the resupply plan were in place.[27]

3

"THEY LOOKED UPON THE GARRISON AS PRISONERS OF WAR"

*D*espite Grant's difficult journey into town, his discussion with Thomas ran late into the evening of October 23. Porter recalled that it was about 10:30 P.M. before Grant "retired . . . to get a much-needed rest. As he arose and walked across the floor," the captain observed, "his lameness was very perceptible." Despite any weariness or his injury, however, Grant had already "made an appointment with Generals Thomas and Smith and several staff officers, to accompany him the next day to make a personal inspection of the lines."[1]

That inspection began early Saturday morning. The party crossed to the north bank of the Tennessee River and traversed the neck of Moccasin Bend to Brown's Ferry, the site General Smith thought best for a crossing and bridge. "Here," recalled Grant, "we left our horses back from the river and approached the water on foot. There was a picket station of the enemy on the opposite side, of about twenty men, in full view, and we were within easy range," but no one tried for a shot at the group, obviously composed entirely of officers. "They looked upon the [Chattanooga] garrison . . . as prisoners of war," mused Grant; there was no need for shooting. Smith had a simpler explanation, recalling that the captain of a nearby artillery battery had earlier informed him "of a tacit agreement that the pickets should not fire on each other." After a short inspection, Grant approved the site, and the group departed.[2]

His morning survey completed, Grant returned to the Walnut Street headquarters. Once there, he issued several consequential orders. The new commander remained concerned that Bragg's army might turn his flank, either by crossing the Tennessee upstream from Chattanooga to interpose a strong force between Thomas and Burnside or by crossing the river downstream from Bridgeport between Sherman and Hooker. Either move would outflank the Army of the Cumberland and threaten Union lines of communication in Middle Tennessee on a much grander scale than that posed by Wheeler's early October cavalry raid. Accordingly,

Grant instructed Thomas to increase the force guarding McMinnville, southeast of Nashville, to about a division and to confiscate as much forage as possible in the less-settled country between McMinnville and East Tennessee, thereby denying its use to Bragg. To Sherman, newly promoted as commander of the Department of the Tennessee, Grant wired urgent new instructions: "Drop everything east of Bear Creek and move with your entire force towards Stevenson until you receive further orders. The enemy are evidently moving a large force towards Cleveland [Tennessee], and may break through our lines and move on Nashville, in which event your troops are the only ones at command that could beat them there."[3]

Here Grant also received an alarming bit of intelligence that, if true, further endangered Burnside. Earlier on October 24, Halleck informed Burnside that "it now appears pretty certain that [Lt. Gen. Richard S.] Ewell's corps [of the Army of Northern Virginia] has gone to Tennessee" via southwest Virginia. He also informed Grant of this development. If accurate, this reinforcement of some "20,000 to 25,000" Confederates could more than double the number of enemy troops operating against Knoxville (Bragg then had approximately 15,000 men at Cleveland) and potentially overwhelm the Federals there. There was no way of knowing if that threat was real, however, nor could more Union troops be rushed to reinforce Knoxville. In response to an inquiry from Thomas, Burnside pointed out that he already had all the troops he could keep supplied. The Federals would just have to remain alert, see what developed, and hope for the best. In fact, Knoxville would never be far from Grant's thoughts during the entire campaign.[4]

Concerning the reopening of Chattanooga's supply line, Grant liked what he saw and heard; he now gave final approval to the Thomas-Smith plan of operations. As he informed Halleck on the twenty-sixth, "Gen. Thomas had also set on foot, before my arrival, a plan for getting possession of the river from a point below Lookout Mountain to Bridgeport. If successful, and I think it will be, the question of supplies will be fully settled."[5]

Thomas's first instruction on the matter had gone out on October 19, prior to Grant's arrival, alerting Hooker "to use all possible dispatch in concentrating your command." This was followed by a more detailed message on the twenty-third, sent singing along the telegraph wires between Chattanooga and Stevenson even as Grant was torturously descending Walden's Ridge. After directing one division to remain in Middle Tennessee to guard the railroads, Thomas apprised Hooker that "the remainder of the Twelfth Corps will . . . move with the Eleventh Corps on the south side of the Tennessee River." At 2:30 P.M. on the twenty-fourth, with Grant now on board, Thomas provided the final details for the operation, instructing Hooker to move first to the site of Rankin's Ferry, near Shellmound, where two brigades from Chattanooga were to meet his column on Monday, October 26. These reinforcements were to help protect Hooker's trains and the army's new intended line of communications. From Shellmound, Hooker was to move to the locality of Whitesides in Running Water Gorge (the narrow passage between Sand and Raccoon Mountains) and thence to Brown's Ferry. "The object," concluded Thomas, "is to hold the road and gain possession of the river as far as Brown's Ferry."[6]

The Rankin's Ferry mission was assigned to the First and Third Brigades of Brig. Gen. Charles Cruft's First Division, IV Corps. To say the least, Cruft's men found the orders unwelcome. In his journal entry for October 24, Lt. Chesley Mosman of the 59th Illinois recorded that he had just finished a brick chimney for his winter shanty and had lit his first fire when the "orders came to . . . march to Shellmound. My aren't the boys mad. . . . We were just getting ready to live, and off we must go, and go at once." When the company bugler tried to sound a call, "the boys start to yelling and cursing him, shouting at him unmercifully. It ain't his fault, but the men must vent their anger and disgust on someone."[7]

Departing at 2:00 A.M. on October 25, Mosman recorded three days of difficult marching, sometimes following the river road on the north bank of the Tennessee, at other times up and over Walden's Ridge, repeatedly encountering incoming supply convoys and the carcasses of dead mules. "The stench was awful." Cruft's brigades reached Jasper on the twenty-seventh, with Mosman's regiment continuing on to cross the river and camp at Shellmound on the twenty-eighth. Ominously for the intended Union timetable, they were already two days behind schedule.[8]

Hooker's men were also delayed. They set out on October 26, filing across the pontoon bridge at Bridgeport, marching the seven miles to Shellmound, and then turning east to follow Running Water Creek toward Whiteside. The two understrength divisions of Howard's XI Corps led the way, followed by Brig. Gen. John W. Geary's division of the XII Corps, with two companies of horsemen drawn from the 5th Tennessee (Union) and 1st Alabama (Union) Cavalry Regiments acting as guides and scouts.[9]

Hooker and his command posed something of a problem for Grant. As noted earlier, Hooker was a former commander of the Army of the

Potomac, now somewhat in disgrace after his poor showing at Chancellorsville, and he had poor relations with both of his senior subordinates. He blamed General Howard and his XI Corps for much of the disaster that befell him at Chancellorsville, and Howard returned the dislike, which made things uncomfortable. But this tension paled in comparison to Hooker's relationship with Maj. Gen. Henry W. Slocum, the XII Corps commander. Like Howard, Slocum had led his corps at both Chancellorsville and Gettysburg. After the army's stinging defeat at the first battle, during which the XII Corps took heavy losses, Slocum began to agitate actively for Hooker's replacement. Perhaps no one in the Union army was more delighted than Slocum when Hooker resigned on the eve of Gettysburg. It was no surprise, then, on September 24, when Slocum learned that he was going to be sent west to Chattanooga as part of Hooker's command, that he immediately wrote a letter of resignation to President Lincoln. "Our relations are such," Slocum penned, "that it would be degrading [to me] if made to accept any position under him." Letter in hand, the general then immediately set out for Washington to deliver his missive in person.[10]

Curiously, Lincoln neither accepted that resignation nor offered Slocum an alternative. He did write to General Rosecrans, imploring that officer to transfer Slocum out from under Hooker's authority as soon as it could be arranged. Then, having dumped the problem on someone else's desk, the president sent Slocum back to the army.

Grant inherited this problem. Rosecrans, though reluctant to place a "Potomac general" in command of a corps of westerners, was in any case out of the picture before the matter could be resolved. On October 19 Slocum renewed his complaint, this time in a highly questionable message to Thomas, which that general then handed off to Grant soon after the latter's arrival in Chattanooga. Grant, clearly frustrated by the squabble, blamed both Hooker and Slocum for the unseemly dispute. In an October 29 wire, Charles Dana informed Stanton that "Hooker has behaved badly ever since his arrival, and Slocum has just sent in a very disorderly communication. ... Altogether, Gen. Grant feels that their presence here is replete with both trouble and danger." But feeling constrained by the fact that Hooker had been appointed directly by the president, Grant was loath to take matters into his own hands. He hoped that either Lincoln or the War Department would step in to resolve the matter, but nothing happened.[11]

Thomas's decision to leave one division of the XII Corps as a railroad guard offered a temporary solution. Slocum could be left behind in

Nashville to command the force assigned to that duty while Hooker and the rest of his command went on to Chattanooga. This arrangement made for minimal contact between the disgruntled subordinate and his equally unhappy superior, but even that limited exposure proved to be too much. Slocum's continued insubordination and barely concealed disdain for Hooker never abated. The problem would continue to irk Grant throughout the fall.

With combat in the offing, Howard and Hooker were able to at least temporarily shelve their differences. According to Howard, Hooker thought the new mission fraught with peril. Upon reaching Bridgeport, he conferred with Howard, who decades later recalled his commander's obvious apprehensions: "Why, Howard, Longstreet is up on that Lookout range with at least 10,000 fighting men. We will be obliged to make a flank march along the side and base of the mountain. I shall have scarcely so many men, and must take care of my trains. It is a very hazardous operation, and almost certain to procure us a defeat." He telegraphed similar thoughts to Thomas. Early the next morning, Dana informed Stanton that "Hooker . . . is in an unfortunate state of mind, . . . fault-finding, criticizing, [and] dissatisfied. . . . He is quite truculent toward the plan he is now to execute."[12]

Truculent or not, Hooker's column departed early on October 27. Already shorn of one division from the XII Corps, Hooker now shed additional regiments along the way to guard strategic locations in his immediate rear. It would do no good to merely traverse the country between Shellmound and Chattanooga; the Federals had to retain control of the entire route or no supplies could follow. As a result, Hooker's combat power diminished with each step eastward.

The head of the column halted that night at Whiteside, where a trestle and then a tunnel carried the Nashville & Chattanooga tracks first over Running Water Creek and then through part of Raccoon Mountain. Running Water Gorge, the passage between Raccoon and Sand Mountains, was narrow, the terrain surrounding it impressive—especially to these easterners, seeing such country for the first time. "It will always be a mystery," marveled Hartwell Osborn, an officer in the 55th Ohio, "why General Bragg did not occupy the terraces of Raccoon Mountain. It was the key to the situation, and had it been boldly occupied, the fate of the Army of the Cumberland would have been soon decided." Only a smattering of Rebel cavalry offered up any opposition, however, and were soon driven away. On the twenty-eighth the column debouched into Lookout Valley.[13]

For the most difficult mission, Grant turned to Baldy Smith. That general commanded the combined amphibious and bridging operation necessary to seize Brown's Ferry. Smith's force consisted of Brig. Gen. William B. Hazen's brigade, drawn from the IV Corps; together with Brig. Gen. John B. Turchin's brigade of the XIV Corps, augmented by the 18th Ohio, acting as pioneers; and, finally, Brig. Gen. Walter C. Whitaker's brigade, which was already garrisoning Moccasin Bend. Hazen's miniature fleet included fifty of the newly built pontoons and two flatboats, enough to transport 1,600 men. Once this flotilla landed at Brown's Ferry, the pontoons were to ferry over the rest of the infantry, then be assembled into the needed bridge. The remaining bridging elements were hauled overland overnight across Moccasin Bend to meet the naval component at dawn. It was a complex plan, with multiple moving parts, all of which had to come together at precisely the right time.[14]

The boats departed at 3:00 A.M. on October 27. Surg. Albert Hart of the 41st Ohio accompanied the flotilla. "It is a moonlight night, but fortunately cloudy, and we gladly see the fog, which hangs over the river. . . . [T]he dark shadow of the forest, skirting the . . . north bank of the river" also helped conceal the movement; the boats and crews would not be silhouetted as they drifted past enemy pickets. "We . . . descended nine miles by the river in just two hours." Then, "there is the sharp rattle of musketry as we turn towards the left bank."[15]

To the Federals' surprise and delight, they met only feeble resistance. The force defending Brown's Ferry amounted to only one-half of the 15th Alabama. Pvt. William C. Jordan of Company B recalled: "We had about half the regiment in picket on the river, our picket line was about ten miles long, from three to five men at a post, at intervals from two hundred to four hundred yards apart. . . . Five of the eleven companies . . . were on picket. Colonel [William C.] Oates had six companies in reserve with him, about a mile from us." The 15th belonged to Brig. Gen. Evander M. Law's brigade, but only it and the 4th Alabama were stationed west of Lookout Mountain; Law's other three regiments were farther east on the slopes of the mountain. It was a thin line with which to hold all of Lookout Valley, as even Private Jordan noted: "Surely a great mistake was made. . . . There should have been at least a division stationed in said territory."[16]

Of course, neither Ohioan Osborn nor Alabamian Jordan fully understood the limited nature of the Army of Tennessee's logistical capacity, which explains why no more than a handful of Confederates were stationed in Lookout Valley. There was also at least one additional complication contributing to the paucity of the Rebel defenses at Brown's Ferry. Problems of jealousy and command rivalry were not solely confined to the Federal army.

Lieutenant General Longstreet was charged with defending the Rebel left, which included Lookout Mountain and Lookout Valley. Longstreet, however, believed that the real threat would come from the south, expecting Hooker's column to ascend Lookout Mountain at Johnson's Crook, near Trenton, and then attack north along the crest. By doing so, the Federals could isolate any Rebels stationed west of the mountain. Bragg, with perhaps a better understanding of the logistical problems posed by this difficult terrain and having been forced to campaign in it for the past few months, felt that such a Union move was impractical. By late October, however, Longstreet had grown increasingly frustrated with his new commander in Chickamauga's aftermath and was paying very little attention to Bragg's opinions. He had joined an earlier effort by many of the Army of Tennessee's senior officers to remove the commanding general, and though the scheme failed, it left deep resentments unresolved. While a personal visit by Pres. Jefferson Davis papered over the rift, affairs were far from congenial within the army's senior ranks. Longstreet and Bragg now had as little as possible to do with each other.

A similar problem roiled the command structure in one of Longstreet's divisions. Maj. Gen. John Bell Hood had been badly wounded at Chickamauga and—assuming he lived—was likely to be promoted to corps command: both Longstreet and Bragg, who could agree on few things, recommended his promotion wholeheartedly. Either way, Hood's fate left permanent command of his division open. General Law temporarily had led the division in action when Hood fell wounded at Gettysburg and again at Chickamauga. Now Law wanted that job permanently, along with the promotion it entailed. Longstreet, however, favored another man for the job: Brig. Gen. Micah Jenkins of South Carolina. Jenkins was senior to Law by two months and, sensing a promotion opportunity, engineered a transfer into Hood's Division for just that reason. Law and Jenkins were not just contenders for the same promotion but also rivals from before the war. Law deeply resented being superseded.[17]

On October 25 Law took a short leave of absence to go and visit the badly wounded Hood, then recuperating at a private house in North Georgia, likely to petition for his support. Hood had initially supported him for the job, but now endorsed Jenkins once he was available. While Law was absent, Jenkins ordered the 44th, 47th, and 48th Alabama Regiments of Law's own brigade out of Lookout Valley and back east of the mountain into Chattanooga Valley. Law later believed that the move "was made 'without rhyme or reason.'" Jenkins, who was killed in action the next year, never offered an explanation, though the ongoing Confederate supply difficulties might have had something to do with the relocation. In any case, the move stripped 1,000 veteran Rebel infantrymen from Lookout Valley at exactly the worst possible time.[18]

Leading his six remaining companies, Colonel Oates attempted to counterattack at Brown's Ferry but was defeated handily; Oates himself fell wounded. The Federal assault force suffered four men killed and seventeen wounded, a far lower cost than anyone expected. By dawn on October 27, Brown's Ferry was secure, and the pontoniers were hard at work. "By ten o'clock the bridge was laid," recalled Grant, delighted at the ease of the victory, "and our extreme right, now in Lookout Valley, was fortified and connected with the rest of the army."[19]

Hooker's column departed Whiteside at 4:00 A.M. on the twenty-eighth, marching first for Wauhatchie Junction, where the Nashville & Chattanooga tracks joined a spur line from Trenton, before angling northeast around the face of Lookout Mountain. Howard's XI Corps led the way. Col. Adin B. Underwood of the 33rd Massachusetts recalled emerging from the folds of Raccoon Mountain to catch the first glimpse of "old Lookout . . . looking down from his couple of thousand feet of crag. . . . Somebody else had their eyes upon [our] column too," he noted, "masses of little Lilliputians . . . eyeing with their telescopes the strange Potomac banners . . . and reporting with their miniature signal flags particulars about [our] movements."[20]

The New Englanders' appearance drew more attention than telescopes and signal traffic; very soon artillery rounds began to drop onto the XI Corps men from the far-off crest. That long-range fire was ineffective since the distance was too great and the elevation too high for accurate gunnery, but it did serve notice that the Confederates would contest control of the valley below.

Both Bragg and Longstreet were among the Confederates watching Hooker's progress. On the morning of October 28, Bragg elected to pay a personal visit to Longstreet after a day's worth of unsatisfactory correspondence between the two generals on the twenty-seventh. Upon hearing word of the Union crossing at Brown's Ferry, he ordered Longstreet to counterattack immediately. Longstreet demurred, still insistent that the real threat was a move against his rear via Trenton and Johnson's Crook. The more of his command placed in Lookout Valley, therefore, the more forces he would expose to isolation and capture. And, as Longstreet again explained, the men in his corps "have such indifferent transportation that [they] will not be able to subsist . . . so far off." When he first received word of Hooker's movements on the twenty-seventh, Longstreet interpreted the Federals as heading to Trenton, just as he feared. Given the apparent conflict between the two Confederate generals over how to best defend Lookout Mountain, Longstreet requested, "I would like the commanding general to give me the benefit of his views in more detail." Bragg now intended to do exactly that.[21]

While the two men were observing the Union bridgehead at Brown's Ferry, Confederate signalmen drew their attention to Hooker's column, which hove into view sometime that afternoon. Longstreet estimated the Federal strength at 5,000 troops; Bragg, somewhat less. This was the XI Corps. It was followed shortly by another 1,500 men—Geary's division of the XII Corps—acting as rear guard. The head of the column joined the Union defenders around Brown's Ferry around 5:00 P.M. Yet both Bragg and Longstreet were surprised to see the rear-guard halt around 4:30 at the rail junction of Wauhatchie, a couple of miles short of the Brown's Ferry defenses, and prepare their own camp.[22]

Bragg's views were simple: he ordered Longstreet to attack and destroy the Union bridgehead, using up to four divisions (Longstreet's own corps plus Major General Breckinridge's division) to do so. For good reasons, Longstreet believed this to be impractical. Passing four divisions over the face of Lookout Mountain on a road that could only be used after dark due to enemy artillery interdiction would take a long time—certainly more than a single night. Nor would that movement go unnoticed by the Federals, who would have plenty of time to respond. It also bears repeating that even a portion of such a large force could not be supplied in Lookout Valley while waiting for everyone to arrive. The orders were logistically impossible, a fact to which Bragg remained oblivious throughout this entire period. Instead, Longstreet decided to use just one division (Law's) to strike the exposed rear guard at Wauhatchie and to do so in that rarest of Civil War actions, a night attack.

To some observers, Hooker's decision to halt Geary three miles short of Brown's Ferry appeared overconfident, perhaps even foolhardy. But that decision was made for Hooker, not by him. Thomas's orders instructed him to "command the road from Kelley's Ferry to Brown's Ferry," which required some sort of force at Wauhatchie. Grant was focused on getting "the steamer Paint Rock [and her cargo of rations] . . . down to Brown's Ferry" not later than October 29, "even if a house has to be torn down to provide the necessary fuel." He also voiced another concern: "there is every probability that the enemy will make every preparation possible . . . to prevent our accomplishing this." This meant that some force must be left at Wauhatchie to guard the road back through Running Water Gorge to Kelley's Ferry.[23]

By the evening of October 28, Grant had every reason to be satisfied with the resupply operation. Both the crossing and the link-up were completed successfully and with minimal loss. At 8:00 P.M. he informed General Halleck that "Gen Thomas' plan for securing the river and south side road hence to Bridgeport has proven imminently successful. The question of supplies may now be regarded as settled." Already he was thinking aggressively. "If the rebels give us one week more time I think all danger of losing territory . . . will have passed away, and preparations may commence for offensive operations." Dana, who accompanied Hooker on the march, made his way into Chattanooga to send his own assessment direct to Secretary of War Stanton: "Everything perfectly successful. The river is now open, and a short and good road in our possession along the south shore. . . . The great success, however, is General Smith's operation at the mouth of Lookout Valley. Its brilliancy cannot be exaggerated."[24]

Officers on the ground were less sanguine. Both Smith and especially Hazen grew alarmed at Hooker's seeming nonchalance, urging him to deploy Howard's men more effectively and do something about Geary's exposed rear guard. Smith even argued his case personally with Major General Reynolds (the Army of the Cumberland's chief of staff) only to discover later that he had not relayed these concerns up the chain of command to Thomas. Gloomily, Smith recalled, "I did not doubt that an attack would be made on Hooker that night and if he was beaten we would lose all we had gained." Dana, already no fan of Hooker's, informed Washington that "Hazen . . . went to . . . Hooker and endeavored to get him to take up a compact line . . . and bring all his forces together. But being confident the enemy would not disturb him, Hooker refused to change his dispositions."[25]

The Confederates were planning an attack. After all, Bragg had ordered one. Longstreet, however, was equally gloomy about the outcome;

he settled on a plan to attack only Geary, not the larger Union force now at the bridgehead. He sent just Hood's Division, under Jenkins, since one of its brigades was already on the west side of Lookout Mountain.

Near dark, Jenkins met with Law and explained that the purpose of the operation was "to cut off the enemy's trains and capture the rear guard." Law's mission was to take two brigades—his own command and the Texas Brigade, commanded by Brig. Gen. Jerome B. Robertson—to a position where he could block the Brown's Ferry road, thus ensuring that neither Howard's XI Corps nor any of the troops defending the bridgehead could interfere. Jenkins also intended to leave Brig. Gen. Henry L. Benning's Georgia brigade on a hill to protect his line of retreat over Lookout Creek, which left only his own brigade of South Carolinians, under Col. John Bratton, available to attack Geary. Law thought the whole operation was too dangerous, but Jenkins insisted he had "positive orders" from Longstreet.[26]

Ironically, by the time Bratton finally attacked shortly after midnight, Longstreet himself was having second thoughts. Jenkins's men took so long crossing Lookout Mountain that Longstreet, who feared that his troops would be stuck on the wrong side of the mountain "during daylight," called off the operation, an order that reached Jenkins too late to halt Bratton. The resulting action at Wauhatchie was intense, bloody, and marked by severe confusion, the last characteristic being hardly unusual for a nighttime assault. The Federals repulsed Bratton's South Carolinians after some desperate fighting, during which Geary's son Edward was killed. Geary suffered 216 casualties, while Bratton lost about 400 men, roughly a quarter of his engaged force, before other events forced Jenkins to order a recall.[27]

When the firing began, Hooker ordered the XI Corps into action. Two surprising results came of this move: a successful nighttime assault and a court of inquiry. While marching south along the Brown's Ferry road, the Federals bumped into skirmishers from Law's two brigades, and elements of the XI Corps immediately faced eastward to deal with that threat. Two regiments, the 33rd Massachusetts and 73rd Ohio, moved against Law's Texans and Alabamians, perched on a hill (afterward known as Smith's Hill after Union colonel Orland Smith, whose brigade assaulted the position) overlooking the road. Charging uphill in the dark against a numerically superior foe was usually a recipe for disaster, and it was almost so this time; the men of the 33rd Massachusetts, who made the first effort, were staggered by a defensive volley. Regrouping however, they and the

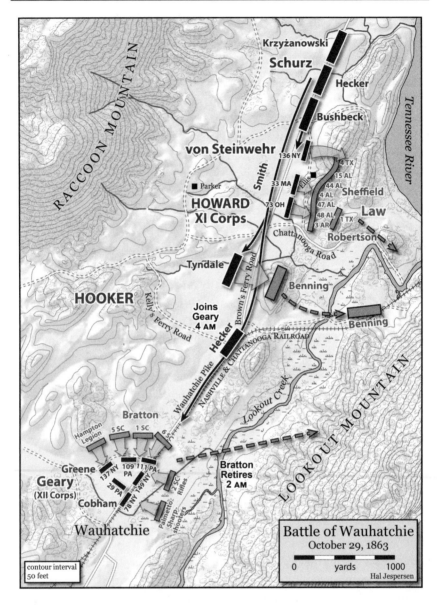

Battle of Wauhatchie
October 29, 1863

contour interval
50 feet

0   yards   1000
Hal Jespersen

Ohioans surged up the slope and effectively routed both the Texans and Alabamians. Their retreat prompted Jenkins to recall Bratton.[28]

The court of inquiry arose later. Excited, Hooker had bypassed Howard and the XI Corps chain of command to issue orders directly to divisional commander Maj. Gen. Carl Schurz, which did more to confuse things than set them in motion. In his report of the affair, Hooker accused Schurz of not responding promptly to the crisis, since no elements of the XI Corps reached Geary until near dawn, well after the fighting concluded. The court found this accusation to be groundless. Doubtless embarrassed by being caught unprepared, Hooker needed someone to blame for something, but his reckless accusation only further embittered him to the men of the XI Corps.[29]

Though he expected little—he had, after all, tried to call off the attack about an hour before it began—Longstreet was disappointed by the night's performance. He blamed Law for retreating so precipitously and hinted at a failure of leadership. "As General Law's troops were veterans, I can only attribute the want of conduct with his troops to a strong feeling of jealousy among the brigadier-generals." For his part, Bragg was now so thoroughly disillusioned with Longstreet that he wanted nothing less than to see the other man gone from his army.[30]

4

"RECOLLECT THAT EAST TENNESSEE IS MY HORROR"

*T*hat part of the Great Appalachian Valley known as East Tennessee, with its cultural and economic center at Knoxville, was never far from President Lincoln's thoughts. This was almost equally true for his Confederate counterpart, Jefferson Davis. For Lincoln, the region represented a part of the South that rejected secession, remaining loyal to the old flag. For the Confederacy, East Tennessee represented vital geography, connecting the war's eastern and western theaters via rails running from Lynchburg, Virginia, to Chattanooga. Thousands of troops and vital supplies flowed eastward to feed the Confederate war effort in Virginia. The railroad company that operated between Bristol, Tennessee, and Lynchburg reported moving an astounding 40 million pounds of foodstuffs in 1862, then more than 25 million pounds in the first eight months of 1863 until Major General Burnside's troops interdicted that flow by occupying Knoxville in early September. The loss of this route badly damaged the southern war effort, reflected in the decline in west–east traffic to less than 11 million pounds over that same stretch of road during all of 1864.[1]

Yet East Tennessee was also a hotbed of Unionist sentiment. Home to only a small number of slaveholders, enthusiasm for secession was largely absent in this portion of the South. One of President Davis's earliest internal crises came in the form of a coordinated assault on the rail bridges traversing the region, a series of guerrilla attacks orchestrated by pro-Union residents in the fall of 1861. The uprising was meant to trigger an early Union occupation of the area. On the night of November 8, the "Bridge Burners" destroyed or damaged six of the nine targeted spans. But despite their efforts, no Union advance into the region was forthcoming. The Confederacy responded harshly with arrests and hangings.[2]

The man responsible for that lack of Federal response was Brig. Gen. William T. Sherman, commanding the Department of the Cumberland, then headquartered at Louisville, Kentucky. Sherman, new to his command and feeling very outnumbered in 1861, suffered a crisis of confidence that fall. Just a few weeks before the Bridge Burners struck, Sherman informed then–Secretary of War Simon Cameron that he would need 60,000 men just to secure Kentucky and at least 200,000 troops to undertake any offensive. Though events would eventually bear out his assessment, at the time Sherman was ridiculed and called crazy for making such preposterous estimates. That fall, he saw no way of sending Union forces into East Tennessee, though he felt personally responsible for the hanged guerrillas. "That the men . . . suffered death has been the chief source of my despondency," Sherman later admitted to his brother (and U.S. senator) John; the executions "weighed on me so that I felt unequal to the burden." Nevertheless, Sherman never viewed East Tennessee as anything but a strategic blind alley for Union forces. Even two years later, wrote Sherman to Grant: "Recollect that East Tennessee is my horror. That any military man should send a force into East Tennessee puzzles me."[3]

Deeply disappointed, President Lincoln replaced Sherman with Major General Buell (himself later replaced by Rosecrans) on November 15, 1861, and reiterated the strong imperative to send forces into East Tennessee. Not only did Lincoln wish to succor the region from reprisal and sever a critical Confederate lifeline, but he also saw East Tennessee as a fertile source of recruits—as indeed it was. Over the next couple of years, tens of thousands of Tennesseans joined Federal armies in the West. Lincoln also saw the area as an early testbed for reconstruction efforts. As such, it remained an important Union objective throughout 1862 and 1863. Thus, when the first of Burnside's men finally entered Knoxville at 4:00 P.M. on September 1, 1863, "the loyalists in town . . . [went] wild with joy. . . . [T]he merry-making continued into the night."[4]

From his perch in East Tennessee, Burnside had no rail connection to any Union supply base, at least not until the Federals rebuilt the bridge over the Tennessee River at Bridgeport, reestablished a rail connection between Nashville and Chattanooga, and restored the rail lines from Chattanooga to Knoxville. Until all of that happened, for sustenance he had to rely on local resources and supplies hauled by wagon from Crab Orchard, Kentucky, approximately 150 miles away through the mountains via the Cumberland Gap. Even for Burnside's small force of about 26,000 men, it was a precarious lifeline. When Rosecrans was defeated at Chickamauga, the Union hold on East Tennessee suddenly seemed very tenuous indeed.

If East Tennessee and Knoxville were important to Lincoln, then they were important to Grant. His mission was not just to relieve Chattanooga but to defeat Bragg and ensure that East Tennessee remained in Union hands. As a result, Grant updated Burnside constantly. At 11:30 P.M. on October 28, after the successful arrival of Hooker's column (but before the fight at Wauhatchie), he outlined his current thinking. "I would like if you [Burnside] could [hold] the line of the Hiawassie [River]. It is particularly desirable that all the territory you now have should be held, but if any portion must be given up, let it be to the east, and keep your Army so that it and Thomas['s] Army can support each other. . . . Thomas is in no condition to move from his present position," Grant admitted. But now that the supply line was restored, he reassured Burnside, "it is to be hoped that with this line open and Sherman up here . . . Thomas will be able to place one division at McMinnville [Tennessee] and the remainder of the corps between here and you." On the morning of October 30, Grant further assured Halleck that as "soon as supplies reach us I will turn my attention to destroying all chance of the Enemy's attacking Burnside from the south west."[5]

Grant had reason to be concerned, for President Davis was also thinking about East Tennessee. In early October 1863 General Bragg dispatched 10,000 men to the region. These two divisions were under the overall command of Maj. Gen. Carter L. Stevenson, who had been released from his Vicksburg parole in late September to join Bragg's army. Stevenson's force was concentrated near the small town of Athens, about fifteen miles northeast of Charleston, Tennessee, and already across the Hiwassee River. Their presence ensured that Burnside could not hold the line of that river, especially since he could not concentrate his whole force against this threat. Only about 10,000 of his men faced Stevenson at this time. Another 9,000 Federals defended against a potential Rebel approach from southwestern Virginia, while 2,000 more troops garrisoned the vital Cumberland Gap, leaving a small reserve of about 5,000 men grouped around Knoxville.[6]

Grant later recalled that Stevenson's "presence there . . . alarmed the authorities at Washington, and, on account of our helpless condition at Chattanooga, caused me much uneasiness." Indeed, Lincoln and Stanton were troubled by this. "Dispatches were constantly coming, urging me to do something for Burnside's relief; calling attention to the importance of holding East Tennessee; saying the President was much concerned for the protection of the loyal people . . . , etc." Grant found he could do little, at least in the short term. "We had not at Chattanooga animals to pull a single piece of artillery, much less a supply train. Reinforcements could not help

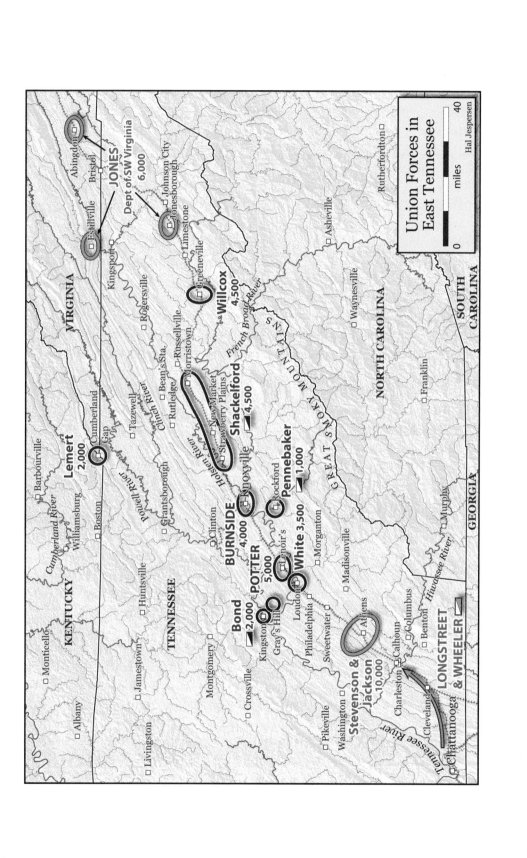

Union Forces in
East Tennessee

Hal Jespersen

miles
0   40

JONES
Dept. of SW Virginia
6,000

Abingdon
Bristol
Estillville
Kingsport
Johnson City
Jonesborough
Limestone

VIRGINIA

Greeneville

Willcox
4,500

French Broad River

Cumberland
Gap

Lemert
2,000

Barbourville
Williamsburg
Boston

Cumberland River

Tazewell
Clinch River
Bean's Sta.
Rutledge
Rogersville
Russellville
Morristown

New Market
Strawberry Plains

Shackelford
4,500

Powell River

Grantsborough

Clinton

Holston River

Knoxville

Rockford

Pennebaker
1,000

GREAT SMOKY MOUNTAINS

BURNSIDE
4,000

Huntsville

KENTUCKY

Monticello
Albany
Jamestown
Livingston

TENNESSEE

Montgomery
Crossville
Pikeville
Washington

Kingston
Gray's Hill

Bond
2,000

POTTER
5,000

Lenoir's
Loudon

White 3,500

Philadelphia
Sweetwater

Madisonville

Morganton

Asheville

Waynesville

NORTH CAROLINA

Franklin

Rutherfordton

SOUTH
CAROLINA

Athens

Stevenson &
Jackson
10,000

Charleston
Calhoun
Columbus
Benton
Hiwassee River
Murphy

GEORGIA

Cleveland

LONGSTREET
& WHEELER

Chattanooga

Tennessee River

Burnside, because he had neither supplies nor ammunition sufficient for them.... There was no relief possible," he concluded, "except by expelling the enemy from Missionary Ridge and about Chattanooga."[7]

Though neither general intended it except as a last resort, both Grant and Burnside discussed the possibility of retreat from the region. As an alternative to the lengthy supply line up into Kentucky, Grant suggested switching to a new a route originating from McMinnville, Tennessee— where a spur of the Nashville & Chattanooga Railroad terminated—to Kingston, Tennessee, at the junction of the Tennessee and Clinch Rivers. The distance from McMinnville to Kingston was about ninety miles. Kingston was another thirty-five miles from Knoxville, but for that leg Burnside could rely on a small amount of river transport at hand and a functioning local rail line from Knoxville to Loudon, upstream from Kingston. At worst, Grant suggested, if Burnside had to retreat, he should do so via Kingston, "which should be held if you have to concentrate all your force there. Should the enemy break through below Kingston [between that town and the Hiwassee] move in force to Sparta and McMinnville." General Thomas offered the opinion that if a Rebel offensive was in the offing, such as occurred in 1862 when Bragg invaded Kentucky, by holding Kingston Burnside would "force the enemy to march for Kentucky via Cumberland Gap[.] In the mean time," he continued, the Federals should "send two divisions of Sherman's corps by rail" to a point on the Cumberland east of Nashville "to intercept his farther advance." Thus, thought Thomas, "Burnside would be on the enemy's flank, and the forces here [in Chattanooga] so far in his rear that he could not hope to escape."[8]

Few generals were as offensively minded as Grant, and it galled him to think strictly of defense. Not surprisingly, on November 3 he wired Burnside to propose a more aggressive gambit: a cavalry raid from East Tennessee into Georgia aimed at Bragg's lifeline, the Western & Atlantic. "What condition is your cavalry in . . . ? Have you the right sort of commander . . . for such an expedition?" If not, Grant proposed sending another trusted subordinate, Maj. Gen. William Sooy Smith, or alternatively, Lieutenant Colonel Wilson, assuming he was promoted as Grant had already requested. Burnside was amenable. Even though his "cavalry [was] much broken down," he felt he could organize "twelve to fifteen hundred men." As for leading such a raid, Grant need have no worries: Burnside assured him, "I have some first rate cavalry commanders." He also noted that he had offered to make just such a raid back in September, but the idea was quashed by Halleck.[9]

In proposing this mission Grant no doubt recalled the success Col. Benjamin Grierson achieved during the Vicksburg Campaign. This time, however, the circumstances of such a raid would be considerably different. Grierson had traversed the length of Mississippi, but he did so in conjunction with the rest of Grant's army moving at the same time and had a Union-held city—Baton Rouge—as his ending point. Burnside's men would have no such advantages. Col. Abel Streight and 1,500 men had tried a similar effort against the Western & Atlantic in May, only to be captured entirely, which seemed a likely outcome for any effort Burnside might have mounted that November. Given these concerns, the idea came to naught.

While the Federals might fret about another invasion of Kentucky, and certainly feared a strike at Burnside, Bragg lacked the logistics to make all but the smallest of those fears real. Moreover, he had internal problems to address.

The Confederate failures in Lookout Valley capped a month of military discord within the Army of Tennessee. In the wake of the successful (but extremely bloody) Battle of Chickamauga, many of Bragg's subordinates had grown increasingly discontented with his leadership—or the lack thereof. Longstanding quarrels between Bragg and many of his subordinates came to a head. He relieved both Lt. Gen. Leonidas Polk and Maj. Gen. Thomas C. Hindman from command, intending to court-martial them for insubordination during the Chickamauga Campaign, and expressed profound disappointment with several other senior officers. In early October a de-facto mutiny emerged when a number of the army's generals signed a secret letter addressed to President Davis petitioning for Bragg's removal. Corps commanders Longstreet and Lt. Gen. Daniel H. Hill both signed the petition, along with several divisional and brigade commanders. Polk, absent in Atlanta, did not sign, but he sent a separate communication directly to the president urging Bragg's replacement. The crisis forced Davis to pay a personal visit to the troubled command. Ultimately, Davis brokered an arrangement allowing Polk to leave the army to assume a new command in Mississippi, replacing him with Lt. Gen. William J. Hardee, and agreed to remove Hill. Though Bragg eschewed charging Hill with any formal wrongdoing, Hill was relieved of command and sent back east to await orders. Ironically, he had come west in July to replace

Hardee, who, equally disgusted with Bragg from earlier campaigns, had been transferred to the Mississippi command that was now given to Polk. To make matters worse, Hill's replacement was Major General Breckinridge, who had his own longstanding disagreements with Bragg. Of the five men who had commanded Confederate infantry corps at Chickamauga, only Longstreet now remained, the others being transferred, demoted, or relieved. The Georgian's prestige and his recent success at Chickamauga meant that Bragg could find little excuse to remove Longstreet, but any admiration the commanding general felt for the other man had long since turned to animosity.[10]

Longstreet's failure to prevent the opening of the Cracker Line only increased Bragg's dissatisfaction with the once-vaunted arrival from the Army of Northern Virginia, and he now saw a way to rid himself of that problem as well. On October 29, while in Atlanta, President Davis heard the news that Hooker had crossed the Tennessee. He sent Bragg a lengthy missive urging him to attack Hooker or move directly against Bridgeport. If quick results could not be had there, however, Davis suggested an alternative: "It has occurred to me that if the operations on your left should be delayed . . . that you might advantageously assign Genl. Longstreet with his two divisions to the task of expelling Burnside, and thus place him in position, according to circumstances, to hasten or delay his return to the army of Genl. Lee."[11]

Clearing East Tennessee of Federals and ridding himself of Longstreet at the same time sounded good to Bragg. For Davis, returning Longstreet's men to Lee's badly outnumbered command in Virginia was equally desirable. Nor did it seem like anything further would be accomplished in Lookout Valley. On October 31 Bragg ordered Longstreet, Hardee (newly arrived to take over Polk's corps) and Breckinridge (now commanding Hill's old corps) "to examine this position with a view to a general battle." All agreed that a major counterattack in the valley was out of the question. "The only route by which our troops could reach the field was a difficult mountain road, only practicable for infantry and entirely exposed to the enemy's batteries" on Moccasin Bend. "Our position was so faulty," concluded Longstreet gloomily, "that we could not accomplish that which was hoped for."[12]

Worse yet, as noted earlier, sustaining a large force west of Lookout Mountain for any length of time was simply not possible. Even the limited Confederate forces already there found it difficult to subsist. Until

November 4 Lt. George Knox Miller of the 8th Confederate Cavalry was stationed at Trenton, Georgia, keeping an eye on Federal movements. An educated Alabama lawyer who attended the University of Virginia, Miller described Trenton as "of all places the one I wished to see less. Just picture to yourself a high range of mountains on each side, almost within speaking distance and a miserable, sterile valley between, poor in its palmiest days, but now a barren waste from the ravages of two armies.... How long we will remain here I have no idea, but from the scarcity of subsistence for both man and horse I predict that our stay will be necessarily limited."[13]

On November 3 Bragg, Longstreet, Hardee, and Breckinridge all met to discuss their options. After agreeing that any strike at Bridgeport was logistically impossible, talk turned to East Tennessee. Since November 1, when Longstreet first got wind of Davis's suggestion, he had been working on a plan. He wanted to take his two divisions, unite them with Stevenson's command, and then strike for Knoxville. Stevenson reported that Burnside had only 23,000 men in all of East Tennessee—not a bad assessment of the actual Union strength—and Longstreet reasoned that with a combined force of 20,000 Rebels, he could defeat Burnside in detail. To prevent the Federals from capitalizing on his absence, he also suggested that the remainder of the Army of Tennessee abandon its siege lines around Chattanooga and fall back to a more defensible position "behind the Chickamauga." Once Burnside was defeated, Longstreet offered that he could "retire to meet the enemy at Chattanooga, or, better, to operate rapidly against his rear and flank."[14]

Bragg agreed with all except the idea to fall back behind Chickamauga Creek. Any retreat would be viewed as failure, and any failure he could ill afford. The next day Bragg ordered Longstreet to move, augmenting his force with Major General Wheeler's cavalry corps, some 4,000 men. "The success of the plan depends upon rapid movements and sudden blows. ... Your object should be to drive Burnside out of East Tennessee first, or better, to capture or destroy him." Yet Bragg cautioned that Longstreet must also "see to the repair and regular use of [the] railroad.... The latter is of the first importance, as it may become necessary in an emergency to recall you temporarily."[15]

Of course, these orders were inherently contradictory. Longstreet could not make "rapid movements" and strike "sudden blows" while at the same time repairing the railroad, all of which he pointed out to Bragg. Worse yet, on November 5 he discovered that Bragg intended to recall Stevenson once Longstreet reached East Tennessee, leaving him with only about half the force he was counting on. Longstreet immediately protested these new developments: "If I am to move along the line of the railroad," he wrote, "it is not at all probable that I shall even overtake the enemy." As for recalling Stevenson, "I think you greatly overestimate the enemy's force . . . around Chattanooga. . . . I . . . cannot think it exceeds your force without Stevenson's division." Furthermore, thought Longstreet, the Army of the Cumberland was still enfeebled from the recent defeat at Chickamauga and living on half rations for a month. The real danger, he thought, was not sending sufficient strength into East Tennessee from the start. "If I am [outnumbered] my movements must be slow and cautious. This would give the enemy warning and time to strike at you." Bragg would hear none of it.[16]

In the days after the fight in Lookout Valley, General Grant spent time inspecting the rest of the Union line. East of Lookout Mountain, Union and Confederate pickets were separated by Chattanooga Creek, swollen from the recent rains. Grant recollected that he took no escort on these jaunts, only "a bugler, who stayed some distance to the rear." The new Federal commander soon discovered that "the most friendly relations seemed to exist between the pickets of the two armies." He approached a man in blue, drawing water from the creek from the perch of a fallen tree that bridged the stream. "I rode up to him," wrote Grant, "commenced conversing with him, and asked whose corps he belonged to. He was very polite, and touching his hat to me, said he belonged to General Longstreet's corps. I asked him a few questions—but not with a view of gaining any particular information—all of which he answered, and I rode off."[17]

Within days that anonymous Rebel was gone from the Chattanooga front, headed to East Tennessee with the rest of Longstreet's command. Such a move, of course, was one of the things Grant feared the most. In his memoirs he recalled that the departure occurred on November 4, though in reality Longstreet's men did not start disengaging until that night, the pickets remaining in place until at least the fifth. "The situation seemed desperate," Grant recalled, "and was more aggravating because nothing could be done until Sherman should get up." Still, *something* must be done. On November 7, despite the Army of the Cumberland's myriad problems, he "ordered Thomas to peremptorily attack the enemy's right, so as to force the return of [Longstreet's] troops."[18]

The genesis of this order could be found in a much more limited move proposed by Baldy Smith on November 5, hoping for a similar result. Smith suggested advancing the Union picket line "about a mile" to Citico Creek "to threaten the seizure of the northwest extremity of Missionary Ridge." He believed that this move, along with the army's "present demonstration in Lookout Valley, will compel [Bragg] to concentrate and come back from Burnside to fight here."[19]

Grant's November 7 order followed. Not content with a mere demonstration, he ordered Thomas to attack "the northern end of Missionary Ridge, with all the force you can bring to bear against it, and when that is carried, to threaten, and even attack, if possible, the enemy's line of communications between Dalton and Cleveland." The order was emphatic: "Where there are not horses to move the artillery, mules must be taken from the teams or horses from ambulances; or, if necessary, officers dismounted and their horses taken. . . . The movement should not be made one moment later than tomorrow morning." With a nod toward Thomas's much greater understanding of the terrain, he concluded that "the details are left to you." As Smith later observed, this order was far more ambitious than his own proposal.[20]

According to an article Smith penned for *Century Magazine* in the 1880s, "the order staggered Thomas." Smith, equally alarmed, later recalled, "after the order had been issued I sought a conversation with General Grant for the purpose of inducing a modification, and began by asking General Grant what was the plan proposed by Thomas for carrying out the order. To this General Grant replied, '*When I have sufficient confidence in a general to leave him in command of an army, I have enough confidence in him to leave his plans to himself.*' This answer seemed to cut off all discussion."[21]

The answer dismayed Smith. In an 1894 account of his time in Chattanooga, he recollected that "the whole idea seem[ed] to have a crudeness entirely out of place in the mind of a general commanding an army," and it "did not accord with my idea of what a great captain would do." As for Thomas, "he seemed very much disturbed." Smith also related that the burly Virginian told him, "you must get that order for an advance countermanded; I shall lose my army." Smith hastened to assure Thomas that this newly expanded offensive was not his doing and suggested that they undertake a more in-depth reconnaissance. Thomas agreed, and along with Brig. Gen. John Brannan (the Army of the Cumberland's chief of artillery, formerly a division commander in the XIV Corps), the men rode to a hill overlooking the northern end of Missionary Ridge. There, according to

Smith, "we satisfied ourselves that Bragg extended too far north for Thomas to hope to outflank him." When he returned that evening to inform Grant that "it was impossible for Thomas to attack . . . with the force he then had; and that everything must wait for Sherman[,] General Grant at once countermanded the order."[22]

At 10:00 A.M. on November 7, Assistant Secretary Dana provided a contemporary view of the proposed movement in one of his daily updates. He informed Secretary of War Stanton that just that morning, "Grant had ordered Thomas to execute the movement on Citico Creek . . . as proposed by Smith. Thomas, who rather preferred an attempt on Lookout Mountain, desired to postpone the operation until Sherman could come up, but Grant has decided that for the sake of Burnside the attack must be made at once; and I presume the advance on Citico will take place tomorrow morning." At 11:00 A.M. on the eighth, Dana reported the cancellation: "Reconnaissance of Citico Creek and head of Missionary Ridge made yesterday by Thomas, Smith, and Brannan . . . proved *Smith's* [emphasis added] plan of attack impractical. The creek and country are wrongly laid down on our maps, and no operation for the seizure of Missionary Ridge can be undertaken with the force which Thomas can now command for the purpose."[23]

While the Army of the Cumberland's lack of healthy horseflesh was a crippling impediment, Thomas also remained concerned with the situation in Lookout Valley. Yes, supplies were getting through and the condition of the army was improving, but the general was not one to neglect details out of complacency. Previously, on November 5, Thomas had crossed Moccasin Bend and ridden over the bridge at Brown's Ferry to inspect newly established Union positions in the valley. He was not pleased with what he saw, as relayed by yet another of Dana's informative dispatches. "Lines very negligently placed," complained Dana, "and work on rifle pits badly done. Apparently this is the first time Howard has ridden the lines of his [XI] corps. Hooker seems to pay little attention to his duties."[24]

For Thomas, the problem was more fundamental than one of inattentive commanders. Work on restoring rail communications into Chattanooga could not begin until Lookout Mountain was wrested from the Rebels. Better still, if the Federals took control of the mountain, not only could that work begin but also the Union defensive lines would be considerably shortened, freeing up many more troops for offensive action. "Thomas," argued biographer Francis F. McKinney, "expected [Hooker's] operation to give him control of the railway and wagon road from Bridgeport to Chattanooga. When it failed to do so it became a makeshift substitute rather than a remedy for [Thomas's] ruptured supply line. Grant was satisfied with the makeshift but Thomas felt that the railway and wagon road should be made secure by breaking the Rebel grip on Lookout Mountain" once and for all.[25]

This fundamental disagreement over strategy was never really resolved. In his official report Grant merely reported that he was forced to cancel the November 7 attack because "it was deemed utterly impractical to make the move until Sherman could get up," citing both "the inadequacy of our forces and the condition of the animals." Thus, claimed Grant, "I was forced to leave Burnside for the present to contend against superior forces of the enemy."[26]

Privately, he was unhappy for the lack of action and blamed Thomas. In his memoirs Grant recollected that the general "persisted in the declaration that he could not move a single piece of artillery, and could not see how he could possibly comply with the order." Grant made no mention of misleading maps, difficult terrain, or the lack of available forces for the mission. In their massive history of President Lincoln, presidential aides and confidantes John G. Nicolay and John Hay asserted that Grant "never thoroughly forgave General Thomas for this difference of opinion." Though Thomas died in 1870, leaving no memoir or other public utterances, former comrades rallied to his posthumous defense, which helped fuel accounts of the grudge between the two men—real or imagined—well into the postwar decades.[27]

Longstreet's lunge against Burnside stumbled from the beginning. The Army of Tennessee's logistics were so broken that it took his 10,000 men more than a week to move sixty miles to Sweetwater, Tennessee—and that was with what passed for a working railroad to that point. The Federals were unaware of those difficulties, so much so that in his memoir Grant merely noted that "Longstreet, for some reason or other, stopped at Loudon until the 13th. . . . [I]t was probable he was directed to remain there awaiting orders." In reality Longstreet's halt was a logistical necessity. He was crippled by lack of supply wagons, by a barely functioning rail line, and by the failure of Bragg's quartermasters to gather supplies at Loudon in anticipation of his arrival. As a result the correspondence between Bragg and Longstreet soured to the point where they exchanged little but mutual recriminations. Col. George Brent, a staff officer at Bragg's headquarters, thought that Longstreet "looks as if he were preparing for a failure and seeking in advance grounds for an excuse." In reality Bragg and his staff had done almost nothing to ensure his success.[28]

Open hostility from Bragg's headquarters did nothing to mitigate the very real challenges Longstreet's men faced in East Tennessee. Those challenges all but guaranteed that, far from conducting a lightning campaign, Longstreet would be forced to move slowly and ponderously, giving Burnside plenty of time to consolidate his own forces and react effectively. The Confederate column did not even have a pontoon train to carry on the march, which greatly limited the options for advance. Instead of moving along the south bank of the Tennessee and crossing somewhere closer to Knoxville, Longstreet could only affect a crossing close to Loudon. Individual pontoon boats had to be hauled on railcars to the destroyed rail bridge, slid down the bank into the river, and then floated to the chosen crossing site. Leading elements of Longstreet's command crossed the Tennessee on the night of November 12 and threw up a bridge on the morning of the thirteenth. The resulting span was so rickety, however, that staff officer Moxley Sorrel described it as forming "a huge letter 'S,'" bowed by the current.[29]

Six more days were consumed before Longstreet's forces reached the outskirts of Knoxville. The Federals fought a series of delaying actions along the way, the largest of which was a spirited fight at Campbell's Station on November 16. Longstreet's effort to cut off the retreating Yankees at this place floundered amid a cold, driving rain and the failure of his two key subordinates—Maj. Gen. Lafayette McLaws and Brigadier General Jenkins, each leading a division—to coordinate effectively. General Wheeler led 3,000 Confederate horsemen on a rapid strike upstream along the south bank of the Tennessee River to try and seize Knoxville while Burnside was busy with Longstreet. Although his horsemen reached the river bank opposite the city on the sixteenth, they were unable to overwhelm the local Union garrison defending that approach, much less enter the city. Wheeler fell back to rejoin Longstreet's infantry that same day. On November 19, with his 13,000 men facing 12,000 Federal defenders well entrenched behind Knoxville's extensive earthen fortifications, Longstreet paused. He would try and lay siege to the city as best he could, but he had far too few troops to fully isolate Burnside's command.[30]

With nothing more he could do but await Sherman and watch developments, Grant grew increasingly agitated. Throughout his military career, when faced with moments of crisis, the general developed a reputation for external calm. His demeanor the night after the first day of the Battle of Shiloh and his whittling during the Battle of the Wilderness have both been used often as examples of Grant's sangfroid, even if he also sometimes displayed signs of tension. In each case, however, his fate was ultimately in his own hands. At Knoxville, in contrast, his fate lay with others, and that fact very much wore on Grant. In November that frustration boiled over.

One who experienced Grant's temper was Maj. Gen. Orlando B. Willcox. On November 16 Burnside ordered Willcox, who commanded a division of mostly raw troops in the IX Corps (including several six-month regiments of newly recruited Indianans) to fall back and defend the Cumberland Gap if telegraphic communications with Knoxville were cut. By the nineteenth Willcox had secured the gap, gathering a force of about 6,000 infantry and cavalry for its defense.[31]

Grant, annoyed that Willcox had retreated, urged a different strategy. In a wire dated November 20, though he agreed that Willcox should follow Burnside's orders, Grant could not help but ask, "Can you not concentrate your forces and raise the siege of Knoxville?" It was a risky, perhaps even desperate proposal, as even Grant admitted when he added, "this I know would close the route to Cumberland Gap for us, and would probably not compensate unless entirely successful in expelling Longstreet," thus making it an all-or-nothing gamble. In a follow-on communique he downplayed those risks, insisting that "Longstreet passing through our lines into Kentucky need not cause alarm. He would find the country so bare that he would lose his transportation and artillery . . . and would meet such a force . . . that he could not return."[32]

Of course, any new Rebel offensive into Kentucky would likely be met with hysteria verging on panic in Washington, making Grant's glib assertion problematic. Moreover, Willcox's small, untrained force was almost as unready to attack as Thomas's Army of the Cumberland. Understandably, no such thrust occurred. None of that logic helped Grant's mood when he received yet another message from Halleck on November 21 reporting "rumors that Burnside is surrounded in Knoxville. At any rate, we [in Washington, D.C.] have no communication with him. The President feels very anxious that some immediate movement be made for his relief."[33]

In replying, Grant gave full vent to his feelings.

> I ordered an attack here two weeks ago, but it was impossible to move artillery. Now Thomas' chief of artillery says he has to borrow teams from Sherman to move a portion of his artillery to where it is to be used. . . . Thomas can take about one gun from each battery, and can go as far with his infantry as his men can carry rations. . . . I have never felt such restlessness before as I have at the fixed and immovable condition of the Army of the Cumberland. General Meigs states that the loss of animals here will exceed 10,000.

The only bright spot, as far as Grant was concerned, was Sherman, who "has used almost superhuman effort to get [to Chattanooga] even at this time, and his force is really the only one that I can move."[34]

This highly illuminating dispatch, sent at 8:00 P.M. on November 21, reveals the extent to which Grant was frustrated with the apparent inaction of George Thomas, Ambrose Burnside, and now Orlando Willcox. To make matters worse, Willcox inadvertently spurred on the general's rising frustration with a dispatch he sent to Halleck on the evening of the twenty-second. In it he commented: "I do not hear from Grant. Will you decide whether I should run the risk of sacrificing all my cavalry in a demonstration . . . in an attempt to aid Burnside? If so, I am ready. Please answer tonight. Firing at Knoxville heard up to 11 o'clock [A.M.] today."[35]

When Grant received a copy of this message, he exploded. On November 23, in a separate wire to Halleck, he complained that "from the time communication with General Burnside was cut off till the present, I have been sending dispatches to Willcox, giving him all the instructions necessary. He has been retreating too fast to get them at the points to which they were directed. His dispatch to you was for effect," Grant sneered. To Willcox he was even blunter: "If you had shown half the willingness to sacrifice yourself and command at the start [that] you do in your dispatch, you might have rendered Burnside material aid." Additionally, Grant hectored, while Willcox was "not expected . . . [to] try to sacrifice [his] command," it was expected that he would "take proper risks." He was directly questioning Willcox's courage.[36]

Nothing came of Grant's imputation, primarily because Willcox, unlike so many Civil War officers, proved thick-skinned enough to simply let the matter slide. He did insist that the "reproof was unjust" based on Burnside's orders, a fact that he claimed Grant "soon afterwards fully acknowledged."

Another officer might have demanded a court of inquiry to clear his name, but Willcox proved remarkably generous. In his memoirs he recalled that "it must be borne in mind that General Grant was already more or less worried and anxious over his impending battle with Bragg . . . that he ignored . . . Burnside's repeated orders for me to 'hold the gap at all hazards.'" Although magnanimous in overlooking Grant's impugnation, Willcox still could not resist getting in one dig: In the context of another conflict of orders, during which Grant ordered him to threaten the Confederate salt works at Abingdon, Virginia, while Burnside simultaneously ordered him to use his cavalry against Longstreet's "rear and left," Willcox pointed out that another Federal general, Brig. Gen. William W. Averell, was in West Virginia and in a much better position to threaten Abingdon. "I have often wondered how that little blunder of the great strategist [Grant] got 'mixed' in his dispatches."[37]

At least two people did not share Grant's anxiety: Thomas and Burnside. On or about November 22, as Grant was chafing for action, Thomas opined that "Longstreet's move is a raid upon our line of supplies. Burnside, at this moment has three men to Longstreet's one. We [Thomas and Sherman] greatly outnumber Bragg's army, and if in our attack we can bring the crushing weight of our full force to bear, we are sure to win." Thomas overestimated Burnside's advantage—there were 25,000 Federals in East Tennessee, while Longstreet had between 13,000 and 15,000 Rebels—but he clearly grasped the logistical realities and constraints of operating in the area far better than did Grant.[38]

Based on his disastrous turn at command in Virginia, culminating in a bloody defeat at Fredericksburg, Burnside had his share of detractors and outright enemies. None of that history deterred him now. On November 18 he informed Secretary of War Stanton that his men were now concentrated at Knoxville and "expresse[d] confidence in the strength of his position." In a second note he told the secretary of his "ability to repel [an] attack if made" and "conjecture[d] that Longstreet's feeble advance may be with design to cover [a] movement into Kentucky."[39]

After the loss of telegraphic communications, Burnside continued to relay messages out of Knoxville, usually via the Cumberland Gap or by secret courier. Two of those messages, sent on November 21 and 23, updated Grant on the state of his supplies. In the first Burnside reported: "We have on hand eight days' bread, half rations; fifteen days beef, and of fresh pork, full rations, and an abundance of salt. Our forage trains cross the [Tennessee]

River daily, and have so far been successful." On the twenty-third he added, "we have provisions for, say, ten or twelve days longer, and will hold out as long as we can." Based on these reports, Grant knew that Knoxville had food enough at least through the first week of December. Burnside's only fear seemed to be that, with only about 12,000 of his men concentrated in Knoxville proper, if Longstreet were heavily reinforced, the Rebels might overwhelm the defenders before other Federal forces could react. So far, however, Longstreet lacked the numbers for that sort of effort.[40]

Thus, Grant had time to both defeat Bragg and save Knoxville, but the window for success was limited. All now depended on Sherman's arrival.

5
"WE WENT IN A ZIGZAG"

$\mathcal{A}$nd where was Sherman, upon whom so much now depended? Through much of October, his command was working its way across northern Mississippi, tasked with repairing the Memphis & Charleston Railroad. Ultimately, Grant intended that road to provide an alternative to the overworked Nashville & Chattanooga line. The two sets of rails converged at Stevenson, Alabama, already a bustling supply depot, where (along with the smaller depot at Bridgeport, five miles farther on) material could be shipped upriver to Chattanooga. Sherman remained personally dubious of the idea to directly reinforce the town. He still favored a two-pronged approach, with his men striking toward Mobile, but "since he had 'abundant faith in Halleck,' . . . he would 'play [Halleck's] game' and move to relieve" Chattanooga. His progress was bedeviled by Confederate cavalry, and he dispatched infantry to clear the Rebel horsemen from as much of the route as possible.[1]

Sherman's lack of enthusiasm for the new mission was probably also linked to the devastating personal loss he and his family had just suffered: the death of son Willy on October 3. Willy, Sherman's favorite child and namesake, died of typhoid fever at the Gayoso Hotel in Memphis as the family was returning home from spending time with the general around Vicksburg. Convulsed with grief and guilt for having let his family visit him in the unhealthy climate of Mississippi that summer, Sherman was devastated. On October 6, in a letter to wife, Ellen (who continued on home to Ohio after Willy's passing), an anguished Sherman confessed: "I can hardly trust myself. Sleeping—waking—everywheres I see Poor Little Willy. His face & form are as deeply imprinted on my memory as were deepseated the hopes I had in his Future." On the tenth, still in Memphis, Sherman informed Ellen: "The moment I begin to think of you & the children, Poor Willy appears before me as plain as life. . . . Why should I ever have taken them to that dread Climate? It nearly kills me to think of it. Why was I not killed at Vicksburg and left Willy to grow up to care for you?" His son's untimely departure would continue to haunt Sherman for many months.[2]

On October 11 Sherman departed Memphis for Corinth via special train, accompanied by his staff and 260 men of the 13th U.S. Infantry. At Collierville, barely twenty-five miles down the track, they stumbled into a fight. Brig. Gen. James R. Chalmers's division of Mississippi cavalry was attempting to overwhelm the Federal garrison at that town: Col. De Witt Clinton and 250 men of the 66th Indiana. Sherman's train pulled to a stop, whereupon the general ordered the 13th Regulars to reinforce the Hoosiers. Sgt. P. J. Carmody, one of those regulars, recorded that Chalmers then demanded the immediate surrender of Sherman, the train, and Colonel Clinton's garrison—an obvious move, given that the Rebel general put his own strength at 3,100 men. "What do you think your 'Uncle Billy' said?" recollected Carmody with evident pride. "'Give my compliments to General Chalmers,' said he, 'and tell him that the government pays me to fight, not to surrender.'"[3]

Sherman was throwing down a bluff, hoping his odds would soon improve, since he had also just wired to Germantown, nine miles back, for reinforcements. Those were soon on the way: the 90th Illinois, 100th Indiana, and three Illinois artillery pieces, all under command of Irish-born Col. Timothy O'Meara of the 90th. Though only twenty-seven, O'Meara already had considerable military experience and had been handpicked by Chicago's ethnic Irish community to lead that regiment, which was also known as Chicago's Irish Legion. He certainly seemed full of fire now. Capt. E. O. Hurd of the 39th Ohio, present with the relief column, described O'Meara as "a genuine fighting man" who pressed forward with all dispatch.[4]

In the meantime, Sherman, his staff, the 13th Regulars, and the local garrison all retreated to the relative security of what Chalmers reported as "a strong earthwork." From there they mounted a stiff defense. The Rebels swarmed over the train, disabling the engine and burning much of the 66th Indiana's camp, but they failed to dislodge the entrenched Federals. Sherman took an intense interest in the fight. "He was mad as a march hare at being trapped in such a manner," marveled Sergeant Carmody, but as the fight progressed, "he became . . . calm and resolute," ordering noncombatants to take up arms as they became available from the dead and wounded. At one point Carmody offered a mild rebuke to his overexposed commander: "General, these men are being killed from the trees and you will surely be hit if you don't keep under cover. . . . 'Sergeant,' said the General, 'attend to your business, sir; attend to your business. I will take care of myself, sir.' I stopped at once," recalled the abashed Carmody, "making suggestions to the General as to his safety."[5]

After about four hours, during which Chalmers could not leverage the Federals out of their fort, the Rebel commander withdrew upon learning of the approach of "heavy reinforcements." O'Meara's column arrived in time to see off the last of the Mississippians. When he arrived at the fort, the colonel, with "his sleeves rolled up, slaughter-house style," and "an ugly-looking" sword "more like an elongated bowie-knife than a field officer's saber," impressed Sherman with his combativeness. "Being an Irishman myself," Carmody took special note of the 90th's green regimental colors. "I naturally felt proud that the flag of the Emerald Isle had led the way to help save Sherman."[6]

The Collierville fight was just one of a series of small actions Chalmers conducted against the railroad. Though the immediate damage inflicted was minor—aside from nearly capturing Sherman—Chalmers's raid convinced the already dubious Sherman of the impossibility of securing the entire length of the Charleston & Memphis Railroad across Mississippi and northern Alabama. He knew he could not spare the thousands of troops needed to defend the line even if it were fully restored. Hence it came as a great relief when, on October 24, Sherman received Grant's order to "drop everything east of Bear Creek [Mississippi] and move with your entire force toward Stevenson until you receive further orders."[7]

On October 19 Sherman had formally accepted command of the Department and Army of the Tennessee, the position vacated by Grant's elevation. By the end of the month, he had gathered a large force between Corinth and Florence, Alabama. Of those units, he intended to bring four divisions to Chattanooga: Brig. Gen. Peter J. Osterhaus's First Division, Brig. Gen. Morgan L. Smith's Second Division, and Brig. Gen. Hugh Ewing's Fourth Division, all belonging to his own XV Corps; and Brig. Gen. John E. Smith's Second Division of the XVII Corps. On October 31 these commands reported a total of 17,283 men present for duty and an aggregate of 21,020 rank and file. Maj. Gen. Frank P. Blair was temporarily elevated to command the XV Corps due to Sherman's own upward bump to head the Army of the Tennessee.[8]

Notably absent from this expedition were some of the Army of the Tennessee's best and most promising officers. Osterhaus, a German émigré who had amassed a solid combat record since joining the Union forces in 1861, took an emergency leave between November 3 and 22—his wife lay dying in Saint Louis. Osterhaus would return on the very eve of battle at Chattanooga, but (as will be seen) additional circumstances would conspire to prevent his division from fighting alongside the rest of Sherman's command.[9]

Interestingly, Maj. Gens. James B. McPherson and John A. Logan were also left behind. McPherson commanded the XVII Corps, in which Logan led a division; both were stationed at Vicksburg. Their absence was surprising since, next to Sherman, McPherson was probably Grant's favorite corps commander and very much a fast-rising star in the Army of the Tennessee. Logan was also a Grant favorite, one of the army's best and most aggressive divisional commanders.

First in his USMA Class of 1853, McPherson joined Grant's staff as a lieutenant colonel of engineers in January 1862, rose to brigadier general after Shiloh, and was given command of the XVII Corps a year later. Described as careful and cautious, "the antithesis of Sherman in temperament," McPherson owed much of his success to the close friendships he forged with both Grant and Sherman because his battlefield record, though admirable as far as it went, was limited. "When told of his major-generalcy, McPherson honestly replied, 'I don't know what [it is] for.'" Grant apparently knew: He retained unlimited confidence in the younger man. "When the assignment required brashness and risk, Grant could turn to Sherman . . . , who loved nothing better than stirring up a fight, no matter what the consequences. But when consequences did matter, he sent in McPherson, who approached everything in Grant's more methodical, practical style."[10]

Instead of joining Sherman, McPherson's only field duty that fall came when Grant ordered him to conduct a raid against Rebel-held Canton, Mississippi, twenty-five miles northeast of the state capital, Jackson. The mission's stated purpose was, in the words of historian Edwin C. Bearss, "a forced reconnaissance" aimed at "capturing this vital railroad center." Doing so would also divert Rebels away from Sherman's eastward march. McPherson's column of 8,000 men, which included Logan, set out on October 14 and began skirmishing with Confederate cavalry the next day. Five days later McPherson was in retreat, never having reached his objective. Though he did divert some Rebel troops, he inflicted no substantial loss on the enemy while suffering "only five killed and fifteen wounded" of his own. Bearss judged the general harshly, noting that "during the course of the Canton expedition, certain weaknesses in McPherson's military character—lack of initiative, a willingness to believe exaggerated reports of the foe's strength, and an unaggressive and passive spirit—became all too apparent." McPherson returned to Vicksburg, remaining there until the next spring. His star—at least in Grant and Sherman's eyes—remained undiminished, for he would take command of the Army of the Tennessee in 1864.[11]

Logan was something of a McPherson protégé, though he was an unlikely candidate for that role. Two years older than his corps commander, Logan was another politician-turned-general, a type often denigrated by West Pointers like Grant and Sherman, but Logan had consistently proven himself in combat. By the fall of 1863, he was perhaps the finest divisional commander in Sherman's army, though he was given little chance to shine on the road to Canton.[12]

Another politician in uniform was Francis P. "Frank" Blair Jr., youngest son of the immensely powerful Blair clan. Blair was a prewar Missouri congressman who now led the XV Corps—at least temporarily. Even though the Blairs were close friends with President Lincoln, and Frank's older brother was a member of the cabinet, Grant did not intend to leave the XV Corps in Blair's hands. On October 27 General Order No. 349 was issued by the War Department, in which, "at the direction of the President, Maj. Gen. William T. Sherman is appointed to command of the Department and Army of the Tennessee, headquarters in the field, and Maj. Gen. John A. Logan to the command of the Fifteenth Army Corps."[13]

The decision to elevate Logan in place of Blair was entirely Grant's. In his memoirs Grant recalled that "Blair joined me at Milliken's Bend a full-fledged general, without having served in a lower grade. . . . I had known Blair in Missouri, where I had voted against him." The reason for that vote, however, was not the main problem as he saw it. The real question was whether Blair could be content to submit to the chain of command. Even though Grant regarded him "as a frank, positive and generous man, . . . [he was] always a leader. I dreaded his coming: I knew from experience that it was more difficult to command two generals desiring to be leaders than it was to command one army officered intelligently and with subordination." As it turned out, Blair adapted well to soldiering, leading Grant to soon revise his opinion: "There was no man braver than he, nor was there any who obeyed all orders of his superior . . . with more unquestioning alacrity. [Blair] was one man as a soldier, another as a politician."[14]

But if Blair overcame Grant's reservations, Logan, also a politician, impressed Grant still more. After the Battle of Raymond in May 1863,

Grant described Logan and Brig. Gen. Marcellus M. Crocker "as being as competent division commanders as could be found in or out of the army and both equal to a much higher command." After the conclusion of the Vicksburg Campaign, he lavished additional praise, opining that "Logan and Crocker ended the campaign fitted to command independent armies." Unfortunately, Crocker also suffered from tuberculosis, and though he remained on duty in Natchez that fall, he was not healthy enough for active campaigning. Thus, Logan's path was cleared for command of the XV Corps.[15]

Logan, however, was still in Vicksburg. It would take time for him to receive his new orders and effect a change of command. Nor, apparently, was there any sense of urgency to the new arrangement. Not until November 13 did the general depart upriver, after a grand review of his old division that proved to be an emotional farewell. Still en route, Logan would not be present to lead his new command into the attack at Chattanooga ten days later. Would the Army of the Tennessee live up to Grant's expectations, bereft of these trusted officers?[16]

At the end of October, Sherman began crossing the Tennessee River at Eastport, Mississippi, a once-prosperous trading town on the Natchez Trace, now in a bit of a decline with the advent of the railroad. Bridgeport lay 175 miles distant; Chattanooga, 206. By crossing to the north bank of the Tennessee, the Federals could expect considerably less resistance from Rebel cavalry, which would have to also venture across the Tennessee to harass the marching troops. But the crossing was no easy task. Capt. Charles Wills of the 103rd Illinois, in Ewing's Fourth Division, was responsible for his brigade's wagons: "I think I never worked harder than I did from 7 o'clock that night (October 27) until 6:30 o'clock the next day, A.M. It occupied two days and nights crossing the whole train." Each division took its turn. Three Federal steamboats ferried the men, wagons, and livestock across, protected by the gunboat *Lexington*. Osterhaus's First Division, now sans its commander, brought up the rear, with the last two regiments, the 12th Missouri and 13th Illinois, completing their crossing at 4:00 A.M. on November 4.[17]

From there the men began a fortnight's hard marching. Capt. Henry Kircher, who commanded Company E of the 12th Missouri, detailed the trek in a letter home on November 18, the day he reached Bridgeport. "On an average, we went 15–16 miles a day: in all, close to 200 miles in 14 days." The country north of the Tennessee was largely desolate, stripped by two years of war. Most of the places he passed through, thought Kircher, "until 3 years ago . . . were probably quite busy, nice little towns of 1000–1500 inhabitants. But now there are few people . . . , and many houses stand empty or are burned down. . . . On the whole march, we didn't see a single enemy. The gorillas [guerillas] don't serve as well when it gets cold and the leaves are off the trees." Kircher found the "region . . . really, really beautiful in places[,] but for a farmer it is not an Illinois by far. . . . [W]here the ground doesn't consist chiefly of gravel or sand . . . the way is boggy and marshy, so that our pioneers always had to spend a lot of time before our trains were able to pass."[18]

Kircher was also bewildered by the choice of path taken by the army. "With out any sense or reason," he complained, "we took the longest and the worst route. . . . We went in a zigzag." He was referring to a detour northward into Tennessee, via Pulaski and Fayetteville, before the column turned back southward into Alabama. The reason for this move was the flooded Elk River. The Elk flows down from the north into the Tennessee River just west of Athens, Alabama. On November 7 a staff officer reported that in Alabama, the river, "containing 4 feet [of] water and 200 yards wide, is impassable." Rather than spend days ferrying the army over the Elk or trying to bridge the obstacle, Sherman elected to detour, adding miles but saving time.[19]

The general's own journey was not completely adventure free, though he had no encounter as exciting as the one at Collierville. Sherman recalled an incident near Florence, where the son of Maj. Ezra Taylor, then serving as an aide, wandered away from the line of march and was taken prisoner by Rebel partisans—some of Kircher's "gorillas." Taylor, who was the XV Corps chief of artillery, appealed to Sherman for help. "I had no cavalry to send in pursuit," wrote the general, so instead he threatened a few of the locals with like treatment. "Young Taylor and his comrade were brought back the next day." Additionally, Sherman instructed Maj. Gen. Stephen Hurlbut, commanding the XVI Corps, to hurry forward Brig. Gen. Grenville Dodge's division as far as Athens per Grant's orders of November 5.[20]

For the time being, Grant intended Dodge's men to both help secure northern Alabama and begin work to restore the railroad running north from Decatur (on the south bank of the Tennessee opposite Athens) to Nashville, which Grant thought would be a useful supplement to the Nashville & Chattanooga line. "It is not my intention to leave any portion of your [Sherman's] army to guard roads," he wrote, "particularly not Dodge who has been kept constantly on that duty ever since he has been subject to my orders. Your army being the smallest army . . . , it should not be broken up guarding railroads." Still, Dodge was not only a talented volunteer officer but also a skilled prewar railroad surveyor and engineer, making him the likely choice for the mission—at least for the time being.[21]

Grant could only wait for Sherman to arrive. In the meantime, business at headquarters was slow. On November 20 Asst. Adj. Gen. Ely S. Parker noted, "when we reached here the Generals staff had but little to do . . . and a Genl William F. Smith came and wanted to borrow me." Parker avoided being transferred but did assist Smith on a temporary basis.[22]

This left Grant with only matters of routine correspondence. In addition to the ongoing communications concerning East Tennessee, from the very first, Grant's days in Chattanooga were occupied with the myriad small details of administration, logistics, and personal affairs. One of those details would prove problematic. On October 27, based on a message from Halleck, Grant hastily arrested Thomas Crutchfield, one of Chattanooga's most prominent citizens, for being a "pretended Union" man and in reality spying for Bragg. Crutchfield and one other man, Dean Thompson, were both sent to Louisville under guard. Crutchfield was in fact an *actual* Union man, not pretend. Former co-owner of the Crutchfield House Hotel in Chattanooga, he had been staunchly Unionist even in the early years of the war, when any Federal troops were far away, and he had been of great help providing intelligence to General Rosecrans during the Chickamauga Campaign. His brother William swam across the Tennessee River on August 31, 1863, to join Rosecrans's army as a scout. Thomas Crutchfield sold his hotel in 1862 and now lived at his expansive farm, Amnicola, upstream from Chattanooga on the south side of the Tennessee. General Thomas should have known him well, and perhaps he tried to vouch for him, for upon hearing of the arrest, Halleck immediately backtracked. "I have no evidence against Crutchfield and Thompson, only a rumor. I did not desire their arrest . . . but merely to put you on your guard against them." Matters were eventually put right, and both men were cleared: By the following spring, Grant described Crutchfield as "a Tennessean of undoubted loyalty . . . [who] has made large sacrifices of property on account of his opinions and has been of great service to the [U]nion cause." But in the meantime, Crutchfield's detention would prove to be a significant mistake, depriving the Federals of important local knowledge for the fighting to come.[23]

On November 2 Grant had to fend off a visit from his wife, who wanted to come at least as far as Nashville to be nearer her husband. He was appalled at the idea under the circumstances. "I do not know what in the world you will do there [in Nashville]. There is not a respectable hotel and I leave no one of my Staff there. You will be entirely among strangers and at an expensive and disagreeable place to live." As for her coming to Chattanooga, "This is just as unsuitable a place for you to be as [was] Millikins Bend." As much as he missed Julia, she could not be with him now.[24]

Other correspondence cluttered his desk. Some of it was personal. Others, like George W. Childs, a Philadelphia publisher and newspaperman, wrote asking for "drawings, plans, &c." pertaining to Vicksburg, a request Grant had to decline since "all books, papers, maps, &c., having no bearing on what is before me" were in storage at Cairo. The general could at least provide an autograph to a young German American, Lt. M. R. W. Grebe of the 4th Missouri Cavalry, who wished to forward the trophy to his father overseas in Hanover.[25]

On the tenth of November, Grant received a pair of interesting requests from his Confederate counterpart, Braxton Bragg. One was an inquiry into the whereabouts of "a young man, John Bowen Brabson," who traveled from his school in Marietta to visit family in Chattanooga and was left behind when Confederate forces abandoned that city on September 8. "It is now understood," continued Bragg, "that he was arrested . . . and is held as a prisoner. He does not belong to our army." But young Brabson (who was either sixteen or eighteen, depending on the source) was not in Union hands. He was found living in Chattanooga at the home of "a Mrs. Whitesides," making him for all intents and purposes a free citizen of the town.[26]

Bragg's other inquiry was far less trivial. The Rebel commander informed Grant that "Mrs Emily [sic] Helm, widow of the late Brig. Genl. B. H. Helm, C.S.A. killed at the battle of Chickamauga, desires to pass through your lines to her home in Kentucky. Will you give her permission to go by way of Chattanooga, under a flag of truce?" Emilie Todd Helm was not just any war widow. She was half-sister to Mary Todd Lincoln, which meant that she was sister-in-law to no less a figure than the president of the United States. Following her Rebel general of a husband south for the war, Emilie had been living in Selma, Alabama, until notified of his death. She and her three newly fatherless daughters, fresh from the general's graveside funeral in Atlanta, now wished to go home to Union-held Kentucky.[27]

Numerous historians have written that Grant rejected Helm's application based on a curious letter Bragg sent to her on November 9. In it Bragg stated as much and described himself as "greatly surprised by the answer." Both the timing and the sentiment expressed in this communique are peculiar. His missive to Grant is dated November 10, the day after Bragg's letter to Helm; Grant responded promptly, also on the tenth. Nor did the Union commander refuse to issue a pass. Instead, he wrote, "Mrs Helm and three children will be received at our lines and furnished a pass to her friends in Kentucky on her obligating herself . . . not to communicate with the enemies of the Government of the United States any thing prejudicial to the Government . . . and that she will send no letter South of our lines except open, and then only through proper Federal officers."[28]

Perhaps these conditions were off-putting, but in any case Grant was not Helm's only recourse. Her father-in-law, John L. Helm, was a former governor of Kentucky. He was induced to write to her stepmother, Betsy Todd, asking her to seek help from a higher source: "Could you or one of your daughters," asked Helm, "write to Mrs. Lincoln and through her secure a pass?" Todd could and did. Within days the required document arrived, signed by President Lincoln, authorizing Todd to fetch Helm north. On November 20 Bragg wrote Grant that "Mrs. Genl. Helm informs me that in consequence of the arrival of her mother . . . she has postponed her trip to your lines." Instead Emilie Helm and her family traveled via Virginia, entering the Union lines at Fort Monroe, and then traveled on to the White House, where they resided as guests of the Lincolns for some weeks.[29]

On November 15 a much more anticipated arrival occurred. Sherman reached Bridgeport, hastening on ahead of his troops at Grant's orders. He caught a supply boat to Kelley's Ferry and by that evening was in Chattanooga.

Sherman, recollected General Howard, "came bounding in after his usual buoyant manner. General Grant, whose bearing toward Sherman differed with that from other officers, being free, affectionate, and good humored, greeted him most cordially." Grant offered him a cigar and, gesturing, "said, 'Take the chair of *honor*, Sherman,' indicating a rocker with a high back. 'The chair of honor? Oh no, that belongs to you, general.' Grant, not a whit abashed by this compliment, said, 'I don't forget, Sherman, to give proper respect to age.'—'Well then, if you put it on that ground, I must accept.'" Banter finished, the generals began to discuss their options.[30]

Howard also observed the three top commanders—Grant, Thomas, and Sherman—as they hashed out strategy. "Sherman spoke quickly, but evinced much previous knowledge and thought. . . . Thomas furnished them the ammunition of knowledge, positive and abundant, of the surrounding mountainous regions. . . . Grant appeared to listen with pleasant interest, and now and then made a pointed remark. Thomas was like the solid judge, confident and fixed in his knowledge of the law; Sherman, like the brilliant advocate; and Grant rendering his verdicts like an intelligent jury."[31]

In his memoirs Grant later claimed that his "orders for battle were all prepared in advance of Sherman's arrival, except the dates, which could not be fixed while troops to be engaged were so far away." This was probably true in outline, since Grant's basic concept remained unchanged from the plan of November 7: Sherman would strike the north end of Missionary Ridge, turn the Rebel right, and drive a blue wedge between Bragg and Longstreet. But a thousand details had to be hashed out, and his draft attack orders were revised several times before they reached final form.[32]

The next two days were taken up with field observations. On the sixteenth, Sherman, Grant, and Thomas rode to Fort Wood, from where they could see virtually all the terrain in question. They surveyed the Rebels atop Lookout Mountain, the Confederate camps lining Missionary Ridge, and the "rebel sentinels . . . in plain view, not a thousand yards off. 'Why' said [Sherman], 'General Grant, you are besieged'; and he said, 'it is too true.'"[33]

Someone pointed out the Moore House on Missionary Ridge, indicating "a group of tents" as Bragg's headquarters. "Bragg, Thomas, and I were stationed at Fort Moultrie, S.C., together for four years from 1842 to 1846," remembered Sherman, "and were as intimate and friendly as possible," a friendship that continued for Bragg and Thomas when the latter served in the former's artillery battery during the Mexican War. "As we rode along," Sherman continued, "I inquired, 'Tom, have you seen Bragg or had any communication with him?' He answered quickly and warmly. 'Damn him, I'll be even with him yet!'" Sherman was taken aback. "'What's the matter now?' 'Why some time ago a parcel of letters unsealed came from the north, addressed beyond the lines, with a request to send it out by flag of truce.'" Since the letters contained no military secrets, Thomas complied, attaching "a note asking Bragg to forward the letters to the addressee—the same parcel was returned by flag of truce, with Genl. Bragg's endorsement:

Respectfully returned to Genl. Thomas. Genl. Bragg declines to have any intercourse (or dealings) with a man who has betrayed his state.' Thomas narrated this event," wrote Sherman, "with deep and earnest feeling, [and] with many threats of what he would do [to Bragg] when the time came."[34]

Sherman also recalled that at some point during the day, Grant shared another concern, presumably out of Thomas's earshot. "The mules and horses of Thomas's army were so starved that they could not haul his guns," which was certainly true and the reason for the lack of any attack on November 7, but Grant now felt the real problem was much more serious. He informed Sherman "that the men of Thomas's army had been so demoralized by the battle of Chickamauga that he feared they could not be got out of their trenches to assume the offensive." His next words, as Sherman recalled them, reflected the commander's ongoing concern for East Tennessee. "Bragg . . . detached Longstreet . . . up into East Tennessee," Grant explained, "that Burnside was in danger, etc.; and that he (Grant) was extremely anxious to attack Bragg" and defeat the Rebels or "at least force [Bragg] to recall Longstreet." If Sherman's troops were "to take the offensive *first*," Grant reasoned, then he "had no doubt the Cumberland army would fight well."[35]

Clearly Thomas's and Smith's unwillingness to attack on the seventh still rankled him, no matter how justified their reasons had been. The incident would continue to bother Grant for years to come, but his low opinion of the Army of the Cumberland's morale would soon be proved wildly off the mark.

The next day, November 16, the command group rode across the Chattanooga bridge to the north bank of the Tennessee River and then upstream to a point opposite the mouth of South Chickamauga Creek. Sherman recalled that the group included himself, Grant, Thomas, Baldy Smith, John M. Brannan (the Army of the Cumberland's chief of artillery), and some unnamed "others." One of those others was William Wrenshall Smith, a civilian cousin of Grant's wife. Smith was a successful Pennsylvania businessman who decided to visit his famous cousin-in-law and to whom Grant had issued a pass on October 4. He arrived in Chattanooga two days before Sherman. Grant immediately extended Smith the courtesy of his headquarters and invited him to ride along on this outing.[36]

The goal of the reconnaissance was to examine Bragg's defenses (or lack thereof) along the north end of Missionary Ridge. Grant intended Sherman's divisions to make a night crossing, much as had been done at

Brown's Ferry, throw up a new pontoon bridge, and be across the river before Bragg could react. Sherman and Baldy Smith "crept down behind a fringe of trees . . . to the very point selected for the new bridge, where we sat for some time, seeing the rebel pickets on the opposite bank, and almost hearing their words." There they agreed that the site was acceptable.[37]

Grant's cousin recalled that while Sherman and Baldy Smith were down at the riverbank, the general "was in a fine humor, and as he leaned against the fence, was telling us about the former great speculations in Real Estate in Chicago and Millwaukee." When Sherman and Baldy Smith returned, Grant and the engineer went down to the river so General Smith could point out the selected crossing site. Here, noted Cousin Smith, the party feared that "they were getting to[o] near the rifles of the pickets on the other side," but no shots rang out. On the way back Grant's ebullience continued, with him and " [Maj. Gen. David] Hunter telling stories of old army acquaintenses some of which were very rich and were hugely enjoyed. Grant is in high spirits—and tells a story admirably. In general he is extremely reserved, but with one or two friends he is very entertaining and agreeable."[38]

Sherman's arrival had clearly energized Grant. At last it seemed like events were being set in motion. On the fourteenth he wrote Julia that "things will culminate here within ten days in great advantages with one or the other parties. I am certainly happily constituted." A few days earlier, on November 9, Grant dispatched Assistant Secretary Dana and Col. James H. Wilson to Knoxville, both to get a better read on Burnside's character and intentions and to stiffen his resolve. The two arrived at that place on the thirteenth and immediately met with the general. On the fourteenth Halleck informed Grant that, based on information from Dana, Burnside was thinking of retreat. "Cannot Thomas move on Longstreet's rear and force him to fall back? . . . I fear further delay may result in Burnside's abandonment of East Tennessee. This would be a terrible misfortune." In response, Grant fired off a missive to Knoxville, which both indicated his expectations of impending movement and reflected his confidence in the outcome: "Can you hold the line from Knoxville to Clinton for seven days? If so, I think the whole Tennessee Valley can be secured from all present dangers."[39]

At 10:00 A.M. on the fifteenth, Grant offered up the most detailed summary of his plans yet. Writing to Halleck, he informed the general in chief that "Sherman is now at Bridgeport. He will commence moving tomorrow or the next day" to march to the preselected crossing site, where "it is intended Sherman's force and one Division of Thomas shall pass. This force will attack Missionary Ridge with . . . Thomas supporting it from here [Chattanooga].—In the mean time Hooker will attack Lookout and Carry it if possible. If Burnside can hold . . . for six days I believe Bragg will be started back for [the] South side of [the] Oostanaula [River] and Longstreet cut off." The Oostanaula, just south of Resaca, Georgia, was fifty miles from Chattanooga, and if Bragg were driven that far south, then Longstreet would be completely cut off from the Army of Tennessee. It was an ambitious, optimistic goal.[40]

The next day, as Sherman headed back to Bridgeport to bring up his command, Halleck warned Burnside "that it is of vital importance that you hold your position for a few days, till he [Grant] can send you assistance. If you retreat now, it will be disastrous to the campaign." Halleck reiterated his worry (again based on Dana's information) to Grant that "Burnside was hesitating whether to fight [at Knoxville] or retreat. I fear he will not fight, though strongly urged to do so. . . . Immediate aid from you is not of vital importance." That afternoon he wired Halleck back with reassurance: "I am pushing everything to give General Burnside early aid. . . . Sherman's troops are now at Bridgeport. They will march tomorrow, and an effort will be made to get a column between Bragg and Longstreet as soon as possible."[41]

As part of that plan, on the sixteenth Grant also ordered Brig. Gen. George Crook, commanding the Army of the Cumberland's Second Cavalry Division, to "select from your command a brigade of 1,500 to 2,000 men under command of Col. E. Long and start them so as to reach [Chattanooga] by Saturday next [November 21] at noon. They are wanted for an important raid." Long's objective was Cleveland, Tennessee. The cavalry was to follow Sherman across the river and then strike out across country for the town of Cleveland, where the East Tennessee & Georgia Railroad met a spur of the Western & Atlantic extending to Dalton. Eleven miles to the northeast of Cleveland lay Charleston, where the East Tennessee & Georgia tracks crossed the Hiawassee River over a bridge the Confederates were returning to service to support Longstreet. Long's mission was simple: damage the tracks enough to ensure that Longstreet's detachment could not use these rails to rejoin Bragg quickly once Grant's main effort was underway.[42]

On November 18, having been reassured that Burnside would indeed hold Knoxville, Grant issued final orders to Thomas: "All preparations should be made for attacking the enemy's position by Saturday morning [November 21], at daylight." Grant made only one important change— Hooker's attack on Lookout Mountain was deemed unnecessary. In order to "mass all the force possible against . . . Missionary Ridge," Grant decided to strip Howard's XI Corps from Hooker, to "be held in readiness to act either with you [Thomas] . . . or with Sherman." Likewise, Thomas was to organize "a moveable column of one Division" to move upstream along the south bank of the Tennessee "to form a junction with Sherman" after the Army of the Tennessee secured its own lodgment on the south bank. Thomas then expanded on Grant's plan, ordering Major General Granger and his two divisions in Chattanooga to be ready "to co-operate directly with Major-General Sherman." Granger was "to bridge Citico Creek" and, after crossing that "deep narrow stream . . . , [move] toward the north end of Mission Ridge . . . , marching so as to arrive at that point simultaneously with . . . Sherman." Grant's long-desired hammer blow against Bragg now seemed imminent.[43]

6

"THE ELEMENTS WERE AGAINST US"

*T*he man least pleased with General Grant's plans had to be Joseph Hooker. The loss of the XI Corps left Hooker with only two small divisions, those of Maj. Gen. John W. Geary, from the XII Corps, and Brig. Gen. Charles Cruft, from the IV Corps. With perhaps 6,000 men total, Hooker's remaining command was too small to assault Lookout Mountain. Instead, he was left to shadowbox against the Confederate left while all the real fighting occurred elsewhere, reduced to the status of onlooker in the great battle expected to unfold any day. At best Hooker might divert some of Bragg's attention away from the real blow to be delivered by Sherman.[1]

As for Sherman, he departed Chattanooga for Bridgeport late on November 16. He traveled downriver in a skiff, since he missed the last steamboat to head for Bridgeport that day, even taking a turn at the oars, and only arrived near dawn on the seventeenth. His four divisions were still widely scattered. Brigadier General Ewing's Fourth Division of the XV Corps and Brig. Gen. John E. Smith's Second Division of the XVII Corps were both present, having reached Bridgeport on November 15, but Brig. Gen. Morgan L. Smith's Second Division of the XV Corps was not yet up (though it would arrive that afternoon), while Brigadier General Osterhaus's First Division of the XV Corps was still two days away.[2]

Sherman immediately ordered Ewing's division to cross the river and head for Trenton, Georgia, a short distance up Lookout Valley to the south but in the opposite direction from Chattanooga. This was yet another deception, worked out between Grant and Sherman. Ewing was "to act as though you were the head of a strong column," with the aim to convince the Confederates—who could easily see that movement from the west brow of Lookout Mountain—that Sherman's men were going to outflank Bragg to the south, much as Rosecrans had done back in September and as Longstreet feared when his command held the mountain. On the eighteenth, noted a diarist in the 103rd Illinois, the troops "camped at Trenton. Lookout Mountain was in plain view, and from the number of signal lights seen, it was well garrisoned." The next day Brig. Gen. John M. Corse's brigade, to which the 103rd belonged, pushed on as far as Johnson's Crook, a bend in Lookout Mountain where Newsom's Gap offered access to the crest. After a brief skirmish with Rebel cavalry, Corse's men camped at the mouth of the crook, building fires enough to simulate "the entire 15th A.C." and having "enough drums and bugles sounded to justify that opinion."[3]

Ewing's men were convincing enough for Bragg to communicate to President Davis on November 20 that "Sherman's force has arrived, and a movement on our left is indicated. The same game may have to be played over," meaning a repeat of the Chickamauga Campaign, in which the Army of Tennessee fell back into North Georgia until it could be reinforced sufficiently to deal with the Union threat. But would those reinforcements be forthcoming a second time? Bragg expressed his frustration over Gen. Joseph E. Johnston's reluctance to send troops from Alabama and Mississippi. "Mobile could certainly spare some [men]," he continued. "Our fate may be decided here," warned Bragg, "and the enemy is at least double our strength."[4]

The rest of Sherman's movements were not going as well. John E. Smith's division followed Ewing over the pontoon bridge at Bridgeport on November 18 but trudged only another eleven miles to Shellmound before halting. Shepherding the divisional trains over the pontoons was especially irksome. Col. Green B. Raum, commanding Smith's Second Brigade, recalled that "the river was overhung with a dense fog. We could scarcely see 10 feet ahead of us. The bridge at its best was not secure. . . . The passage was slow." Morgan L. Smith's division did not start across the Tennessee until the next day, November 19. Osterhaus's men, who only reached Bridgeport on the afternoon of the eighteenth, began their crossing two days later.[5]

On the twentieth the rain that had been threatening for the past few days now set in. Lt. Chesley Mosman of the 59th Illinois, whose brigade in the IV Corps was now assigned to Hooker, watched Sherman's men slog by. "Rained hard enough to bother these huge trains passing along these mountainous roads. . . . General Sherman's Corps was passing our camps all day, and the roads being filled with troops all day as well as with trains, we did not march." Those wagons struggling by on the rutted, miry roads would soon become a bone of some contention. Sherman blundered. While Ewing's division brought forward only their combat trains (ammunition wagons and ambulances primarily), the rest of Sherman's troops marched with full trains, including those hauling camp equipage, behind each formation. The result was immense delay as the wagons passed and their wheels and draft animals churned the road surfaces into a nearly impassable mire. To make matters worse, the cold rain continued overnight and into the next morning, hopelessly disrupting Grant's intended timetable.[6]

Sometime on the twenty-first, Grant caught wind of Sherman's troubles with his trains, for the departmental commander directed his ever-present chief of staff, Brigadier General Rawlins, "to say that, in order to avoid delay, you [Sherman] will have your troops pass your transportation and move up at once, leaving only a sufficient force to guard your trains." By now, however, the damage was largely done; the trains had already created huge bottlenecks at Bridgeport and in the narrow canyon of Running Water Gorge.[7]

While Ewing turned south toward Trenton and Johnson's Crook, John E. Smith's command marched for Brown's Ferry, recrossing the Tennessee River at 3:00 A.M. on November 21. Once back on the north bank and onto Moccasin Bend, however, as recorded by the 4th Minnesota's regimental historian, the troops "got on the wrong road and countermarched." After reversing their steps for a mile, the Fourth Division went into camp near daylight "in a ravine about one mile from the Tennessee River" and upstream from Chattanooga.[8]

On November 21 Assistant Secretary Dana also reported on the difficult conditions: "Heavy rain all night; still continuing. Roads bad; movement of troops difficult. Sherman may be obliged to leave subsistence trains in Lookout Valley." The next day he wired a more optimistic assessment to Washington, noting: "Morning beautiful; cool. Sherman's troops nearly up. Howard ordered to march into Chattanooga [at] 2 P.M. today." But on November 23—two full days past Grant's original timetable—Dana could no longer maintain his positive spin. "The continued movement of Sherman, Thomas, and Howard," he wrote,

> which should have been executed Saturday morning . . . , is still paralyzed by the fact that Woods' [Osterhaus's] division . . . is still behindhand, its advance having scarcely reached the mouth of Lookout Valley. . . . A lamentable blunder has been committed in moving Sherman's forces . . . with the enormous trains they brought from West Tennessee following in usual order in rear of each division, instead of moving all the troops and artillery first. Grant says the blunder is his; that he should have given Sherman explicit orders to leave his wagons behind; but I know

that no one was so much astonished as Grant on learning they had not been left, even without such orders.

Dana made no mention of Grant's own order of November 21, instructing Sherman to do exactly that, presumably because it was issued too late to avoid the problem.[9]

Sherman's own words, however, penned in a letter to his wife, Ellen, on November 17, suggest that the decision to bring along his subsistence wagons was intentional, not an oversight. "Great difficulty has existed to Supply Chattanooga . . . and I hate to take my troops & horses & mules up into that mountain Gorge, where our men will be half starved and horses totally so." Sherman was clearly worried that his men and animals would go wanting once across the Tennessee and perhaps chose to travel with as much food and fodder as he could haul. It is worth noting that so far he had traveled to and from Chattanooga via the river and had not seen the state of the roads between Bridgeport and Wauhatchie firsthand. If he had traversed the road through Running Water Gorge, Sherman might have reached a different decision concerning his divisional and corps trains.[10]

Grant's willingness to excuse the blunder, much less take responsibility for it, seems surprising. But the Army of the Tennessee was his own army, first and foremost, and Sherman was his handpicked successor. Moreover, both Hooker, an eastern general with an easterner's disdain for western Federals, and Thomas, perhaps still smarting from Grant's displeasure over the failure to move on November 7, would be watching closely (and likely critically) as Sherman's men toiled these last few miles into Chattanooga. Certainly, both Grant and Sherman underestimated how difficult operations in this region could be. Regardless, Sherman was not held to account for the error, far from it—Grant's praise was effusive. At 8:00 P.M. on the evening of November 21, in a dispatch to Halleck, he wrote that "Sherman has used almost superhuman efforts to get up even at this time, and his force is really the only one I can move."[11]

Nor would Grant find much fault later. In his official report he simply blamed "heavy rains" for the delay, making no mention of the trains in question. Sherman did the same, reporting that he reached "Hooker's headquarters, 4 miles from Chattanooga, during a rain on the afternoon of the 20th, and met General Grant's orders for the general attack the next day." Here Sherman noted that "it was impossible for me to fill my part in time" due to "the terrible road from Shellmound to Chattanooga. . . .

On a proper representation, General Grant postponed the attack." In his memoir Sherman merely reiterated that the poor roads were to blame, omitting any mention of supply trains. Only Dana's agitated telegram of November 23 identified the main source of delay.[12]

In his own memoir Grant provided slightly more detail. The situation as he recalled it was exceedingly tense because, on November 20, "news had been received that the battle had been commenced at Knoxville. . . . The President, the Secretary of War, and General Halleck, were in an agony of suspense. My suspense was also great, but more endurable, because I was where I could soon do something to relieve the situation." But how soon would he act? Grant wanted any delay to be kept to a minimum. When he received the news that "it would be impossible to get Sherman's troops up" in time for the November 21 target date; "I then asked him [Sherman] if . . . they could . . . make the assault on the morning of the 22d, and ordered Thomas to move on that date." Another twenty-four hours still proved to be not enough time. "The elements were against us," Grant recalled. "It rained all the 20th and 21st. The river rose so rapidly that it was difficult to keep the pontoons in place."[13]

Despite the revised orders, there would again be no attack on November 22. A day earlier the 55th Illinois, in Giles Smith's First Brigade of Morgan Smith's division, recrossed the Tennessee "at Brown's Ferry and waded three miles in mire through a steady downpour . . . [and] encamped about noon" behind Stringer's Ridge near John E. Smith's command, all hidden from the Confederates. The 47th Ohio of Brig. Gen. Joseph Lightburn's Second Brigade of the same division followed that afternoon, but then, "on account of the rapid rise" in the river, "the bridge broke and the crossing was interrupted." This break left half of Sherman's force still far short of their intended staging area.[14]

That break was repaired by the twenty-second; the XI Corps filed across it that day. Howard reported that, as per Grant's newest orders of the same morning, his command began crossing at Brown's Ferry "at 2 P.M. . . . and move[d] thence to Chattanooga direct." The reason was simple: Baldy Smith decided "it was practicable to re-enforce Sherman along the south bank of the Tennessee without trusting to the treacherous pontoons" any more than necessary. Watching half of his command march away, Hooker was loath to be reduced to a mere spectator. He appealed to Thomas to be allowed to accompany Howard's force since, he stated, "it was my duty to join that part of my command going into battle." Thomas agreed. In preparation for his departure, Hooker spent the rest of that afternoon surveying his own and the enemy's dispositions around Lookout Mountain with General Geary, who would take charge of the Union defenses in Hooker's absence.[15]

Howard's use of the repaired Brown's Ferry pontoon bridge ate up most of the afternoon. Ewing's division, marching from Trenton, reached Wauhatchie at about 2:00 P.M., four miles from Brown's Ferry. Here, noted the men of the 103rd Illinois, "knapsacks were loaded on the wagons, 3 days rations, to be cooked when the opportunity came, and 100 rounds of ammunition [were issued] to each man." Once the easterners cleared the pontoon bridge, Ewing's men crossed, finally going into camp near the two Smiths' commands about midnight, still "hidden from view of the enemy."[16]

Unfortunately, the "treacherous pontoons" now lived down to Howard's assessment. A further rise in the river due to all the rain, coupled with timber rafts launched by the Confederates upstream, knocked out the Brown's Ferry span again sometime that night, leaving Osterhaus's division—with General Osterhaus only just returned from his emergency leave to resume command—now stranded in Lookout Valley. It was clear that Sherman's force would not be ready for an attack on the twenty-third either.[17]

The great General and Chief of the German General Staff Helmuth von Moltke, a military theorist and practitioner of no small repute, was said to have two aphorisms. The first could be paraphrased as "no plan survives contact with the enemy." So far, Grant's plans had not survived contact with the weather, let alone Bragg's army. Moltke's second dictum stated that, far from being a set of arcane rules to be rigidly adhered to, "strategy is a system of expedients." Though in November 1863 Grant probably had little knowledge of the German general or his thoughts on warfare, the Union commander could certainly embrace the need for expedience. He was forced to do so now. That evening Grant informed Sherman that, "owing to the late hour when Ewing gets up, if he gets up atal [sic] tonight and the entire impossibility of Wood [Osterhaus] reaching in time to participate tomorrow, I have directed Thomas that we will delay yet another day. Let me know tomorrow at as early an hour as you can if you will be entirely ready for Tuesday morning [November 24.] I would prefer Wood should be up, but if he can [not] . . . , I would prefer you should commence without him."[18]

But could Grant afford to wait until the twenty-fourth? On November 20 he received a curious message from Bragg: "As there may still be some non-combatants in Chattanooga, I deem it proper to notify you that prudence would dictate their early withdrawal." On the face of it, this warning suggested that the Confederate commander was contemplating an attack on the city. No Federal officer, however, believed that Bragg would be so foolish as to attack the heavily fortified garrison, testing those defenses with the lives of his much smaller army. Instead, Grant and his generals took it as a ruse to cover a retreat, an opinion further bolstered when a Rebel deserter slipped into Union lines on the night of the twenty-second to report that "Bragg [was] falling back."[19]

But the Confederate general was not contemplating a retreat. He was, however, trying to cover up a major troop movement. If on November 20 Bragg thought that Ewing's movement to Trenton presaged a strike at his left, Ewing's reversal and the easily observed steady stream of blue-clad troops filing across the Brown's Ferry bridge—when it was trafficable—had, by the following day, inclined Bragg to think that Sherman's men were now headed to East Tennessee. That day he advised Longstreet: "We have rumors of some movement on your left and rear. Scout in that direction and keep me advised, that I may counteract them." The very next day, November 22, Bragg informed him that he was sending "General [Danville] Leadbetter [chief engineer, Department of Tennessee] to confer with you, and to express my views more in full than can be well done by telegram or letter. Nearly 11,000 reinforcements are now moving to your assistance." These troops included Brig. Gen. Bushrod Johnson's division (formerly commanded by Major General Buckner) of Hardee's Corps and Maj. Gen. Patrick R. Cleburne's division of Breckinridge's (previously Hill's) Corps. Both divisions saw hard fighting at Chickamauga and could be considered crack troops—especially those under Cleburne. In order to compensate for the loss of these men, Bragg ordered Hardee to send Brig. Gen. States Rights Gist's division from the army's left to Missionary Ridge. Brig. Gen. William B. Bate's division (formerly Breckinridge's) of Breckinridge's Corps was shifted as well.[20]

This was a stunning reversal. After weeks of denying Longstreet reinforcements sufficient to accomplish a quick knockout blow against Burnside, Bragg now was reducing his own force dramatically to double the size of Longstreet's expeditionary force even as the Federals facing the Army of Tennessee were swelled by Sherman's arrival. Bragg's solicitations for reinforcements from other theaters—principally Mobile and Mississippi—had borne little fruit since the arrival of Stevenson's Division of Vicksburg parolees in early October. Now, in late November, a few other commands were authorized to move to join Bragg, but they were only just starting those movements and would not be present for some time. Minus Johnson and Cleburne, Bragg's effectives numbered perhaps 35,000 men.

The Army of Tennessee's morale was now in a precarious state, marked by short rations and disastrous feuding among the army's senior men. With President Davis's help, Bragg had successfully quashed the "generals' revolt" of early October, transferring or otherwise removing those men who seemed most disloyal, but that did not mean that harmony now ruled the day. On November 12 Colonel Brent recorded in his headquarters diary: "It strikes me that it is high time to leave this place. . . . I can see no use in persistently holding on here, when no good is to be gained, & much risk is to be run." To Brig. Gen. St. John Richardson Liddell, a brigade commander in Cleburne's Division, Bragg seemed "infatuated with the hopeless anxiety to take Chattanooga. This caused him to overlook the gathering storm."[21]

Bragg certainly appeared complacent. On November 21 he went so far as to invite a bridal party of fourteen women to visit the army the next day. It was hardly the act of a commander expecting to be attacked momentarily. That complacency went far to explain why he would order away what amounted to another infantry corps. Neither Buckner nor Colonel Brent echoed that complacency. Back on November 5 Buckner felt that Bragg "seemed blind to the state of affairs" at Chattanooga; nothing since had dissuaded him of that assessment. On the twenty-first, with some understatement, Brent journaled, "this distribution of forces seems hazardous."[22]

To prevent what Grant feared was a Confederate withdrawal, the Union commander turned to Thomas and the "demoralized" Army of the Cumberland. "Not willing that [Bragg] should get his army off in good order," wrote Grant, "Thomas was directed, early on the morning of the 23rd, to ascertain the truth or falsity of this report." In turn, Thomas turned to Major General Granger, informing the IV Corps commander to "throw one division . . . forward in the direction of Orchard Knob, and hold a second division in supporting distance, to discover the position of the enemy, if he still remains in the vicinity of his old camp. Howard's [XI Corps] and Baird's [Third Division, XIV Corps] commands will be ready to cooperate if needed." By driving in the advanced Confederate picket line running along Orchard Knob, the Federals should be able to determine if Bragg's main body was still present. Though the effort was only as a probe, Thomas intended to mass enough force—perhaps 20,000 men—to appear to be a real threat.[23]

Up to November 23 Bragg's army was not entrenched atop Missionary Ridge, which at more than two miles east of the town was too far from the Union defenses to deliver effective fire upon the enemy. Instead, the Confederate main line ran along the foot of Missionary Ridge (following modern-day Dodds Avenue) until it turned west to cross the Chattanooga Creek valley and connect with the Rebel positions on and around Lookout Mountain. Twelve hundred yards west of this main line, the Rebels established a forward line that paralleled their primary positions. A key feature of this advanced position was Orchard Knob, a craggy outcropping only a mile from the critical Union bastion of Fort Wood (near modern-day Perkins Park in Chattanooga). Brig. Gen. Arthur M. Manigault, whose mixed brigade of Alabamians and South Carolinians held that segment containing Orchard Knob, described the feature—which the Rebels referred to as "Cedar Hill"—as "the most prominent point between the Ridge and Chattanooga. . . . The 24th and 28th Alabama regiments were on duty that day. . . . The picket line was entrenched with a shallow ditch and low earthwork, with rifle pits a little in advance." Manigault's Brigade was expected to defend eight hundred yards with six hundred men. Other Confederate brigades held similarly long and undermanned positions on Manigault's left and right.[24]

Thomas's demonstration was ostentatious, intentionally so. Early on the afternoon of the twenty-third, Federal troops began filing out of their own entrenchments to form massed columns in the no-man's-land between the opposing lines. A correspondent for the *Chicago Evening Journal* noted that from Fort Wood, "the smooth ground descends rapidly to a little plain . . ., then a fringe of oak woods, then an acclivity, sinking down to a second fringe of woods, until . . . three-quarters of a mile distant rises Orchard Knob . . . , perhaps a hundred feet high, once wooded now bald. . . . Breastworks and rifle-pits seamed the landscape."[25]

A young English tourist was also a spectator that day. Henry Yates Thompson was traveling through the United States that fall and, through the auspices of the Christian Commission, managed to get to Chattanooga. After a breakfast of "cornbread and bacon," he toured the Union lines. Thompson was in Fort Wood when the Union assault commenced and left a vivid description in his diary: "I saw a sight I shall never forget," he wrote. "The whole Union army in the town—about 25,000 men under General Thomas—left their tents and huts and marched out past Fort Wood in long winding columns creeping into the valley and into line of battle round the town. From Fort Wood it all looked like a great review. But it was in deadly earnest."[26]

Granger selected Brig. Gen. Tom Wood's Third Division, IV Corps, to assault Orchard Knob. In turn, Wood chose Brig. Gen. August Willich's brigade to spearhead his column. Willich, a German émigré and former revolutionary, was a good choice for the role; he was a competent, aggressive leader. Pvt. Joseph Buckley of the 89th Illinois described the moment it began: "Just after dinner we were ordered to fall in with 100 rounds of cartridges each. We were then ordered in front where we formed in line of battle, and at two o'clock the word 'Forward' was given. We all started simultaneously, and it was one of the most splendid sights I ever saw."[27]

Manigault did not think it so splendid. As the senior brigadier, he was temporarily in charge of Maj. Gen. Patton Anderson's division while Anderson was away. Upon receiving word of the Union activity, he hurried to the top of Missionary Ridge and was greeted by an alarming spectacle. "All within the hostile lines seemed alive with men, and large masses of troops were pouring out [of] . . . their works. There must have been at least 50,000 (fifty thousand) men . . . under arms." Manigault immediately roused the division. "As the movement was visible to the whole army, in a short time [our] entire force was in the trenches, prepared for an assault."[28]

Most of the Confederates out on that forward line fell back to the main position at the foot of the ridge without putting up much resistance. Given the size and scope of the Federal reconnaissance, that was a reasonable course of action. Only Manigault's two Alabama regiments, the 24th and 28th, made a spirited but ultimately futile and costly resistance. The two units lost 175 men, nearly a third of their numbers, before falling back only to avoid wholesale capture, as "the enemy were getting in their rear." Among the losses were the 28th's battle flag. Cpl. G. A. Kraemer of the 41st Ohio "alone ordered and received the surrender of twenty men with the [28th Alabama's] colors." With the knoll in their possession, jubilant Federals set to work digging their own entrenchments. "We advanced steadily but quickly," recorded Private Buckley of the 89th Illinois, "and drove the REBS one mile before we stopped and took possession of their first line of Breastwork, and also a large knoll which went by the name of Orchard Knobb, but we call it Willick's Knobb now."[29]

Wood reported a Union loss of 29 men killed and 161 wounded in his division, waxing poetic at the grandeur of the advance. Both Grant and Thomas were satisfied with the effort, having observed it from Fort Wood.

Quartermaster General Meigs, also present, was unimpressed by the captured Rebels. "Two Alabamians were the first brought in, very much excited and very stupid. Did not know the name of their Brigade Commanders, but said Hindman's Division, to which they belonged, were all here." Grant and Thomas now had solid evidence that Bragg's army had not abandoned Missionary Ridge, demonstrated when the Army of Tennessee went on full alert to man the main line. That did not mean, however, that Bragg would choose to remain. At 8:00 P.M. that evening, Dana reported: "Nothing shows decisively that the enemy will fight or fly. Grant thinks [the] latter; other judicious officers think [the] former." More alarmingly, he also reported that the Tennessee "River has risen 5 feet since yesterday morning. Enormous quantities of drift. Both Chattanooga bridge and Brown's Ferry bridge [are] broken. [Osterhaus's] division still remains in Lookout Valley."[30]

For Bragg, the day's events proved shocking. His first thought was to recall Johnson's and Cleburne's divisions, now headed for Knoxville. That order found Cleburne at Chickamauga Station, loading troops. His own division had not begun to depart yet, but only one of Johnson's three brigades (that of Brig. Gen. A. W. Reynolds) was still present. Cleburne was directed to shift all these troops to the vicinity of Bragg's headquarters at the Moore House on Missionary Ridge. Bragg also ordered Hardee to take personal charge of this redeployment, shifting the corps commander's responsibility from the Confederate left on Lookout Mountain and in the direction of Trenton to the Army of Tennessee's right flank at the northern end of Missionary Ridge. Finally, according to Manigault, "during the night of the 23rd, orders came to construct a line of defenses on the crest of the Missionary Ridge, and such artillery as was in position in the lines at the foot was brought away." Bragg might not be thinking of retreat, but much of his army was on the move nonetheless.[31]

Grant knew little of these changes, of course, hidden as they were from Federal view by the surrounding heights. But once commenced, he had no intention of halting again. "The advantage was greatly on our side now, and if I could only have been assured that Burnside could hold out ten days longer I should have rested more easily. But we were doing the best we could for him and the cause." Grant also noted that "by the night of the 23rd Sherman's command was in a position to move, though . . . (Osterhaus's) [division] had not yet crossed . . . at Brown's Ferry . . . , but I was determined to move that night even without this division."[32]

7

"IT IS ALL POETRY"

*T*he stranding of Osterhaus's division in Lookout Valley proved a stroke of great fortune for Joe Hooker. At 7:30 P.M. on November 23, in response to Hooker's query if there would be an attack the next morning, Major General Reynolds, the Army of the Cumberland's chief of staff, responded: "the intention is, yes." Further, wrote Reynolds, "General commanding department desires that you remain with the troops in Lookout Valley." At 10:00 P.M. Thomas instructed Hooker that "if Wood's [Osterhaus's] division does not get across the river [at Brown's Ferry] by daybreak, he is ordered to report to you, and in that event the General commanding the Department directs that you endeavor to take the point of Lookout Mountain." Shortly after midnight, again via Reynolds, Hooker was told, "you can take the point of Lookout if your demonstration develops its practicability." By that time, everyone knew the bridge at Brown's Ferry would be out for at least another twelve hours. Hooker's demonstration would proceed apace.[1]

On November 22 Brigadier General Osterhaus rejoined his command after his emergency leave. On the night of the twenty-third, understanding that he was to be under Hooker's orders, Osterhaus rode to that general's headquarters to confer. There, he noted, "I passed the greatest part of the night, in discussing the operations of next morning." Those "operations" paid only lip service to the idea of a demonstration. Hooker was set on a full-scale assault. He also developed a high opinion of Osterhaus, whom he had not previously met, calling the German American general "a glorious Soldier [and] the best representative of the European service it has been my fortune to become acquainted with."[2]

Lookout Mountain's crest looms some 1,800 feet over the surrounding terrain. Its most important military feature, however, is the shelf, about two-thirds of the way up the slope, that adorns the nose of the mountain. Along it passed the main road from Chattanooga over Lookout Mountain past the white clapboard Cravens House, a distinctive landmark. Another steep slope rose from the shelf to Lookout's palisade, the vertical-sided rock walls that formed the mountain's most impassible barrier.

With Hardee's departure, Maj. Gen. Carter L. Stevenson was charged with defending Lookout Mountain. His division was mainly arrayed atop the mountain and oriented south, positioned against a potential Federal thrust up from Trenton via Johnson's Crook. The shelf was defended by Brig. Gen. Edward C. Walthall's Mississippi Brigade of Maj. Gen. Benjamin F. Cheatham's division. Cheatham's lines continued down to the southern bank of the Tennessee River east of Lookout Creek, then eastward across Chattanooga Valley to connect with Bragg's main line at the foot of Missionary Ridge. Stevenson belonged to Breckinridge's Corps, while Cheatham was part of Hardee's command, though neither corps commander was now present to oversee the mountain's defense—both men were on Missionary Ridge.

Hooker's objective—"the point of the Mountain"—was that shelf. If he captured it, Stevenson's men at the crest would be temporarily cut off from the rest of Bragg's army, their only way down via another gap in the palisade several miles to the south. But a direct assault against the shelf would require the Federals to force a crossing of rain-swollen Lookout Creek under fire, then a steep climb to assault Walthall's Mississippians, entrenched behind earthworks and rock walls. Far from promising a spectacular victory, the direct approach seemed more likely to produce a bloody failure, a western Fredericksburg, with heavy Union losses.

Hooker's command was a motley assemblage: three divisions drawn from three different corps from three different armies. Osterhaus's men were Army of the Tennessee veterans. Brigadier General Geary's Second Division, XII Corps, had accompanied Hooker from the East, drawn from the Army of the Potomac. Brigadier General Cruft's First Division belonged to Granger's IV Corps of Thomas's Army of the Cumberland. Cruft, who had been sent to help guard Kelly's Ferry and Shellmound during the operation to secure the Cracker Line, was now brought up to join the attack on the mountain. Only Geary had served under Hooker previously, back east, during the disastrous Chancellorsville Campaign—a stain Hooker was now seeking to erase. "We were all strangers," wrote Hooker in his report, "no one division ever having seen either of the others."[3]

Hooker's plan used Osterhaus and part of Cruft to threaten a crossing and direct attack on the Confederates, while Geary, reinforced by the other of Cruft's brigades, marched up the west bank of Lookout Creek to

Light's Mill. There, Geary was to cross the creek and move up the slope to the palisade, then face north and advance on Walthall's flank. Once Geary was engaged, then Cruft and Osterhaus would cross Lookout Creek in force and join the assault. The whole movement would be supported by Hooker's artillery, which commanded the Confederate positions from a line of hills on the west side of Lookout Creek, and from additional Army of the Cumberland guns on Moccasin Bend, across the Tennessee River.[4]

Grant expected little from the operation; indeed, Thomas favored the move more than he did. If all Hooker achieved was to divert a bit of Rebel attention away from Sherman's predawn crossing of the Tennessee River and subsequent movement against the north end of Missionary Ridge, Grant would be satisfied. Hooker, however, was intent on making the most of this sudden opportunity.[5]

For Grant, everything hinged on Sherman. The objective was still, as first articulated on November 7, to gain the northern end of Missionary Ridge and drive a wedge between Bragg and Longstreet. By November 23 three of Sherman's divisions were camped amid the hills on the north bank of the Tennessee, along with Brig. Gen. Jefferson C. Davis's division of the XIV Corps. Davis's three brigades had been waiting for Sherman's column since November 19, their men spending their time organizing the pontoon boats needed for the crossing. Col. Daniel McCook's brigade handled most of these duties, massing the boats in the waters of North Chickamauga Creek, hidden from Rebel eyes, until needed. Capt. Allan Fahnestock of the 86th Illinois, selected to command one of those boats, heard Thomas's reconnaissance against Orchard Knob: "heavy cannonading and volleys of musketry at Chattanooga[,] extending all along our line." Impatiently, he added: "We intended to cross the river last night on pontoons but it was too clear[,] but tomorrow we will cross. . . . The ball will open soon, and we will dance to the firing line."[6]

The final element of Sherman's operation was Howard's XI Corps, two small divisions amounting to 6,000 men. As first articulated in Grant's order to Thomas, Howard was to move northward along the south bank of the Tennessee once Sherman was across, extending the Army of the Cumberland's reach to link up with Sherman's westerners once they were established on the far shore. From there, Howard could either support the move against Missionary Ridge or rush to its defense should Bragg prove suddenly combative and attempt a counterattack.

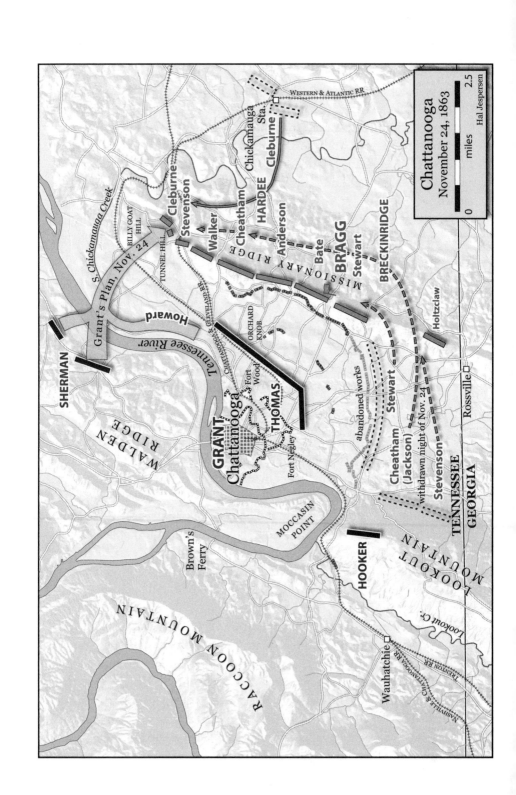

Chattanooga
November 24, 1863

Hal Jespersen

0   miles   2.5

So far, the XI Corps had seen only limited fighting at Chattanooga. In October at Wauhatchie, the brunt of the combat fell on Geary's XII Corps men, not Howard's troops; and though Howard had a limited role on November 23, he sustained very little loss in the move against Orchard Knob. That did not mean a relaxation within the ranks, however. On the twenty-third, when Maj. Gen. Carl Schurz, the German ex-revolutionary who now commanded Howard's Third Division, awoke at daybreak, his "first thought was that on that day, I would be killed." He spent the morning feeling the certainty of his death, nearly even penning a "last letter," but despite a near-miss with an artillery shell that afternoon, Schurz passed the day unscathed. November 24 promised a renewed chance for action.[7]

Sherman's operation by then was already underway. According to the regimental historian of the 55th Illinois, at 11:00 P.M. of November 23, his regiment, the 8th Missouri, and the 116th Illinois, all of Brig. Gen. Giles A. Smith's brigade of Morgan L. Smith's Second Division, made their way to the long line of "one hundred and sixteen pontoons" along north Chickamauga Creek. "Every boat was manned by four oarsmen" and carried "twenty-five men and officers." Muskets were "loaded but not capped." Once the men were on board, the boats made their way down the creek to where it joins the Tennessee. There, they turned downstream and headed for the far shore, aiming for the mouth of South Chickamauga Creek, guided by lanterns on the north bank. The landing was a complete success. The entire Confederate picket post guarding that spot was captured, with only a single musket discharged, and "that by the last sentinel captured, who in his nervous surprise, fired in the air." That report failed to rouse the Rebels, and Morgan Smith's men began the process of erecting a fortified *"tete du pont"* while the boats returned to fetch more troops. John E. Smith's XVII Corps division was the next across, commencing its move at 1:30 A.M.[8]

"By daylight of November 24," Sherman reported, "two divisions, of about 8,000 troops, were on the east [south] bank of the Tennessee, and had thrown up a very respectable rifle-trench." With the dawn, work on a pontoon bridge commenced, while the steamboat *Dunbar* chugged upstream to aid the crossing of Ewing's Fourth Division. At 11:00 A.M., reported a Union signal officer, "Sherman has three divisions across and four guns." But the same officer observed "Rebels moving heavy force to our left." Accordingly, Sherman eschewed any further offensive movement until his whole force was across the river. Davis's men were the last to cross and the first to use the newly completed pontoon bridge—"1,350 feet," according to Sherman—which was ready about noon.[9]

General Howard, who Grant "directed to open communication with [Sherman] by a brigade," now appeared. He reached Sherman's entrenched line close to midday, surprising some of the troops since "they did not expect anything or anybody from that quarter except the enemy." Howard posted Col. Adolphus Buschbeck's brigade on the right of Ewing's division near the Crutchfield farm and rode on up to the bridge, where he reported to Sherman. They met "just as the last pontoon was being ferried into its place. 'How are you General Howard! That's right! You must have got up early,'" exclaimed the buoyant Sherman. His mission complete, Howard left Buschbeck in place to connect with Sherman's right and returned to the rest of his corps, which lacked the strength to form a continuous line connecting the main army with the newly established bridgehead.[10]

Sherman's troops were digging in across the fertile fields and pastures of Amnicola, Thomas Crutchfield's expansive farmstead just outside of Chattanooga. The recently arrested owner was not at home, having been sent off to Nashville, but his family was in residence. The men of the XV Corps apparently treated the farm as if its owner were a confirmed Rebel. At the end of the year, Crutchfield described his property as "a perfect barren waste, farm implements all destroyed, not a rail left, [and] the farm all cut up with rifle pits. . . . Not content with the destruction of everything on the farm, but they plundered all the houses, save the one my family was in." This devastation was unfortunate, as was Crutchfield's arrest. As a local, no one had a better knowledge of the surrounding terrain than he did. Had he been available, his input could have proved invaluable to Sherman.[11]

Grant monitored Sherman's morning activities closely. At 11:20 A.M. he informed Sherman that "Thomas' forces are confronting enemy's line of rifle pitts which seem to be but weakly lined with troops. Conciderable movement has taken place on top of the ridge towards you. . . . Until I do hear from you I am loth to give any orders for a general engagement." He repeated a similar sentiment to Howard at 12:40 P.M., instructing Howard to "resist but bring on no attack until otherwise directed unless troops to the right or left of you become engaged. . . . The open spaces between you & Sherman can not be closed until Sherman advances to shorten it." To Thomas, at 1:00 P.M., Grant explained that "Sherman's bridge was completed at 12. M at which time all his force was over except one division. That division [Davis] was to cross immediately when his attack would commence. Your forces should attack at the same time." If things were rel-atively quiet on the Union left, however, things were certainly progressing elsewhere. To the above note to Sherman, Grant appended, "Hooker seems to have been engaged for some time but how [he fares] I have not heard."[12]

Hooker was indeed engaged. At 3:15 that morning Cruft had received his initial orders. His division was then camped near Hooker's headquarters in Lookout Valley, having just come up from Whiteside Station the day before. Hooker instructed Cruft to send Brig. Gen. Walter C. Whitaker's brigade south to Wauhatchie, there to join up with Geary's flanking col-umn. Whitaker moved out at 6:00 A.M. Cruft, with Grose's brigade, 1,624 strong, awaited additional instructions, which arrived fifteen minutes later. Cruft was to "rapidly seize two bridges over Lookout Creek, in our front, and place skirmishers" across the creek in order to "hold and re-pair them." Grose "moved out at 6:45 A.M." but almost immediately halted again; the equipment needed to affect those repairs was not readily at hand. Cruft admitted to "some time spent in sending back for tools." By 9:00 A.M., however, Grose was in position "just below the railroad bridge across Lookout Creek." There, they soon discovered a strong Confederate picket line holding the east bank of the unfordable stream. Skirmishing ensued, but the Federals were unable to seize either bridge.[13]

Geary's column was waiting for Whitaker at Wauhatchie; they rendez-voused about daylight. Whitaker numbered 1,465 officers and men, while Geary's own small division numbered 2,359. Thus reinforced, Geary led the combined force of just over 3,800 troops toward Light's Mill on Look-out Creek, two and a half miles south of the creek's mouth. There, while making rounds on November 23, Lt. Col. Eugene Powell of the 66th Ohio noted an uncompleted dam. Wooden supports offered the foundations of a footbridge, which, once planked, became Geary's means of accessing the east bank. Powell led a party of Union pickets across first to clear out any Rebels. Finding none, Geary's men commenced work on the footbridge.[14]

At the Cravens House, General Walthall listened uneasily to the various sounds of combat resounding from below. Unlike November 23, when the weather was cold but clear, the twenty-fourth brought cold rain, mist, and fog—perfect attacking weather, shrouding both Sherman's and Hooker's operations. General Stevenson feared an attack on the mountain, having notified Bragg that he expected as much the day before; but where would that blow land? At first light Stevenson visited Walthall at the Cravens House, informing the Mississippian that if he was assailed he would have to fall back to the eastern face of the mountain, defended by Brig. Gen. John C. Moore's Alabama brigade of 1,000 men. Walthall's own five regiments were widely dispersed. The 29th and 30th Mississippi held the brigade's left, defending a rock wall created the month before by Longstreet's men. The 24th and 27th Mississippi manned the extended picket line along the slope down to and along the east bank of Lookout Creek, supported by half of the 34th Mississippi, connecting to Moore's Alabamians, which extended that picket line east along the Tennessee River and into Chattanooga Valley. Walthall retained the other half of the 34th as a reserve. At 9:00 A.M., with Cruft's Federals appearing in force at the rail and road bridges, Walthall dispatched the rest of the 34th down the slope to reinforce his line and notified Stevenson of the developing threat.[15]

By 10:00 A.M. Osterhaus's division was on the scene, and Hooker used these western Federals to reinforce Cruft. Brig. Gen. Charles Woods's brigade moved up to the creek on Cruft's right, upstream, where they engaged the Mississippians and began preparing to throw across a "pole bridge." Cruft ordered Grose to leave the 75th and 84th Illinois Regiments in place at the rail crossing and shift the rest of his brigade south in support of Woods. By late morning, Union pressure was mounting along the entire length of Walthall's front.[16]

All the while, Geary's men were getting into position. Edward Hopkins of the 149th New York later recalled that as each regiment crossed, the division commander, posted at footbridge, "shook hands with [each] colonel . . . and gave him his orders." Then the lines of troops scrambled up the mountain until they reached the foot of the palisade, where they faced left—north—and formed three lines of battle. Geary's own three brigades formed the first line, while Whitaker's men formed in two supporting lines behind Geary's right. "Soon the order passed along the line," recalled Hopkins, whose regiment was in the center of Geary's formation, "and away we went, working our way through the tangled undergrowth and working our way over rocks and fallen trees for nearly half a mile." Then they struck the left flank of the 30th Mississippi, still behind their now-useless rock barricade. "To our joy," wrote Sgt. Maj. Charles Partridge of the 96th Illinois, following along in Whitaker's brigade, "we saw that [their works] had been constructed to resist a direct attack from below, and that from our position we could rake them with an enfilading fire."[17]

Having achieved complete surprise, Geary's attack rolled forward, unstoppable. It was "a sickle of Mars," exulted Sergeant Major Partridge,

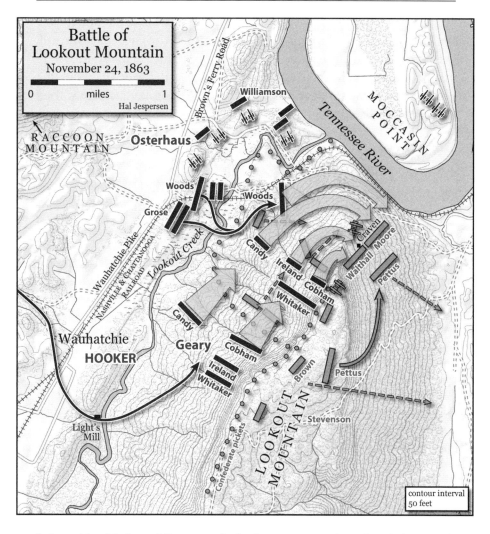

"whose blue blade and fire-tipped edge" swept around Lookout's face, with the mountain's "point as a pivot [to] reap a glorious harvest." Discovering he was flanked, Walthall ordered his men to fall back to the Cravens House, where he hoped to make a stand, but he met with scant success. "I endeavored in falling back to turn the rocks and irregularities of the ground to the best account for the protection of the men, and . . . to yield the ground as slowly as possible." Walthall sought to buy enough time for Moore's Brigade to form a firm line at the Cravens House, where his own men might fall in to aid in the defense, but events outpaced him. "Most of my picket line to the right of the railroad bridge . . . was cut off," lamented

Walthall, with many of those men falling into Union hands. By the time his survivors reached the immediate vicinity of the Cravens farmyard, they were in no shape to reform, under fire from Union artillery arrayed in an arc from across Lookout Creek over to Moccasin Bend. The retreating men kept on going, passing Moore's arriving Alabamians, who now tried to stop the onslaught.[18]

As those Rebel pickets scrambled rearward, Hooker lost no time in sending Osterhaus and Cruft's remaining force across the creek, adding to Walthall's and Moore's woes. Woods's brigade completed their footbridge and crossed, along with most of Grose's troops. At the railroad bridge the 84th and 75th Illinois also managed to span the gaps, allowing Osterhaus to lead Col. James A. Williamson's six Iowa regiments across as well. "I ascended the mountain in as direct a line as possible, in order to reach the right of General Woods's brigade and press the retreating enemy toward him." This attack netted Osterhaus several hundred captured Rebels from both Walthall's and Moore's brigades.[19]

At the Cravens House, where the rest of the Alabamians were struggling to hold firm, another sharply delivered Union attack soon cleared the shelf. Moore's line held the lower part of the shelf, but, as Lt. Samuel Sprott of the 40th Alabama noted, "Walthall's brigade had been practically destroyed before we knew it, and the remnant of his brigade passed to the rear as we moved to the front." This left the upper reaches of the intended Cravens House position open to Union penetration, and though Moore's men repulsed an initial rush against their part of the line, Walter Whitaker's Federals gained Moore's flank. Sergeant Major Partridge recorded the 96th Illinois's actions here: "Colonel [Thomas E.] Champion grasped the situation in an instant . . . and gave orders for a left wheel. The Regiment . . . , gaining a position along a rude fence, poured a destructive fire into the ranks of the enemy." Flanked, the Rebels retreated, allowing another of Whitaker's regiments, the 40th Ohio, to overrun a section of two guns from Capt. Evan P. Howell's Georgia Battery. This section, commanded by Lt. R. T. Gibson, never had a chance to fire; first masked by Walthall's men, they were forced to abandon the cannon when Moore's men retreated.[20]

By 2:00 P.M. Moore and Walthall had fallen back to a point some four hundred yards to the rear and around the eastern curve of the mountain. There, they reformed and were eventually reinforced, first by three Alabama regiments of Brig. Gen. Edmund W. Pettus's brigade, which Stevenson had started down from Lookout's crest at 12:30 P.M., and then that evening by Col. J. T. Holtzclaw's brigade of yet more Alabamians. The Federals followed but did not again attack, contenting themselves with trading periodic volleys with the Confederates. The Southerners did manage to retain control of the Summertown Road, without which Stevenson and the remaining troops atop Lookout would have been marooned. But Hooker decided not to press what would have been a frontal assault against fresh troops; his 10,000 men had accomplished enough. In a mission similar to General Howard's, at 2:00 P.M. Thomas dispatched Brig. Gen. William P. Carlin's brigade of the XIV Corps from Fort Sheridan—part of the Chattanooga defenses—to cross Chattanooga Creek and connect with Hooker's troops. Thus, by early afternoon all three principal Union commands—Hooker's, Thomas's, and Sherman's—were in direct communication along the south bank of the Tennessee River.[21]

Thanks to the clouds and mist, the Battle of Lookout Mountain was only intermittently viewable from Chattanooga or Missionary Ridge, though the fog parted sufficiently at midday to allow Hooker's artillery to play a significant role in the fighting around the Cravens House. The action was sufficiently visible, however, to generate great enthusiasm among the watching Federals. Henry Yates Thompson was again observing from Fort Wood, and he was in august company. Grant was there, as was Quartermaster General Meigs and Stanton's new envoy, Maj. Gen. David Hunter. Thompson saw a bit of Sherman's crossing and heard firing that morning from the vicinity of Lookout Valley, but then things quieted down.

I began to think nothing was doing, [he wrote], when at about midday . . . heavy reports of cannon and musketry . . . made all of us hurry to that side of Fort Wood. I joined two officers looking through telescopes toward Lookout Mountain, and we soon saw Hooker attacking, his men plainly visible . . . , sweeping round the steep face of Lookout. We saw Hooker's men fall back once—then they advanced again. After some little suspense we saw the Rebels run round the face of Lookout near the top and Hooker's line advance after them, rifles popping all along the face of the mountain and guns shelling the retreating Rebels from Moccasin Point and Fort Negley. An officer beside me . . . cried out: "There they are and the Rebels are running!" . . . [A]nd there sure enough . . . we saw a running fight with the Rebels retreating before Hooker's men. Furious cheering soon started on the Federal right . . . , where they could see the action better than we could.

That cheering soon spread throughout the army. "I never saw in my life anything like the excitement on Fort Wood. . . . The only man who seemed unmoved was General Grant himself, the prime author of all this hurly burly. There he stood in his plain citizen's clothes . . . apparently totally unmoved."[22]

Meigs gave the action a name destined to become immortal: "The Battle above the Clouds." Considering the fog, Sergeant Major Partridge thought later, "literally it was a battle *in* the clouds." The commanding general was less charitable. In later years, irritated by Hooker's demeanor and the fuss made over the affair, Grant would dismiss the action casually: "There was no such battle, and no action even worthy to be called a battle on Lookout Mountain. It is all poetry."[23]

Still, to those observing, Hooker had accomplished the spectacular, if not quite impossible. Now, on the afternoon of November 24, what could Sherman accomplish?

Sherman ordered his advance to begin at 1:00 P.M., just about the time the fighting on Lookout reached its climax. The movement, he reported, "had been carefully explained to all division commanders." Each formed their troops in column. Morgan Smith's division was on the left, advancing parallel to and south of South Chickamauga Creek; John Smith's division constituted the center column; and Ewing's brigades moved to John Smith's right. "Each . . . column was covered by a good line of skirmishers. . . . A light, drizzling rain prevailed, and the clouds hung low, cloaking our movement." The first Federals stepped off at 1:30 P.M.[24]

In his memoir James Wilson found Sherman's caution mystifying and inexcusable. Sherman had crossed the Tennessee without opposition and had faced none all morning. "With his three divisions . . . safely landed on the south bank of the river," fumed Wilson, "there was nothing left for [Sherman] to do but move against the enemy. The country was entirely open, and . . . the way both to the enemy's flank and rear was straight out from the river." Instead, "Sherman's movements were slow and ineffective. . . . The fact is that halting to fortify had cost the Federal commander all the advantages of a surprise."[25]

Wilson's criticism had the advantage of considerable hindsight, but he was not wrong. Bragg was unprepared for Sherman's crossing. Shortly after dawn, while riding along Missionary Ridge, the Confederate commander caught sight of the newly crossed Federals digging in, and he hastened to respond. That response, however, was inexplicably ineffectual. Even though Cleburne's Division was lying in reserve near his headquarters, Bragg directed its commander to send only one brigade—that of Brig. Gen. Lucius Polk—"toward the far right; the rest of the division was to stay put." Polk's mission was to defend a railroad bridge over South Chickamauga Creek in order to keep Sherman away from Chickamauga Station. At 8:30 A.M. Bragg ordered the recently detrained Tennessee brigade of Brig. Gen. Marcus J. Wright to march from that same station toward the mouth of South Chickamauga Creek, where Wright was "to resist any enemy attempt to cross" the Tennessee. It was, as historian Peter Cozzens has pointed out, "a bizarre order" since "Sherman already had five times as many troops" as were in Wright's command.[26]

So far, given Bragg's lack of an effective response, Sherman's hesitation cost Grant little. The Confederate flank and rear remained dangerously vulnerable. That window of opportunity, however, would not remain open forever. But Sherman's advance toward Missionary Ridge proceeded with, if anything, even more caution. From the new Union line, the first visible high ground (which the general assumed was the northern end of Missionary Ridge) was a mile and a half distant. It took his lead elements almost two hours to complete that move, though, as Pvt. Joseph E. Walton of the 30th Ohio, which provided the skirmishers for Morgan Smith's column, admitted: "we proceeded without much opposition to take possession of a spur of Mission Ridge." This "spur" turned out to be more of a detached hill, "jut[ting] out to the north at the east end of the ridge proper and . . . somewhat lower than the main ridge, being timbered on the north declivity, with a cleared space on top . . . , exposing us to full view of the enemy, who were posted on the east end of the main ridge."[27]

As Federal skirmishers from the other two divisions joined Walton and his fellow Ohioans on this hill, known locally as Billy Goat Hill, they soon discovered that the lay of the land at the north end of Missionary Ridge was considerably different than supposed. The north end of Missionary Ridge really terminated on a high hill just north of where a tunnel for the East Tennessee & Georgia Railroad passed through the ridge—hence the name Tunnel Hill. Billy Goat Hill was a completely separate elevation, north of Tunnel Hill. Between the two lay a steep ravine. A spur of Tunnel Hill (not to be confused with Walton's spur mentioned above) ran to the east just north of the tunnel. East of Billy Goat Hill, yet another individual hill rose to overlook the valley between Tunnel and Billy Goat Hills. Somewhat farther to the north, the Western & Atlantic tracks ran around the north end of Billy Goat Hill, turning eastward at Boyce's Station to then cross South Chickamauga Creek. To gain the actual north end of Missionary Ridge and thus turn Bragg's right flank, Federals from Billy Goat Hill would have to either attack south across the ravine to Tunnel Hill or east across the same ravine to take the other unnamed hill. Unfortunately for Sherman, both of those features now sported—or soon would sport—Confederates.

These men were the rest of Cleburne's Division, hurriedly deployed to meet Sherman's advance. At 2:00 P.M., spotting the Federals, General Hardee sent an urgent courier to Cleburne, an action mirrored by Bragg a few minutes later. Shifting northward, Cleburne posted an artillery battery on the crown of Tunnel Hill, sent Brig. Gen. James A. Smith's Texas brigade down the slope toward Billy Goat Hill to resist the Yankee advance, and brought up his last two brigades, first to occupy the unnamed eastern hill, then later to secure the eastern spur of Tunnel Hill. A sharp skirmish resulted in the valley between Billy Goat and Tunnel Hills, as Col. Theodore Jones led Private Walton and the rest of the 30th Ohio down the slope in turn. By this time it was after 4:00 P.M., and little daylight remained. When Jones was repulsed, Sherman elected to halt and dig in on Billy Goat Hill.[28]

There was a similar collision and skirmish along the banks of South Chickamauga Creek. Morgan Smith's First Brigade, under Giles A. Smith (the division commander's younger brother), bumped into Wright's Tennesseans, moving toward the riverbank from the railroad station. The encounter surprised both formations, triggered a brief firefight and a somewhat more prolonged exchange of artillery, but produced few casualties. One of those who did fall was Giles Smith, badly wounded, a loss that caused considerable confusion within his brigade. This unexpected appearance of Rebels to his left and rear must have caused Sherman some concern about that flank.[29]

In his report, submitted nearly a month after the fact, Sherman explained what happened. "From studying all the maps, I had inferred that Missionary Ridge was a continuous hill, but we found ourselves on two high points, with a deep depression between us and the one immediately over the tunnel, which was my chief objective. . . . The ground we had gained, however, was so important that I could leave nothing to chance, and ordered it to be fortified during the night."[30]

Sherman's great blunder here was in not securing local guidance. If the maps were indeed wrong (and Civil War maps often were), then securing local guides was essential. Henry Van Ness Boynton, a 35th Ohio veteran and postwar Chickamauga-Chattanooga National Park historian, called this an "astonishing error. . . . [I]t is certainly one of the most remarkable oversights of the war that this position was not thoroughly identified. Even . . . to stop at a farmhouse and ask a citizen would have answered the purpose." Again, Crutchfield's absence while under arrest looms large. And even if his loyalty were suspect, why not consult other proven Unionist citizens or obtain local knowledge drawn from the Union army itself? For example, just two months previously, on September 22 and 23, the 59th Ohio defended the ground around Boyce's Station immediately after the Battle of Chickamauga and had a running skirmish with Confederate cavalry as they fell back into Chattanooga. Now those Ohioans were in Wood's division of the IV Corps. Why did word not go out through the ranks that men who knew the area were needed? In short, there were ample resources available to supplement Sherman's apparently inadequate maps had the effort been made.[31]

Sherman wrote his report with the benefit of hindsight. There is considerable contemporary evidence that he knew none of the details about Billy Goat Hill, Missionary Ridge, or Tunnel Hill on the night of November 24. Certainly, if he did know, he failed to relay that crucial information up the chain of command. That evening Grant informed Thomas that "General Sherman [had] carried Missionary Ridge as far as the tunnel with only slight skirmishing. His right now rests at the tunnel and on top of the hill; his left at [South] Chickamauga Creek." At 7:30 P.M. Assistant Secretary Dana, who spent the day with Sherman's forces, echoed the same news, informing Stanton that "the crest of the ridge was gained without serious opposition or loss, and at 4 o'clock, when I left the ridge, the line extended from the turnpike bridge over the Chickamauga to the tunnel of the Knoxville railroad." Clearly, based on these dispatches, either Sherman did not know he was not on Missionary Ridge, or if he knew, he did not tell Grant. Since Dana was with Sherman and, according to his own dispatch, on Billy Goat Hill—what he deemed "the ridge"—until 4:00 P.M., Dana's message strongly suggests that Sherman did not know.[32]

Almost unnoticed by most participants, one other force had a role to play in the events of November 24. Col. Eli Long's newly assembled cavalry brigade followed the last of Sherman's infantry across the Tennessee River that afternoon, slipping around Missionary Ridge's north end. The force included detachments from the 1st, 3rd, and 4th Ohio Cavalry; the 4th Michigan Cavalry; and elements of the 17th Indiana and 98th Illinois

Mounted Infantry. Long reached Brown's Ferry on November 22 and had been waiting on the north bank of the Tennessee for Sherman since then. If Sherman did not otherwise need him, Long's orders were to make for Cleveland, Tennessee, and there "destroy as far as possible the enemy's lines of communication in that direction." Once across the river, Long's column quickly rode out of sight. It would be several days before they were heard from again.[33]

Ulysses S. Grant.
Major General Grant
rushed to Chatta-
nooga in October
1863, with orders to
restore the mili-
tary situation and
avert an impending
crisis. Courtesy of the
Library of Congress.

George H. Thomas. Major General Thomas reluctantly replaced
Rosecrans at the head of the
Army of the Cumberland, a move
he felt was unwarranted and
unfairly motivated by Secretary
of State Edwin Stanton's personal
animosity toward Rosecrans.
Courtesy of the Library of Congress.

Grant and Thomas. The meeting between these men has been described as difficult, but Horace Porter recalled an affable encounter. *Left to right*, Brig. Gen. John Rawlins, Assistant Secretary of War Charles A. Dana, Brig. Gen. James H. Wilson, Brig. Gen. W. F. "Baldy" Smith, Major General Grant, Major General Thomas, and Captain Porter. Horace Porter, *Campaigning with Grant* (New York: Century, 1906), 4.

The Nashville and Chattanooga Railroad. The railroad skirted the northern foot of Lookout Mountain on a narrow shelf just above the Tennessee River, a perfect chokepoint for Confederate interdiction. Courtesy of the Library of Congress.

Braxton Bragg. The Confederate general commanded the Army of Tennessee at Chickamauga, that army's only significant victory, and now besieged the Federals in Chattanooga. Courtesy of the Library of Congress.

James Longstreet. The Confederate lieutenant general, freshly arrived with his corps from Virginia, proved to be a difficult subordinate for Bragg. Robert Underwood Johnson and Clarence Clough Buel, eds., *Battles and Leaders of the Civil War, People's Pictorial Edition* (New York: Century, 1894), 126.

William J. Hardee. The Confederate lieutenant general, a Bragg critic in the past, was returned to the Army of Tennessee after Chickamauga in a vain hope to bring harmony to that troubled command. Courtesy of the Library of Congress.

John C. Breckinridge. The Confederate major general and former U.S. vice president, though a Bragg foe, persuaded the Confederate commanding general to stay and defend Missionary Ridge on November 25, 1863. Courtesy of the Library of Congress.

William T. Sherman. The Union major general was Grant's most trusted subordinate, but he proved tactically ineffective at Chattanooga. Courtesy of the Library of Congress.

William F. "Baldy" Smith. The Union brigadier general was the Army of the Cumberland's chief engineer at Chattanooga, where he greatly impressed Grant with his determined efforts to restore the army's supply lines. Courtesy of the Library of Congress.

Joseph Hooker. The Federal major general, disgraced at Chancellorsville, was eager to win renewed fame and redeem his military reputation in the western theater. Courtesy of the Library of Congress.

The Cravens House. The site of fierce fighting on November 24, 1863, the house was destroyed during the Battle of Lookout Mountain but was eventually rebuilt. Courtesy of David A. Powell.

The Battle of Chattanooga. This painting by Swedish-born artist Thure de Thulstrup, shows Grant, Thomas, and their staffs observing the fighting on Missionary Ridge, November 25, 1863. Courtesy of the Library of Congress.

Missionary Ridge. Missionary Ridge's western face, near the railroad tunnel, was the approximate area of Sherman's assaults. Courtesy of the Library of Congress.

Sherman's attack on Missionary Ridge. This drawing by Alfred Waud, probably a postwar rendition, shows elements of Sherman's force attacking Tunnel Hill. Courtesy of the Library of Congress.

The 100th Indiana at Missionary Ridge. This image, from the 100th Indiana's regimental history, shows that regiment's assault against Tunnel Hill as part of Loomis's brigade of the XV Corps. Sherlock, *One Hundredth Regiment of Indiana Infantry.*

The 32nd Indiana at Missionary Ridge. This Adolph Metzner illustration of the infantry regiment depicts Lt. Col. Henry Von Treba capturing Confederate artillery on November 25, 1863, at the storming of Missionary Ridge. Courtesy of the Library of Congress.

Captured Confederate artillery. The guns were lined up in Chattanooga for inventory after the Battle of Missionary Ridge. Courtesy of the Library of Congress.

Grant on Lookout Mountain. In the days following the defeat of Bragg's army, Grant, seen at the lower left, visited the battlefields of Chattanooga, Chickamauga, and, pictured here, Lookout Mountain. Courtesy of the Library of Congress.

8
"WE SHALL HAVE A BATTLE ON MISSION RIDGE"

*H*aving spent much of the day on November 24 observing what he could of the fighting, Grant retired to his headquarters, well satisfied with the day's progress. After all, as far as he knew, Sherman had secured Missionary Ridge at least as far south as the rail tunnel, compromising Bragg's entire defensive line. Now the Federals need only complete the victory, assuming Bragg did not retreat. Once again, Sherman was the point of the spear. Via Chief of Staff Rawlins, Grant ordered his most trusted subordinate to "attack the enemy . . . from your position at early dawn to-morrow morning (25th instant). General Thomas has been instructed to commence the attack early tomorrow morning. He will carry the enemy's rifle-pits in his immediate front or move to the left to your support" as needed. On the Union right, Hooker's mission was again limited. With Confederates still atop Lookout Mountain, Grant expected him merely to hold the Summertown Road, thus blocking the escape of any of those lingering Rebels, and then secure the summit.[1]

In contrast to the weather of the previous day, November 25 was "a beautiful clear cold day." At 7:00 A.M. Montgomery Meigs recorded: "Sun appeared just above Mission Ridge—Large bodies of [Rebel] troops moving to our left along the summit gaining a position on the high point." More interestingly, off to his right rear, the quartermaster general could see an "American flag waving from the top . . . of Lookout Mountain. Our troops apparently in possession—no firing. Clear beautiful morning, smoke and mist hang in the valleys [but the] summit [is] clear." Most importantly, thought Meigs, "we shall have a battle on Mission Ridge."[2]

General Bragg had rearranged his forces considerably during the night, but he was still determined not to retreat. He did, however, quickly decide that he could no longer afford to hold Lookout Mountain. As early as 2:30 P.M. on November 24, Bragg ordered Major General Stevenson to withdraw his men to the east side of Chattanooga Creek, "destroying the bridges behind." That movement began deep in the night at 2:00 A.M. The

Rebels withdrew first from the summit; then from the shelf, where they confronted Hooker and still held open the Summertown Road retreat route; and finally from the lines stretching laterally across Chattanooga Creek connecting Missionary Ridge with Lookout Mountain. Bragg ordered the bulk of those forces to the north end of Missionary Ridge, where Sherman had appeared so unexpectedly the afternoon before. At dawn many—if not most—of those troops were still in motion. This was the activity Meigs witnessed.[3]

The Confederate retreat allowed a detail from the 8th Kentucky (U.S.) to cautiously ascend the face of the mountain from the Cravens House and, once they found the summit clear of Confederates, to plant their national colors at the point, visible to all below. "We could occasionally hear," recalled Capt. T. J. Wright of the 8th, "a heavy, rumbling noise on the top of Lookout, above us, that caused us . . . to suspect some movement of the enemy." When brigade commander Whitaker asked the 8th for "a few volunteers to climb that cliff and see if the enemy are still there," the men responded quickly. Capt. John Wilson and six enlisted men made the ascent via "an irregular kind of natural stairway, by which hung a large wild grape vine." The outcome of this climb must not have been all that uncertain because the detail took the regiment's national flag with them, something they certainly would have been loath to do if capture were likely. The remainder of the regiment soon followed and quickly discovered that the only Rebels left at the summit were "over 200 of their sick and convalescent, with a thin line of pickets surrounding their camp at Summertown." Hooker quickly reported, "we have possession of the peak . . . [and] present indications point to the enemy's having abandoned our front; prisoners think they have abandoned the valley entirely."[4]

There was also no immediate fighting on Sherman's front, despite Grant's order for that officer to attack at first light. The retreat from Chattanooga Valley, combined with the lack of action to the north, produced confusion among the Federal commanders. In stark contrast to Meigs's 7:00 A.M. prediction of battle, at 7:30 A.M. Assistant Secretary Dana reported "no firing at [the] front. This makes it pretty certain Bragg [has] retreated. . . . As soon as positively determined Bragg has gone, Granger, with 20,000 men, moves up south bank Tennessee . . . to cut off Longstreet's retreat and relieve Burnside."[5]

Federals were not the only ones who believed the Army of Tennessee would abandon Missionary Ridge. Many Confederates thought similarly.

At 9:00 P.M. the night before, General Bragg conferred with his two corps commanders, Lieutenant General Hardee and Major General Breckinridge, at army headquarters. Hardee argued for a full retreat to the east side of Chickamauga Creek. He reasoned that the Army of Tennessee was badly outnumbered, that both flanks were now threatened, and that with the creek behind them rising due to rains, a defeat risked the army's destruction. Conversely, Breckinridge wanted to stay. He pointed out that there was not time to complete a full withdrawal before daylight, giving Grant a sure opportunity to attack them while moving. Breckinridge also insisted that Missionary Ridge was a position of immense strength, averring that "if troops could not fight there, they could not fight anywhere." Despite his immediate postbattle allegation (redolent with the hindsight that remaining had been a mistake) that Breckinridge was "totally unfit for any duty from the 23rd to the 27th—during all our trials—from drunkenness," Bragg sided with the Kentuckian. The Army of Tennessee would stand fast. He did decide to assign Hardee to the critical right flank, where Cleburne clung to Tunnel Hill, and was given as reinforcements Stevenson's men from Lookout Mountain.[6]

Cleburne was already preparing his departure, assuming too that the army would not stay in the face of such an overwhelming Union threat. After dark he sent Capt. Irving Buck to Hardee's headquarters to ask for orders. When Buck discovered that Hardee was with Bragg, he rode on to the Moore House. The first senior officer he met was his corps commander, Breckinridge, who snarled: "I never felt more like fighting than when I saw those people shelling my troops off Lookout today, and I mean to get even with them." More pragmatically, Hardee instructed the captain that Cleburne was back under his command and to "tell Cleburne we are to fight; that his division will undoubtedly be heavily attacked, and they must do their very best." He rode back and reported all this to Cleburne, who immediately called up his artillery and sent word to place additional troops on the surrounding hills. Personally, Buck was displeased: "What motive Bragg had for remaining on the ridge is inscrutable."[7]

As it turned out, Cleburne would have time to prepare for the expected blow. The Union assault against his position was slow to develop. Sherman reported that "he was in the saddle" before dawn, "attended by all my staff." Starting along the banks of Chickamauga Creek, the party rode up the north face of Billy Goat Hill, along Brig. Gen. Joseph A. J. Lightburn's newly fortified lines, then down the west face of the hill to Col. Jesse I. Alexander's brigade of John E. Smith's division, and then farther west along the lines of Corse's and Cockerill's brigades of Ewing's command, all similarly entrenched. This ride revealed the truth of Sherman's position—that he was not on Missionary Ridge at all.[8]

Despite Grant's explicit orders, it is possible that Sherman did not expect to have to launch an attack that day. If he did indeed hold the north end of Missionary Ridge as he supposed—and having his men spend the night hours entrenching strongly suggests he believed as much—then it would be logical to expect Bragg to either retreat or launch a desperate counterattack of his own. Sherman's entire military career demonstrates that he was not a man to favor a stand-up fight; he always preferred maneuver to assault and to let the enemy fight or flee in turn. Establishing a strong position threatening Bragg's supply line and local supply depot seemed to accomplish that goal. But the Federals were not on Missionary Ridge, and Bragg's troops, not Sherman's, held the key position of Tunnel Hill. Sherman had little choice but to take the offensive.

That said, he determined not to rush into any headlong assault. Sherman had his three Army of the Tennessee divisions immediately available, plus Davis's XIV Corps division in reserve, as well as Buschbeck's brigade of the XI Corps on his right. Of the 20,000 or so Federals available to him, Sherman selected only the 920 men of Corse's brigade to deliver the main blow, approaching Tunnel Hill's narrow confines from the north. Corse was to receive direct support from the 30th Ohio (along with two companies of the 4th West Virginia) from Lightburn's brigade, 200 additional muskets. According to Col. Charles C. Walcutt's postbattle report, Corse began his advance at 7:00 A.M. Curiously, Lightburn reported that it only was much later, writing, "at 9:00 A.M. I received verbal orders from Major General Sherman to send forward 200 men to occupy Tunnel Hill."[9]

Two additional brigades were also tasked with supporting Corse's main effort, though that support would prove halting and uncertain. General Ewing ordered Col. John M. Loomis's brigade to move out of reserve and swing southeast across the open fields to approach Tunnel Hill's western face, coming into action on Corse's right. But Ewing's orders to Loomis can only be construed as mystifying: "push the enemy's skirmishers, but under no circumstances . . . bring on a general engagement." Presumably, he did not want the colonel's four regiments to launch a frontal assault straight up Missionary Ridge from the west, but how else could they really support Corse, atop the ridge if not doing just that? Ewing's injunction seemed to directly contradict the intent of Grant's orders to Sherman.[10]

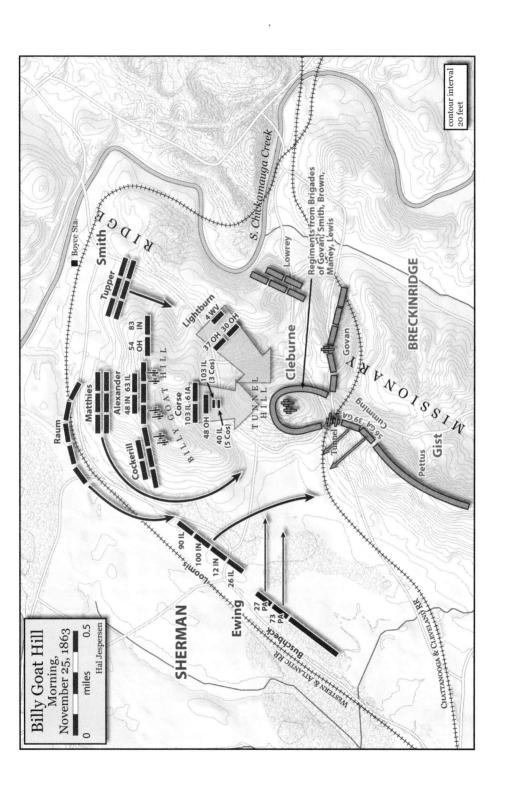

Billy Goat Hill
Morning,
November 25, 1863

contour interval
20 feet

0   miles   0.5

Hal Jespersen

Boyce Sta.

Smith RIDGE

Tupper

Raum

Matthies

48 IN 63 IL

Alexander

Cockerill

83
54
OH IN

Lightburn

4 WV

37 OH 30 OH

BILLY GOAT HILL

Corse

103 IL
(3 Cos)

103 IL 6 IA

48 OH

40 IL
(5 Cos)

TUNNEL
HILL

Cleburne

Regiments from
Brigades
of Govan, Smith, Brown,
Maney, Lewis

Lowrey

Govan

56 GA 39 GA

Cumming

Tunnel

MISSIONARY

BRECKINRIDGE

Pettus

Gist

RIDGE

S. Chickamauga Creek

SHERMAN

Ewing

Loomis

90 IL

100 IN

12 IN

26 IL

27
PA

73
PA

Buschbeck

WESTERN & ATLANTIC RR

CHATTANOOGA & CLEVELAND RR

While Loomis tried to square Ewing's instructions for the job that day, the other brigade's mission has been nearly lost to history, thanks to the lack of reports from that command. With Giles Smith rendered hors de combat on November 24, Col. Nathan Tupper assumed command. His report sketched only a barebones itinerary from November 21 to 30, omitting any mention of either November 24 or 25 entirely. According to the 55th Illinois regimental history, that morning the "brigade was moving directly towards the rear of the Confederate position, unopposed, but also unsupported, and nearing a hazardous position where a massed force of the enemy lay in wait." Here Giles Smith's absence was sorely felt. As explained by Lt. Col. Frank Curtiss of the 127th Illinois, "just as dawn was breaking," Tupper "was [ordered] to take his regiments . . . to Boyce Station and then proceed along the creekside road seeking an approach to Tunnel Hill . . . [that was] less difficult" than Corse's route. They reached the station just as the first firing could be heard to their southwest, where Corse and the 30th Ohio were presumably engaged. A half mile beyond the station, Tupper halted to confer with his regimental commanders. Though they had met with no opposition, the brigade was now well beyond the limit of Sherman's main line, and another large hill loomed off to their left and rear. This height, currently occupied by only two regiments of Brig. Gen. Mark P. Lowrey's mixed Alabama and Mississippi brigade, was potentially the key to turning Cleburne's flank on Tunnel Hill.[11]

But Tupper paid it no heed. Instead, fearing he was on the wrong road, the colonel directed his men to retrace their steps westward to the next road junction, where a farm track ran south from the creek road between Lightburn's position atop Billy Goat Hill and the hill held by Lowrey's Rebels. Tupper moved south into that valley. Again his skirmishers met no opposition, but, as characterized by the 127th Illinois regiment's modern chronicler, "the movement was very slow, tentative, almost hesitant." During their march, Tupper's Federals could hear the swell of more fighting to their right-rear, suggesting that they had "unknowingly outflanked" James Smith's Texans. Then they ran into a smattering of Confederate pickets, most likely Arkansans from Brig. Gen. Daniel C. Govan's brigade, which Cleburne had placed on that eastward-running spur of Tunnel Hill just north of the actual tunnel. Here, Tupper halted for the rest of the morning, until recalled at 1:00 P.M. Despite a considerable gap between Govan's men on the spur and Lowrey's two semi-isolated regiments on their hill, the Federals made no effort to wrest that dominating position from the Rebels. Had they done so, they could have compromised Cleburne's retreat route and gained easy access to Bragg's base of supplies at Chickamauga Station—essentially the two objectives Sherman believed he had accomplished the night before. Two additional Confederate brigades, those commanded by Brig. Gens. Marcus Wright and Lucius Polk, guarded the railroad bridges over Chickamauga Creek on the far side of Missionary Ridge, but Cleburne had too few troops to either substantially reinforce Lowrey or secure a continuous line between Govan, Lowrey, Wright, and Polk.[12]

Meanwhile, the main effort against Tunnel Hill was underway. Based on Lightburn's report, it was well after sunup when the 30th Ohio set off. The delay was not especially significant, for Corse's men were not immediately in position to launch their assault and would need considerable time to get into position. The brigade's overnight line sat atop the western end of Billy Goat Hill, and the men had to move down the southeast slope into the valley below, from where they were to advance up the narrow northern slope of Tunnel Hill, with the aim of sweeping its entirety from north to south. Corse ordered the 40th Illinois forward as skirmishers, 130 men in five companies, and once at the bottom of the hill deployed three companies of the 103rd Illinois as a second skirmish line behind them. His remaining force was formed in support. Then the general ordered Maj. Hiram W. Hall to take the 40th Illinois up the slope and, "if possible, . . . drive the enemy from his position and take possession of his works." Gamely, Hall crested the hill and charged into a line of Confederate skirmishers at its northern end. These were Texans from James Smith's brigade.[13]

Hall's men were not the first Federals engaged that morning. Col. Theodore Jones and the 30th Ohio (plus the West Virginians) claimed that honor. Given his limited numbers, Jones might have wondered at Sherman's initial instructions—"occupy Tunnel Hill"—but the general soon elaborated: "I wish you to go up the point of the hill and assist Corse, who is coming up the side." Then Sherman added, "the sooner you get off the better[,] as Corse is ready to start." Jones wasted no time. By using a more direct route to Tunnel Hill and taking less time to deploy, the 30th Ohio engaged Smith's Confederates well before Hall's skirmishers arrived. How long is hard to tell, but, writing in 1908, Colonel Jones estimated that his men "preceded Corse's brigade for one hour at least."[14]

Smith's brigade included eight regiments of infantry and dismounted cavalry, but their ranks were so depleted they were organized into three tactical formations—the 7th Texas, the 6th and 10th Texas and the 15th Texas Cavalry, and the consolidated 17th/18th/24th/25th Texas Cavalry. They were formed in a semicircular line embracing the crest of the hill just north of the tunnel, upon which also sat Lt. Harvey Shannon's four 12-pound Napoleons of the Warren (Mississippi) Light Artillery, protected by earthworks. Smith's men had initially erected a defensive barricade at the northern end of the hill, about 250 yards from Shannon's position, but abandoned that during the night due to a shortage of troops. Now the forward edge of Tunnel Hill was defended only by a skirmish line.[15]

Jones's Federals drove in the 17th/18th/24th/25th's skirmishers and surmounted the abandoned outer works. From there they could see the Mississippi battery. Essaying an attack, however, proved unwise: Jones's initial attempt failed at a considerable loss and left the colonel to wonder what was keeping Corse. Feeling isolated, Jones sent a request back to his own commander for help; General Lightburn sent him the 37th Ohio as a reinforcement.[16]

The Ohioans were just climbing the hill to report to Jones when, to their right, Hall's Illinoisans surmounted the hill's north slope. The major's men swarmed forward, "scaling the enemy's outer works" (the now-abandoned Confederate forward line), but as Lt. James B. Smith remembered, "this charge was made with a heavy loss."[17]

Corse made his way up the slope just as Hall's first attack was repulsed. He met with both Hall and Colonel Jones, each of whom expressed some frustration at their circumstances. Corse organized a larger attack, using Jones's Buckeyes and Lt. Col. Louis von Blessing's 37th Ohio as well as re-inforcing Hall's 40th Illinois with the 46th Ohio and three companies of the 103rd Illinois from his own command. As the troops were deploying, Jones later recalled that one of Sherman's staff officers "came with orders . . . to make the charge . . . proposed." Curiously, he recollected that at this juncture, Corse, who had had time to examine the situation more fully, suddenly had second thoughts. "Seeing that the situation was different from what he had anticipated, [he] directed me to go to Gen. Sherman and explain the situation."[18]

Once back on Billy Goat Hill, Jones found a now-anxious General Sherman and reported his news. "'Go back and make that charge immediately,'" snapped the general. "'Time is everything. If you want more men, I will give you all you want; if you want artillery[,] I will give you that. General Grant is on Orchard Knob waiting for your assault in order to send up a column from the [A]rmy of the Cumberland.'" Sherman was apparently fed up with delay and feeling pressure from above.[19]

Jones returned posthaste. Corse led the next attack personally. "The several lines rushed over the brow of the hill under a most terrific fire," Colonel Walcutt reported. "Being in easy canister and musket range, it seemed almost impossible for any troops to withstand it. . . . [T]he men . . . charged through it . . . with a fearlessness and determination that was astonishing." The charge surged almost to the foot of the battery's works, during which General Corse fell badly wounded. His loss broke the momentum of the charge, and the Yankees fell back. Following them, Brig. Gen. James Smith and Col. Roger Q. Mills, commanding the 6th/10th/15th Texas, led an impromptu counterattack. "Some fly, others surrender, but others, for a brief space continue to fight, but they are soon overcome," recollected Sgt. Albert Jernigan of the 6th Texas. The Federals rallied at the abandoned line, and now it was the Texans' turn to face a withering fire. Mills and Smith, both mounted, were each badly wounded, and the counterattack effort collapsed. Col. Hiram Granbury of the 7th Texas assumed command of the defense of Tunnel Hill.[20]

Corse's and Jones's men were done attacking, though they would cling to the north end of Tunnel Hill and those abandoned works for the rest of the day. Union efforts now switched to the western face of the hill, where, ultimately, elements of four more Federal brigades would try their hand at taking the heights.

Through the morning's fighting, Cleburne received a steady flow of reinforcements, as more and more troops from Lookout Mountain filed into position. General Gist's division defended the next significant high point on the ridge to the south (the site of the modern-day Delong Reservation), but its three brigades numbered too few to connect with Cleburne's line. At 4:00 A.M. Bragg ordered Stevenson's division of three brigades into position between Cleburne and Gist. Brig. Gen. John C. Brown reported that his Tennesseans took position on the ridge directly over the tunnel "immediately after sunrise." About "two hours later" he advanced again, farther to the left, and deployed skirmishers down off the ridge along the railroad and the Glass farm, nestled at the western foot of Missionary Ridge. Brig. Gen. Alfred Cumming's Georgians then filed into line about 9:30 A.M., with Brig. Gen. Edmund Pettus's Alabamians not far behind.[21]

During the night, Bragg had also directed Brig. Gen. William B. Bate, whose division was then holding the center of the Rebel line, to send Col.

Joseph H. Lewis's Kentucky Brigade (the famous Orphans) to Cleburne as well. Lewis reported to Cleburne about dawn but was initially kept in reserve. His men fired only a few volleys about midmorning, and only the 9th Kentucky suffered any loss; the 9th was briefly engaged either against the 37th Ohio or Colonel Tupper's force and suffered three men wounded.[22]

Many of these troops filing into position that morning could be seen from Orchard Knob, in full view of the Union generals assembled there. Later, the Federals would assume that Bragg, under increasing pressure from Sherman, was stripping his center to reinforce his right. In fact only the Kentucky Brigade came from any of the forces defending the Confederate center, and that move was made overnight, before Sherman attacked, and well before any Federal could observe it. Gist's and Stevenson's men were redeployed from Lookout Mountain and the now-abandoned line across Chattanooga Valley.

These were the Confederates positioned to receive Colonel Loomis's two Indiana and two Illinois regiments as they moved against Missionary Ridge's west face that morning, tasked with supporting Corse's right flank. Though the men were up early, eating breakfast at 4:30 A.M., they moved cautiously. Forming at the base of Billy Goat Hill, Loomis sidled south toward Orchard Knob for some distance before heading east to the base of the ridge. This move widened the gap between his left, below the ridge, and Corse's right, atop it, by several hundred yards. "About 8:30 or 9:00 a.m., it was still foggy on the low land," wrote Sgt. Eli Sherlock of the 100th Indiana, but "the sun shone brightly on the top of Missionary Ridge. . . . [W]e could look up through it and see one long column of rebels after another moving from the Confederate center to their right and being massed directly in our front." At about 9:00 A.M. Loomis halted his men in a tree line opposite the Glass farm, which sat at the foot of the ridge just north of where the Chattanooga & Cleveland Railroad tracks curved to enter the tunnel. Skirmishers from Brown's Tennessee brigade held the foot of the ridge between the farm and the rail embankment, while, noted Loomis, "the abrupt hill-sides in his rear were occupied by three lines of skirmishers or sharpshooters." Above them at the top of the ridge, Confederate cannon were clearly visible. Shortly after Loomis's own skirmishers first appeared beyond the trees, Hardee personally directed Brigadier General Cumming to send two Georgia regiments—half his brigade—to directly occupy the Glass farm buildings and extend Brown's right.[23]

For a while, Loomis dueled with the enemy at long range, accomplishing little beyond setting the farm buildings ablaze with artillery fire and flushing out several badly frightened civilians. At 10:30 A.M. Loomis's orders were changed: word came from Ewing that "Corse was about to assault Tunnel Hill, accompanied with an order to advance simultaneously." Col. Adolphus Buschbeck's brigade of the XI Corps would support the movement. Loomis's line, covered by two lines of skirmishers, surged forward. The Rebels opened fire all along their front. "The mountains lapped each other and formed a kind of half circle," recalled one member of the 90th Illinois, the terrain providing the opportunity to subject Loomis's men to a "heavy direct and cross fire of artillery and the infantry and sharpshooters of the enemy." The Irish 90th, positioned on the brigade's left, suffered severely, losing both Colonel O'Meara and Lt. Col. Owen Stuart in this fight. Stuart would return, but O'Meara, the commander whose timely arrival had saved Sherman at Collierville, was mortally wounded near a large, well-fenced two-acre livestock pen close to the Glass farmyard. The attack now faltered, not the least because Confederates from multiple brigades could rake Loomis's advancing lines with murderous crossfire. Even Colonel Mills of the 6th/10th/15th Texas had time to marvel at the Federal infantry's steadiness while under fire from that portion of his regiment not then engaged with Corse. Stymied, Loomis "plac[ed] the brigade under such cover as the low ground afforded" and called for help.[24]

By midday, Sherman's attacks were blunted. Corse and Loomis had borne the worst of it, their troops suffering heavily for no gain. Sherman also did a poor job of keeping Grant informed of his progress. At 1:00 P.M. Charles Dana composed an update to Stanton, informing him that shortly after 9:00 A.M., the "battle commenced on our left, the attack being made by Sherman apparently, though no report from him yet received. Fight raged very furiously all forenoon, both east of Missionary Ridge and along its crest this way [south] towards . . . railroad tunnel, which," Dana erroneously reported, "we gained about 12 M." At about the time the assistant secretary was composing this missive, Sherman sent his first communique to Grant, though it must have arrived after Dana's message was on its way. Timed at 12:45 P.M., Sherman's note was not informative. "Major General Grant," wrote Sherman, "Where is Thomas?" "I am here [on Orchard Knob]," responded Thomas fifteen minutes later. "My right is closing in from Lookout Mountain towards Missionary Ridge."[25]

At this point the fighting on the Union left might have ended for the day were it not for Buschbeck's brigade. About 12:30 P.M., responding to Loomis's request, Colonel Buschbeck positioned his largest regiment, the untried 33rd New Jersey, behind Loomis as a reserve and moved up his own remaining two Pennsylvania regiments, the 27th and 73rd, on his right. After some heavy fighting, the Pennsylvanians flushed Cumming's Georgians out of the now-wrecked Glass farm. Buschbeck intended to halt them there at the foot of the ridge, but through some confusion, he suddenly saw the 27th Pennsylvania and part of the 73rd continue up the slope toward Cleburne's line and the artillery redoubt at the crest of Tunnel Hill. They made it most of the way up, only to be pinned down near the top, where they would remain for the next couple of hours.[26]

Inexorably, the plight of Buschbeck's Pennsylvanians drew two brigades of John E. Smith's division into the fight, all to Smith's dismay. His First Brigade, under Colonel Alexander, garrisoned Billy Goat Hill, along with Cockerill's brigade of Ewing's division; both commands remained securely ensconced behind their newly dug entrenchments for the duration of the day. Col. Green B. Raum's Second Brigade and Brig. Gen. Charles L. Matthies's Third Brigade of Smith's division, however, were at hand. At 11:00 A.M., with Loomis pinned down in the valley, Ewing asked for a brigade from Smith, who sent him Matthies. An hour later he appealed for more help, and Smith reluctantly released Raum. Both brigades shifted forward, but neither became immediately engaged. Shortly thereafter, when Smith found Raum's men out in front of Cockerill's works, apparently dangerously exposed (though they were not yet under significant enemy fire), Smith remonstrated first with Ewing, who ignored him, and then with Sherman, who deferred to Ewing. Dismayed, Smith returned to Raum's position. As he did so he observed a brigade ascending the west face of Tunnel Hill, which he took to be Loomis's men. Much to his surprise, it turned out to be Matthies, gone forward to try and relieve Buschbeck's Pennsylvanians.[27]

Brigadier General Matthies first reported to Colonel Loomis, who ordered him into position at the Glass farm, the house now blazing merrily. Matthies formed his men in the lane running from the farmhouse northward along the base of the ridge, taking fire from the same semicircle of Rebels that shredded Loomis's earlier advance. At this juncture Col. Holden Putnam of the 93rd Illinois informed Matthies that the 27th and 73rd Pennsylvania, then on the ridge, had sent back word that with "re-enforcements . . .

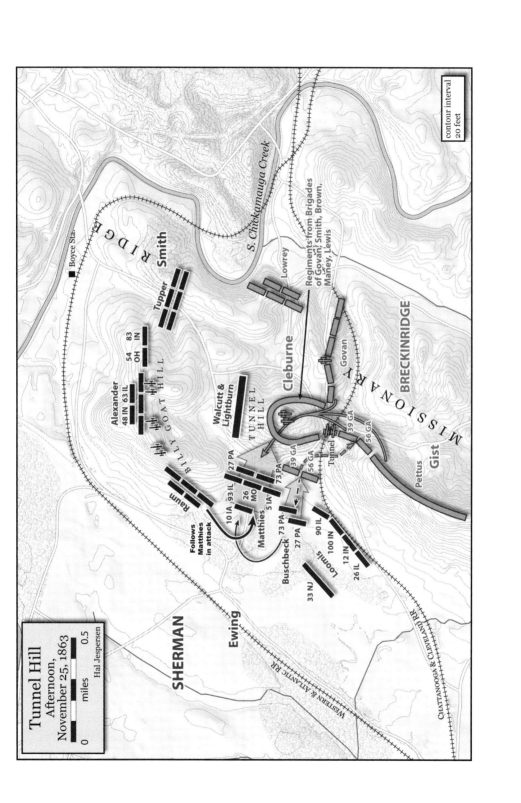

Tunnel Hill
Afternoon, November 25, 1863

0   miles   0.5

Hal Jespersen

Boyce Sta.

RIDGE

Smith

Tupper

S. Chickamauga Creek

Lowrey

Regiments from Brigades of Govan, Smith, Brown, Maney, Lewis

54 OH   83 IN

Alexander
48 IN   63 IL

BILLY GOAT HILL

Cleburne

Govan

BRECKINRIDGE

Raum

Walcutt & Lightburn

TUNNEL HILL

39 GA

56 GA

MISSIONARY

Follows Matthies in attack

27 PA

Matthies
10 IA   93 IL

26 MO   5 IA

73 PA

39 GA

56 GA

Tunnel

39 GA

56 GA

Pettus

Gist

SHERMAN

Ewing

Buschbeck
73 PA

27 PA

90 IL

100 IN

12 IN

Loomis

26 IL

33 NJ

CHATTANOOGA & CLEVELAND RR

WESTERN & ATLANTIC RR

contour interval 20 feet

they could hold the hill." In response Matthies "ordered Colonel Putnam to move up cautiously."[28]

Cautiously or not, the move cost Putnam his life and left the 93rd pinned down on the slope alongside Buschbeck's Keystoners. Shortly thereafter, one of Matthies's aides returned with fresh orders from Ewing "to hold the hill if possible, and [word] that another brigade was coming up to our assistance." Dutifully, Matthies led the rest of his men up the hill. Once there, he found his brigade intermingled with the Pennsylvanians. "I was turning round to caution my men to fire low and sure," the general reported, when "I was struck by a bullet in the head." Briefly unconscious, when Matthies revived, he sent for Col. Benjamin D. Dean of the 26th Missouri, passed command to him, and staggered back down the hill to seek aid.[29]

Colonel Raum had been watching the fight with interest from a position at the foot of Billy Goat Hill when, at 2:00 P.M., Generals Ewing and John E. Smith rode up together. "They stated that Gen. Sherman had directed that I should reinforce Matthies with my brigade." Raum wryly noted, "I had felt for some time that Matthies needed help." After a quick consultation with the two senior generals, he formed his brigade in two lines, moved up to Matthies's former position in the farm lane, and then sent his first line up the hill. Matthies, staggering down the slope, met the colonel and his brigade scrambling up it. Raum recalled that Matthies "was quite bloody, but able to walk. He stated that his brigade was almost out of ammunition [and] that their losses had been very heavy." With that Raum hurried forward to overtake his leading regiments—the 17th Iowa and 80th Ohio—and lead them the rest of the way to the crest.[30]

Raum's men arrived just in time to receive the next Confederate counterattack. So far, General Cleburne was managing his defense masterfully. According to Captain Buck, upon "seeing a column of assault advancing up the hill, Cleburne . . . placed himself at the head of the Texas Brigade, and leaping the works, met and repulsed the charge, returning with a number of prisoners and several stands of colors." Additional help, unlooked for but welcome, came from two regiments of Cumming's Georgians who joined in, whom Hardee had ordered sent over from Stevenson's portion of the line. As he arrived Cumming asked for permission to charge, which was readily granted. Cleburne also reinforced Smith's Texans with the 2nd/15th/24th Arkansas from Govan's Brigade and the 1st/27th Tennessee from Maney's Brigade. Thus reinforced, the charge was successful. Lt. Robert M. Collins of the 15th Texas recalled, "we sailed into them, capturing many prisoners, six stands of colors, and many guidons." Collins "unbuckled his sword, and as we went over the works left it, grabbed a rock and went in."[31]

Raum remembered that he was in the front line when this charge struck and soon realized that the combination of Confederate frontal and flank movements made his current position on the slope untenable. "I must confess I did not stand on the order of my going. . . . I ran down Missionary Ridge as fast as my legs would carry me. . . . The ground was rough and rocky. I fell twice, but hurriedly scrambled to my feet and rushed on to keep out of the way of the determined men who were close on my heels." The colonel was not merely fleeing in panic, however; he knew he still had two regiments in his reserve line at the foot of the hill. "As I jumped down into the road, with a loud voice I shouted, 'Fire!' The . . . Confederates were within 20 yards of our line, but the withering volley . . . brought them to a sudden halt. Four or five volleys were exchanged with deadly effect, when the Confederate troops retired precipitously up the hill."[32]

Cleburne's stroke effectively ended the fight for Tunnel Hill. Sherman still had Corse's and Jones's men clinging to the north end of the hill, but he had nothing else to show for the day's bloodshed. According to XI Corps divisional commander Carl Schurz, who met the general about 2:00 P.M., Sherman "was in an unhappy frame of mind, his hope of promptly overwhelming the enemy's right flank and thus striking the decisive blow of the battle having been dashed by the discovery of the big ravine in his way. It was a stinging disappointment. He gave vent to his feelings in language of astonishing vivacity,—at least it astonished me, as I had never seen or heard him before." Schurz now expected to be ordered into action in support of Ewing, but Sherman instead "preferred that my command should remain in reserve on his left to provide for the emergency of a rebel attack from that quarter."[33]

Including Davis's division, which never moved from its fortified bridgehead position on November 25, Sherman began the day with twelve infantry brigades. He was reinforced by the remaining four brigades of the XI Corps and subsequently offered, but declined, Brig. Gen. Absalom Baird's division of three brigades (more on that later). Of these sixteen brigades, only five brigades and two regiments of a sixth saw serious action, with all their efforts narrowly focused on Tunnel Hill. Each brigade went into action alone and only belatedly supported, allowing the Confederates to deal with each thrust in turn. Why Sherman never launched a more coordinated effort, or more significantly, why he never tried a multipronged attack against Tunnel Hill and the height held by Lowrey's Rebels simultaneously—a move for which he easily had enough force—has never been recorded.

There is some evidence that at least one general wanted to attack in that direction. Writing in 1882, one of Thomas's early biographers stated that "General Davis, chafing under enforced inaction, requested permission to turn the enemy's right flank by moving his division to its rear, but this movement, which might have produced decisive results . . . was forbidden by General Sherman." Henry Aten, the regimental historian of the 85th Illinois, asserted that Davis's "division was fresh and strong in numbers— over seven thousand effective men—and if successful . . . , we would have seized the road over which Bragg retreated during the night. But General Sherman, no doubt wisely, declined the offer of his enterprising subordinate." Instead, Sherman's effort devolved into a series of fruitless frontal assaults.[34]

Brig. Gen. Emerson Opdycke, who commanded the 125th Ohio at Missionary Ridge, felt Sherman stumbled badly here. He insisted that Sherman "was to decide the fortunes of the day" at Chattanooga. "Davis asked of him permission to march to the rear of the enemy's right." By refusing this request "and holding Davis and the 11th corps in idleness, Sherman failed in the part assigned him." Opdycke opined that Davis's movement "certainly would have been immediately and comprehensively decisive."[35]

The Union senior commanders barely show up in the existing accounts of the day's action. Sherman spent the day atop Billy Goat Hill, as did Morgan Smith. John E. Smith saw his division parceled out to Ewing, who for his part, never seems to have gone far enough forward to visit either Loomis or Corse while they were engaged. Completely absent from the picture is temporary XV Corps commander Frank Blair, who, while present, made no official report of the day's fight. Nor does he appear in subordinate reports. Perhaps Sherman's immediate presence rendered Blair superfluous. What can be said is that aggressive leadership was sorely lacking in the Army of the Tennessee that day. Grant expected much from his star performer on November 25, but Sherman accomplished very little.

9

"INSPIRED BY THE IMPULSE OF VICTORY"

*G*rant's morning began in a leisurely fashion. This slow start was somewhat surprising, given that the night before Assistant Secretary Dana had informed Washington: "Grant has given orders for a vigorous attack at daybreak by Sherman on the left and Granger in the center, and if Bragg does not withdraw . . . , we shall probably have a decisive battle." The phrase "if Bragg does not withdraw" explains Grant's relative inaction, for the question of Bragg's presence or absence was still unresolved as the sun rose. At least one man, Dana, believed the Rebels had fled. As noted, at 7:30 A.M. he dashed off a wire to Washington stating that there was "no firing in front. This makes it pretty certain Bragg retreated. . . . As soon as positively determined Bragg has gone, Granger, with 20,000 men, moves up the south bank [of the] Tennessee . . . to cut off Longstreet's retreat and relieve Burnside."[1]

Grant's cousin and Civil War tourist William Smith wrote a lengthy diary entry for that morning, certainly conveying no great sense of urgency or expectation. "A beautiful clear cold day," Smith recorded. "We find the enemy evacuated Lookout during the night and our flag this morning flouts from its top. After breakfast we all go to Fort Wood." Along the way Grant, Smith, and General Hunter, riding together, passed the 15th Pennsylvania Cavalry, which served as the Army of the Cumberland's escort force. Being himself a Pennsylvanian, Smith interjected that the 15th "had been recruited . . . as a body guard for Anderson and afterwards Buell. Hunter said that Fremont had run the escort or body Guard so much into the ground that it was now looked on as a want of sense to have one, and [next] remarked that if Fremont had had charge of the war, the rebellion would have been a success in six months. . . . To which Grant agreed!"[2]

After spending some time at Fort Wood, with no apparent action in the offing, Smith became bored. "As everything appears quiet [Captain] Lagow and I ride back to quarters for a drink. We stay'd but a few minutes and rode immediately back, to the fort, but found the General gone." Grant had gone forward to join other senior officers gathering atop Orchard Knob. Smith followed. "About 11 o'clock," he noted, "Sherman became heavily engaged."[3]

Montgomery Meigs also began his morning at Fort Wood, where, unlike Dana, after spotting Rebels moving north along Missionary Ridge, he expected action. General Howard accompanied Meigs to Fort Wood but did not linger, instead riding on to join his XI Corps. Within a few minutes, Dana appeared and suggested to Meigs that they "should pay Granger's Headquarters a visit." The quartermaster general initially declined: "I told [Dana] that I was waiting for Genl. Grant, near whom I wished to be during the day.... But concluding that we could ride to 'Orchard Knob' and return by the time any serious movement would be made—I consented to visit Granger." The two men rode out, presumably after Dana drafted and sent off his 7:30 A.M. dispatch. Reaching the knob, they "found Gen. Wood" and informed him "that the flag waved on Lookout Crest. This was good news to him." Meigs "remained [at Orchard Knob] 'till Genl Grant was seen approaching." Though he did not specify the time of Grant's arrival, it was clearly not before 8:00 A.M. or so. Wood later recalled only that "quite early in the forenoon . . . General Grant, General Thomas, and General Granger . . . with their staff officers, took position on Orchard Knob."[4]

This coterie of generals, and their interactions as they observed the day's events, proved to be one of the more celebrated and most controversial episodes of the war. Present were Grant, newly promoted to theater command; Thomas, the equally new commander of the department; corps commander Granger, and division commander Wood. Also in attendance were Quartermaster General Meigs, Major General Hunter, and Chief Engineer "Baldy" Smith. Brigadier General Rawlins, Grant's chief of staff, close confidante, and sometimes-minder, was also there, as were a host of staff officers associated with these various commanders. At least two newspapermen joined this group, Sylvanus Cadwallader and William Shanks. Also, Grant's cousin William Smith returned to the knob after his refreshment. Later, Baldy Smith would marvel that, while Orchard Knob "was under close cannon range" of Missionary Ridge and so filled "with officers of all grades . . . , we were allowed to stay there so quietly. Only once did the enemy fire on us and then I think no damage was done though there was some scrambling to change positions[,] which would probably have been amusing to a looker-on in safety."[5]

The number of luminaries in this gathering, as well as the dramatic events of November 25, have combined to produce a rich variety of sources describing the scene. Unfortunately, that multiplicity of accounts has produced confusion rather than clarity: they differ greatly in tone, content, and interpretation. Postwar agendas drove many of those differences, as wartime rivalries hardened over time and everyone jockeyed to take credit for what would prove to be the day's unexpected triumph.[6]

Given its panoramic vantage, Orchard Knob would continue to host the assembled generals through much of the day. Early on there was little to see, which might explain the relatively leisurely pace to the morning, despite Grant's orders for the day to Sherman and Thomas. As we have seen, Sherman's assault unfolded slowly, almost hesitantly. Thomas was also in no hurry to assault Missionary Ridge. Not only was his forward movement dependent on Sherman's advance, but he was also concerned with his army's right flank. Initially it was unclear to the Federals whether Bragg had abandoned Lookout Mountain and the defensive line across Chattanooga Valley; if that line was still in place, any Union advance against Missionary Ridge would be enfiladed by a potentially devastating flank fire, especially Baird's division of the XIV Corps. Thus, Hooker's original instructions of the night before were to "advance as early as possible . . . into Chattanooga Valley and seize and hold the Summertown road and cooperate with the Fourteenth Corps by supporting its right." Both missions—holding the Summertown Road and cooperating with the XIV Corps' right—supposed that Rebels would still be on Lookout Mountain and well entrenched in Chattanooga Valley the next morning. These orders were still in force at 7:00 A.M., as evidenced by Thomas's order of that time instructing Hooker "to immediately move forward, in accordance with instructions of last evening." A bit later, once it was clear that all the Confederates had fallen back to Missionary Ridge, Thomas still wanted Hooker in position to flank the Rebels via Rossville, connecting with the right of Maj. Gen. Philip Sheridan's division, before sending Granger's men, including Sheridan's, forward.[7]

Col. Joseph S. Fullerton, then serving on Granger's staff, later wrote that, early on the morning of November 25, Grant suspended Thomas's attack order once he "learned that the ridge had not been carried as far as Tunnel Hill." While this suspension would make sense given the changed circumstances, there is no written evidence of that suspension in the records or in either commander's battle reports; presumably in their verbal discussions, both Grant and Thomas always understood the order to be conditional based on Sherman's success, or perhaps Grant simply told Thomas to wait and see what developed.[8]

Though the day dawned clear, a pervasive ground mist interfered with Union signals, and it was not until 9:20 A.M. that Hooker was able to definitely report: "[We] have [a] regiment on Summertown road; one on summit of Lookout. Enemy reported picketing Chattanooga Creek. They appear to be burning camps in valley; I await orders." Thomas replied at 10:10 A.M. After instructing Hooker to send Carlin's brigade back to Johnson's division of the XIV Corps and leave two regiments to secure the mountain, Thomas ordered him to "move with the remainder of your force . . . on the Rossville road toward Missionary Ridge, looking well to your right flank." Eventually, this order would put pressure on Bragg's left flank, but that move would take time. Hooker faced a major water obstacle at Chattanooga Creek and had approximately four miles to traverse before he reached Rossville Gap.[9]

To the gathered observers, it seemed that serious fighting developed along Sherman's front only after 11:00 A.M. This was because Corse's and Jones's movements were made slowly and their initial efforts were directed against the north and northeast sides of Tunnel Hill, not visible from Orchard Knob. The movement of Loomis's brigade toward the Glass farm, however, was clearly in view, as were the follow-on actions of the afternoon.

Dana's dispatches offer the most contemporaneous window into the thinking at Grant's headquarters that morning, especially since, with no direct word from Sherman concerning his progress, the observers were left to draw their own conclusions. As noted, at 7:30 A.M. Dana was all but certain Bragg had retreated during the night. By nine o'clock he was able to more definitively report that "Bragg evacuated . . . Lookout Mountain last night and our troops occupy it, but he [Bragg] still holds to his rifle-pits along base Missionary Ridge, and has been moving troops all the morning toward front of Sherman's position." Dana cautioned, however, that "what force he can mass there [is] still undetermined." While dubious that Bragg intended to fight, he was hinting that the general might only leave a strong rear guard to mask his larger retreat.[10]

At 8:45 A.M. Thomas took the first concrete step to support Sherman. He ordered Howard to "move your force toward General Sherman's, looking well to your right flank and in readiness to form line on your right in case you should be attacked on the march." This essentially reestablished the connection made yesterday, but instead of leaving only a brigade, the whole of the XI Corps would join the Army of the Tennessee. It also reflected Thomas's underlying caution in warning Howard of the possibility that

Bragg might suddenly leave the line of Missionary Ridge to attack him. Howard received this directive an hour later, at 9:45, and probably did not get started moving until after ten o'clock.[11]

Howard was not the only reinforcement sent Sherman's way. On November 24 Major General Baird and his men, forming the rightmost division of Thomas's line facing Missionary Ridge, were still concerned with the line of entrenched Confederates stretching laterally across Chattanooga Valley to connect with their comrades on Lookout Mountain. But with that valley now evacuated of Rebels and Hooker now supposed to be moving up on the right, Grant decided Baird's men could be more useful elsewhere. "Orders were brought to me, direct from departmental headquarters, directing me to pass with my division to the extreme left, to the assistance of General Sherman, then hotly engaged in the vicinity of Tunnel Hill." This was a curious decision, necessitating a march of several miles for Baird and effectively duplicating the XI Corps move. It also reduced Thomas's force confronting Missionary Ridge to a mere 19,000 men while boosting Sherman's combat power to something like 35,000 troops—and Sherman already had many more men than he was using in the fight. Once he became aware of Baird's orders, "Sherman sent word that he had all the force necessary," allowing Thomas to redirect the division into line on Wood's left, filling part of the gap between Thomas and Sherman. This redeployment allowed the massing of four divisions against Missionary Ridge; but Baird's movement would not be complete until midafternoon.[12]

Dana's 1:00 P.M. wire stated that "soon after my dispatch of 9 A.M., battle commenced on our left, the attack being made by Sherman apparently, though no report from him yet received." Here was another curious tidbit: why had Sherman not updated Grant on his situation that morning? The historical record indirectly suggests that Grant communicated with Sherman, evidenced by Colonel Jones's recollection of Sherman's peevish rebuke: "General Grant is on Orchard Knob waiting for your assault." But if so, that communication must have been verbal, for no written record survives. It is also possible that Sherman's comment merely echoed his previous understanding of the overall plan. Dana's next words were even more perplexing: the "fight raged very furiously . . . toward [the] Knoxville railroad tunnel, which we gained about 12 M." Aside from being incorrect—Sherman never gained control of the railroad tunnel—this detail also directly contradicted Dana's report on the evening of the twenty-fourth, which stated that Sherman had already reached that tunnel. At some point that morning, it became obvious to everyone that Sherman's report of the night before was incorrect since they could see Rebels on the ridge above the tunnel and combat "raging" along the crest to the north. Yet in both his battle report and his memoirs, Grant ignored this discrepancy. Finally, Dana also reported that "in our front . . . [the] Rebel rifle-pits are fully manned, preventing Thomas gaining [the] ridge."[13]

Sherman's first terse and uninformative written communication came at 12:45 P.M. "Where is Thomas?" It did nothing to enlighten Grant as to the day's progress. And by now, it was beginning to be apparent that there was very little progress indeed. Meigs described the visible action in some detail, encompassing both Loomis's first advance and the subsequent engagement of Buschbeck's, Matthies's, and Raum's brigades:

A line was seen deployed in a cleared field on Sherman's right—a blue line which went steadily up the steep ascent. Soon another followed in support. How gallant an assault, It is impossible for them to succeed where the exclamations. I watched them with my telescope . . . saw them pass the fence on the upper edge of the field, enter the oak woods, climb to the edge of the crest of the hill . . . and stop. A sputtering musketry fire broke out. The men sought shelter from the deadly fire of the log breastworks above them. I saw the [Confederate] reserve brought up to resist the assault, filling the terrepleine of the entrenchment with a mass of gray. I saw officers leaping into the air and waving their swords urging and calling their rebel soldiers to the front. I saw the reserve fall back again out of fire.

I saw a great body of troops move from a Camp between our front and Sherman and pass steadily along the ridge to assist in repelling the assault. I saw the men again urged forward slowly, step, first a few, then more, then the whole body over the breastworks, and advance pouring fire into our men, who stood fast and returned it.

Then the rebels nearer to us advanced and taking our men crowded under the shelter of the hills in flank, poured into them a murderous fire, and the right flank of the group dissolved, and the open field below was filled with men running down the hill. The rebels cast stones from their rifle pits into our men thus wounding some, so near were the two hostile bodies during the half hour or hour they thus stood in deadly array before the rebel charge.[14]

In 1866 William Shanks described both Grant and Thomas as "passive, cool, and observant" while watching this action. In his journal William Smith recorded that Grant took lunch with him and several others at about this time (Smith put the time at 2:00 P.M., but it could have been sooner) and seemed unruffled. "We go down under the hill," wrote Smith, and "sit on down on a log near a fire and open the lunch which is divided between the General [Grant], Gen. Hunter, Dr. Kittoe and myself. . . . After smoking and talking pleasantly for half an hour more we go again to the top of the Knoll."[15]

Grant must have returned from that meal in time to watch Sherman's attack falter. In his 1868 presidential campaign biography of Grant, Albert D. Richardson penned the following exchange between Grant and an unnamed staff officer:

GRANT.—"They seem to be driving our boys."
OFFICER.—"Yes."
GRANT.—"Driving them pretty badly."
OFFICER.—"Yes."
The columns rallied, charged, and were again repulsed.
GRANT.—"They are driven again; but it is all right now. You see that signal flag?"
OFFICER.—"Yes."
GRANT.—"Well that's Sherman. Sherman is there and he will make it all right."[16]

In 1876 and again in 1896, Wood recalled a similar exchange, only with Grant addressing him instead of an anonymous staffer. As Wood recalled it, "every eye on Orchard Knob was turned on General Sherman's operations. . . . Assault after assault was repulsed. About half past two P.M. it was plainly and painfully evident . . . that General Sherman's attack . . . had been hopelessly defeated." Here, added Wood, "General Grant . . . approached me and said: 'General Sherman seems to be having a hard time.' I replied, 'He does seem to be meeting with rough usage.' To this General Grant said, 'I think we ought to try to do something to help him.' I said, 'I think so, too, General, and whatever you order we will try to do.'" That order, said Wood, was for him "and Sheridan . . . to advance . . . and carry the rifle pits at the base of the Ridge." Doing so, Grant reasoned, would cause Bragg to recall troops to his center, and "insure the success of General Sherman's attack."[17]

The nature of that order, how it was issued, how it was executed, and even Grant's intent in issuing it have all been hotly debated ever since. It ultimately produced a result so unexpected that everyone observing was caught by surprise, and not a little shocked.

Thomas merely stated that once Baird took up his position on "Granger's [Wood's] left . . . about 2:30 P.M., orders were then given him . . . to move forward on Granger's left, and within supporting distance, against the enemy's rifle pits on the slope and at the foot of Missionary Ridge." In the face of that advance, "the enemy, seized with panic, abandoned the works at the foot of the hill and retreated precipitately to the crest." Following closely, Thomas concluded that the "troops . . . apparently inspired by the impulse of victory, carried the hill simultaneously at six different points." These words make it seem as if the assault were executed first by Baird, starting on the left, and as part of a general movement against the base of the ridge. Granger reported something similar, though not identical. "General Sherman was unable to make any progress in moving along the ridge . . . therefore, in order to relieve him, I was ordered to make a demonstration upon the works . . . directly in my front, at the base of Mission Ridge."[18]

After the fact, Grant's report suggested more was afoot than a demonstration. For one thing, he mentioned Hooker's engagement on Bragg's left—expected momentarily—to be the signal for Thomas's movement. "[Hooker's] approach," wrote Grant, "was intended as the signal for storming the ridge in the center with strong columns." No mention was made of the need to help Sherman. He did write that it was the "discover[y] that the enemy in his desperation to defeat or resist the progress of Sherman was weakening his center on Missionary Ridge, [which] determined me to order the advance at once." Grant further added that he intended for Thomas to "carry the rifle pits at the foot of Missionary Ridge, and when carried to reform his lines . . . with a view to carrying the top of the ridge."[19]

Thomas's report is dated December 1, 1863, submitted just six days after the events in question. Grant's report is dated December 23, drafted, as was customary, after most subordinate reports were handed in. But Granger's report was not submitted until February 11, 1864, completed while the IV Corps was stationed in East Tennessee. Since Granger and his men departed Chattanooga immediately after the battle for Missionary Ridge to go to Burnside's aid, some delay in filing his and his subordinate commanders' reports was to be expected; it is also likely that Granger had a chance to review or at least catch wind of what Grant had written. While both Thomas's and Granger's reports differ from Grant's in key areas, Granger's is the most explicitly contradictory. Neither he nor Thomas mentioned "storming the ridge." Going further, Granger described merely a "demonstration," not a real attack.

Thomas wanted no part of a frontal assault on Missionary Ridge. Such an approach was not his style of warfare. Moreover, things had become quite lively atop Orchard Knob in the intervening hours. While "Baldy" Smith recalled hardly a rebel cannon shot aimed at them earlier in the day, Meigs now noted that "a battery of [Rebel] 10 pdrs. rifled fired at the 'Knob' all day. Head Quarters remained there 'till about 4:00 P.M. and every few minutes throughout the day, a shell whizzed past." That enemy shellfire intensified as more of Bragg's guns went into position along the crest through the late morning. With little else to do, Thomas personally directed the fire of various Union batteries in response, his messages sent back to the Union artillery in Fort Wood. At 11:00 A.M., for instance, he observed: "You are firing in the wrong direction. Fire near the tunnel north of Orchard Knob." But as biographer Francis F. McKinney wrote: "Bragg's center was numerically equal to Thomas' storming columns and had the tremendous advantage of position. The risk of ordering" a forward movement "under these conditions seemed to Thomas unparalleled. He opposed such a movement until Bragg's flanks had been shattered." Until then, with five of its nine divisions either assigned to Sherman or with Hooker, the rest of the Army of the Cumberland had little to do.[20]

Having reached a decision, noted Wood, "Grant walked directly from me to Gen. Thomas, who was standing a few paces distant, and a short talk occurred between them." Despite being out of earshot, Wood "was satisfied they were conversing out the movement against the Confederate intrenchments." That supposition was soon borne out. "Gen. Thomas called Gen. Granger . . . to him and gave him some directions. Granger came immediately to me, and said substantially, 'We are ordered by Gen. Grant to take the rifle pits at the foot of the ridge, and there halt. Get your division ready to move as soon as you can.' He added, 'I will send the order to Gen. Sheridan, and the two divisions will move together.'" It was also Wood's "impression" that Grant initially only intended to send Granger's two divisions forward "and that Baird's division on my left, and Johnson's division on Sheridan's right—both of the Fourteenth Corps were included in the movement at the suggestion of Gen. Thomas."[21]

Wood's account is relatively straightforward, free of any accusation of delay or distraction. Other accounts are less charitable. Albert Richardson paints a disturbing, almost dysfunctional scene, leveling harsh criticism at Granger:

> He was at the battery on Orchard Knoll, in the zeal of an old artillerist, forgetting his soldiers, but sighting the guns, and shouting with delight when they did good execution. For hours our infantry had been lying in line, just in rear of their breastworks, ready for the expected assault, and Granger's men were still waiting.
>
> [Chief of Staff] RAWLINS.—"Why are not those men moving up to the rifle pits? I don't believe they have been ordered forward."
> GRANT.—"Oh yes, I guess the order has been given. General [Wood], why is not your division moving up?
> WOOD.—"We have had no orders to."
> GRANT.—"General Thomas, why are not those troops advancing?"
> THOMAS.—"I don't know. General Granger has been directed to move them forward."
> GRANT.—"General Granger, why are your men waiting."
> GRANGER.—"I have no orders to advance."
> GRANT (sharply).—"If you will leave that battery to its captain, and take command of your corps, it will be a great deal better for all of us."
>
> Granger, never lacking in enthusiasm if there was fighting to be done, obeyed promptly, and six cannon shots, fired at intervals of two seconds, gave the preconcerted signal for the Union soldiers to advance.[22]

Here Granger is portrayed as the main culprit of the delay, but Thomas is also inattentive; only Grant's prodding, instigated by Rawlins, triggers the advance.

Writing in 1912, James Wilson conveyed a similar impression, though he amplified the degree of uncertainty exhibited by Grant.

> At first, everybody seemed hopeful, but as the day wore on towards noon and afternoon, with nothing done, the situation became exceedingly embarrassing. Rawlins, always an anxious and questioning observer, grew sullen and finally indignant, first at Granger and next at Thomas himself. . . . Grant seemed anxious but undecided, and gave no positive

orders, but as time continued to drag on with nothing done Rawlins finally, at my suggestion, urged Grant to silence Granger and give Thomas positive orders for a general advance . . . to begin at the firing of six guns at regular intervals. . . . All thought at the time that the enemy was moving troops constantly from his left and center toward his right, where Sherman was believed to be pressing him. . . . [I]t was a strong conviction to that effect which at last caused Grant to order Granger to rejoin his corps and then turn with equal firmness to Thomas and direct him to advance his whole line against the rifle trench at the foot of the Ridge in front. Thomas, recognizing at once the difference between a suggestion and a positive order, sent his aid[e]s-de-camp to the various division commanders.

In 1916 Wilson published a biography of Rawlins in which he further amplified the chief of staff as the driving force behind Grant's final order:

[Rawlins] stepped up to Grant, and in a low voice made the suggestion; whereupon Grant walked over to Thomas several steps away and in a conversational tone said: "Don't you think it is about time to order your troops to advance against the enemy's first line of rifle pits?" To this Thomas made no reply whatsoever so far as could be heard, but stood silent with uplifted glasses, scanning the enemy's position on the ridge. . . . He was evidently in doubt. So far as the eye could determine there was nothing to indicate the slightest success on Sherman's front, and so the deadlock continued. Our little group became more and more serious as time passed slowly on. Minutes seemed like hours. Granger kept up the noisy fire of his battery and this added to the annoyance and the embarrassment of the situation. . . . [F]inally at or about three o'clock, Rawlins again pressed Grant to issue a positive order. . . . Grant, who had by this time also become thoroughly aroused, turned to Thomas . . . and with a blazing face . . . said: "General Thomas, order Granger to turn that battery over to its proper commander and take command of his own corps." After a pause, he added in the same tone of authority: "And now order your troops to advance and take the enemy's first line of rifle pits."

Of course, by the time Wilson published these recollections, virtually everyone else involved was long dead, incapable of providing refutation, thus leaving him the last word.[23]

Both Richardson and Wilson paint unflattering pictures of Granger and Thomas, but Wilson goes further to portray Thomas as all but completely ignoring Grant, who he shows as unwilling to take decisive action until shamed into it by Rawlins. Wood's account of the exchange, however, seems the most credible. It is worth noting that neither Meigs's nor William Smith's journals—the two most contemporaneous accounts of that day on Orchard Knob—mention any such tension or recalcitrance. As a civilian, Smith might not have picked up on such, but Meigs, a professional soldier of long standing, certainly would have taken note.

The timing of this order is important and often overlooked. Wood put his conversation with Grant sometime after 2:30 P.M., by which time Sherman's attack had clearly foundered. Per both Wood and Wilson, Grant's order was probably issued close to 3:00 P.M., though in all other respects the two accounts differ markedly. The attack commenced a short while later, at about 3:30 P.M.

And what was the Army of the Cumberland doing before that order was issued? The army was far from inactive up to that point. At 8:45 A.M. Howard's XI Corps was detached to join Sherman. At 9:30 a.m. Thomas ordered Hooker to close up on the right toward Rossville. At midday Baird's division was also sent to Sherman, necessitating a march of several hours, only to be redirected. Baird's departure required the redeployment of Johnson's division, first to try and connect with Hooker, then to "form in two lines" on "the right of General Sheridan's division, and to conform to his movements." Baird's return, as described in an 1888 letter to "Baldy" Smith, ate up more time. Baird explained that, by the time the head of his column reached a position opposite the railroad tunnel, "all heavy fighting on Gen. Sherman's front had ceased" and that he was no longer needed there. Directed to reposition his command to Wood's left, Baird continued, he had only just got into position when he "met [Smith] with the verbal orders for the attack."[24]

Despite Richardson's dismissive claim that the Army of the Cumberland had been "for hours . . . lying in line, ready for the expected assault," in reality, at least half of Thomas's force had spent that time marching and countermarching at Grant's direction. Of the four divisions that ultimately made the assault, the last of them (Baird's) was not in position until moments before Grant ordered Thomas to attack. The Army of the Cumberland simply was not ready for a grand assault much before 3:00 P.M. Further, the rapidity with which that assault was finally organized and how it stepped off strongly suggests that Wood's version of the day's events is the correct one. No one was hesitating or pouting on Orchard Knob, except maybe Wilson and Rawlins.

It is certainly possible, even probable, that Granger was annoying everyone by playing at being a battery commander—a widely noted peccadillo—but it is also highly unlikely that his antics did anything to delay any attack. Even after the order was issued, time would inevitably elapse between issue and execution. Couriers had to go out to the divisional commanders, who then had to disseminate those orders through the ranks to their brigade and regimental commanders. If four divisions totaling 24,000 men massed across a front of more than two miles were all to advance on one signal, that advance required a level of coordination that would take time to arrange. It is also worth noting that the battery Granger was fooling with was the same battery that would fire the signal shots. This meant the general was where he was supposed to be, at a place from where he could observe his command and order the signal fired when all was ready. His demeanor might have been annoying, but he was not neglecting his duties.

The Confederates tasked with defending Missionary Ridge in the face of this onslaught amounted to three divisions: those of Maj. Gen. Alexander P. Stewart, Brig. Gen. William B. Bate, and Brig. Gen. J. Patton Anderson. Bate and Anderson were temporary commanders, elevated by absence or promotion. Bate commanded Breckinridge's Division since Breckinridge now commanded what was formerly D. H. Hill's corps. Anderson commanded Maj. Gen. Thomas C. Hindman's division since that officer was indisposed, both ill and recovering from a Chickamauga wound. Bate and Stewart belonged to Breckinridge's Corps, while Anderson was part of Hardee's Corps. These three divisions numbered approximately 15,000 officers and men. Additionally, Brig. Gen. Alexander W. Reynolds's brigade of two North Carolina and two Virginia regiments, orphaned when the rest of Buckner's Division joined Longstreet, were now stationed in reserve near Bragg's headquarters. Reynolds added perhaps another 1,000 men to the available defenders.

All three intact divisions were stretched thin, but Stewart, tasked with defending the entirety of the ridge from Rossville to nearly Bragg's headquarters, was stretched exceptionally thin. Like many men on both sides, Stewart believed that his own retreat from Chattanooga Valley on the night of the twenty-fourth was only the first step in a larger retreat: "Although the position [on Missionary Ridge] was naturally strong, it *seemed* like folly to attempt to hold it in the face of the immense force concentrated in its front." When it became clear that Bragg was staying put, and with his division unable to defend the whole of its assigned part of the ridge, Stewart posted two Georgia regiments at Rossville to hold that pass. This left a gap of nearly a mile between the Rossville force and his next brigade in line to the north, Col. Randall Gibson's Louisianans, which was sketchily filled by the remainder of Stovall's men, deployed in an extremely extended order.[25]

The Rebel defenses entailed at least two lines of entrenchments, though in some places intermediate lines had been constructed midslope. The main defenses consisted of a strong line of well-dug trenches at the base of the ridge and new works at the crest. Those crest fortifications, hastily constructed mostly in the dark, were only partially complete and in many cases not properly sited at the military crest but instead at the geographic crest. Initially, most of the artillery that should have formed the backbone of Bragg's defenses was absent, recalled to the ridge only on the morning of the twenty-fifth after the general's last-minute decision to stand firm. The Army of Tennessee eventually deployed 96 cannon atop the ridge (out of an army total of 145 guns), but many of those pieces did not get into position until very late in the day. The crews of the Fifth Company of the Washington Artillery, for example, reached their designated positions only at 3:20 P.M., approximately ten minutes before the Union signal guns were touched off. "A number of batteries," noted historian Larry Daniel, "lacked [any] protective earthworks" at all.[26]

To further complicate matters, General Breckinridge decided to divide his forces in order to hold both lines. Commands were directed to leave half their manpower at the foot of the ridge and the other half at the crest. Divisional, brigade, and even some regimental commanders were forced to try and direct formations bifurcated between the bottom and the top of the ridge, separated by a steep slope. Inevitably, control became confused and uncertain. As a further complication, some of those below thought they were to hold at all costs, while others thought they were only to delay the Federals and then scramble up to the top. Perhaps 6,000–7,000 men, possibly a bit more, were posted at the foot of the ridge; leaving 8,000–9,000 men atop the ridge. As a defensive scheme, it was a recipe for disaster.

Brig. Gen. Arthur Manigault, whose mixed Alabama and South Carolina brigade defended Anderson's center, recalled that "the instructions to the officers in the lower line were . . . to await the approach of the enemy to within two hundred yards, deliver their fire, and then retire to their works above[,]," a strategy he regarded as "most injudicious." Col. William F. Tucker, who commanded the brigade of Mississippians on Manigault's left, reported that "one half the brigade [was] in one rank in the trenches & the other half busy engaging at the top of the Ridge. Around midday, noted Tucker, "orders were received that if the enemy advanced in force, the men at the foot of the ridge *were not to fight where they were*, but fall back skirmishing." Inconsistency in implementing these instructions would soon produce additional chaos amid the Confederate ranks.[27]

And what, specifically, was the Federal objective? Wood succinctly reported that he "was ordered to advance and carry the enemy's entrenchments at the base of Mission Ridge and hold them." In 1888 Baird stated that Baldy Smith told him that upon the signal, "the whole line was to advance and carry the enemy's line of works at the foot of the ridge. I then asked," added Baird, "what we were expected to do after we had taken them, and you [Smith] replied that was the extent of the order; that we were simply expected to hold the works and await further orders, or words to that effect. Soon afterwards Gen. J. H. Wilson came to me and repeated . . . exactly the same orders." Curiously, in his official report, Baird suggested that Wilson added a codicil of his own: "This," said Wilson, "was intended as preparatory to a general assault on the mountain, and that it was doubtless designed by the major general commanding that . . . I would be following his wishes were I to push on to the summit." Wilson's remarks must have raised some confusion in Baird's mind: was he to halt and wait for additional instructions or keep going to the top? Presumably Wilson was anticipating his boss's next move, for none of the other three divisional commanders received any suggestion to carry the crest.[28]

Sheridan, whose division was next in line to Wood's right, reported that his orders were "to carry the enemy's rifle pits at the base of Mission Ridge." Johnson, whose division was on Sheridan's right, merely reported that he "was ordered . . . to conform to [Sheridan's] movements." None of the four divisional commanders claimed to have any instructions to take the crest: this attack was understood to be a demonstration, aimed at relieving the pressure on Sherman, not the decisive blow of the battle.[29]

To Sheridan, the orders seemed clear enough: "to carry the enemy's rifle pits at the base of Mission Ridge." But, thought Sheridan, "the first line of pits . . . would prove untenable after being carried . . . , [and] doubt arose in my mind whether I had properly understood the original order."

He dispatched an aide to go find Granger and clarify. Before that officer returned, six evenly spaced cannon shots from Bridges's battery on Orchard Knob rang out. The signal to attack had sounded.[30]

"Our advance to the base of the Ridge was the grandest sight I ever saw," wrote Maj. James A. Connelly, a member of Baird's staff, on November 26. "Our line stretched across the valley for miles, in the open field, in plain view of the rebels on the mountain top, and at a given signal all moved forward as if on parade." Lt. Marcus Woodcock of the 9th Kentucky in Wood's division noted: "The moment our boys emerged . . . into the open ground they attracted the attention of [Rebel] batteries which immediately turned their whole fire on our advancing line. Then was presented a scene for painter and poet that defies all description. The whole line of the summit of the Ridge seemed to be the continuous crater of one immense volcano."[31]

Fortunately for the attackers, the Rebels were ordered to avoid a stand-up fight in front of the ridge. "About three hundred yards in front of the enemy's works," noted Woodcock, the "occupants delivered a scattering volley . . . and immediately broke and fled up the hill." The Kentuckians chanced to be facing Manigault's and Tucker's Rebels, striking the seam between those two brigades. Manigault, atop the ridge (his forward line was commanded by Col. James F. Pressley of the 10th South Carolina), watched as his men "gave them their volley, and a well-directed and fatal one it proved: but then followed a scene of confusion rarely witnessed." Instead of retreating in good order, the forward line began a mad scramble up the slope. "All order was soon lost." Manigault then witnessed the Federals, heartened by this unexpected collapse, surged forward into the lower works.[32]

Next in line to the south, Tucker's Mississippians had already retreated. As accounts from within the ranks of the 7th Mississippi make clear, they fell back well before the Federals closed and failed to deliver any fire into the oncoming enemy ranks. "We rejoined our command at the top of Missionary Ridge about a half an hour before the general advance of the enemy," noted the commander of consolidated Companies E and K. Another member, writing home on December 2, explained that the men, exhausted from the climb, "were only able to rest for about thirty minutes when all eyes went to the plain below where five lines of battle were advancing."[33]

The Union troops soon seized the entire line of Confederate trenches at the base of the ridge. Here, however, that blazing Rebel artillery now

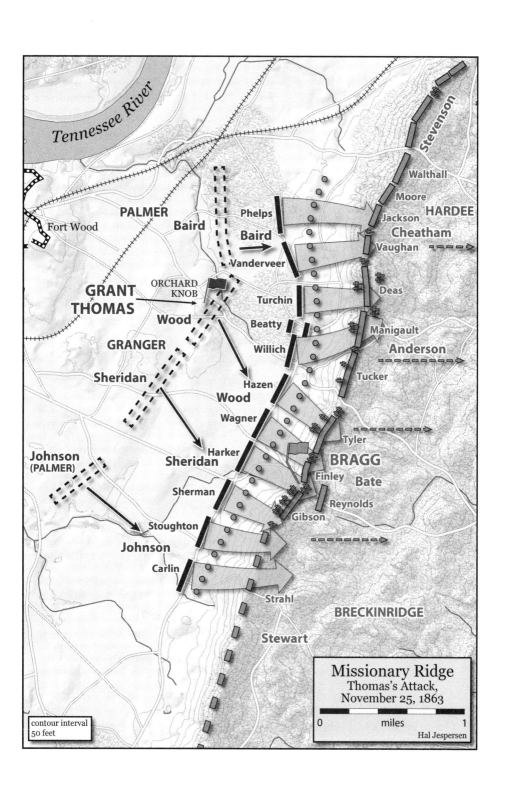

Tennessee River

PALMER
Fort Wood
Baird

Phelps
Baird
Vanderveer

Stevenson

Walthall
Moore
HARDEE
Jackson
Cheatham
Vaughan

GRANT
THOMAS
ORCHARD
KNOB

Turchin
Beatty

Deas

Wood
GRANGER
Sheridan

Willich

Manigault
Anderson

Hazen
Wood
Wagner

Tucker

Johnson
(PALMER)

Harker
Sheridan

Tyler
BRAGG
Finley
Bate
Reynolds
Gibson

Sherman

Stoughton
Johnson
Carlin

Strahl
BRECKINRIDGE

Stewart

Missionary Ridge
Thomas's Attack,
November 25, 1863

0   miles   1
Hal Jespersen

contour interval
50 feet

played upon them freely, a stationary target—and those captured works offered no protection from plunging fire. As the regimental history of the 41st Ohio of Wood's division recorded: "No fight could be made from that insufficient . . . shelter. It was destruction to remain, it was impossible to withdraw without confusion and great loss." Quickly, men began to go up the slope after the fleeing enemy. More followed them. Wood was amid the troops of his second line as he watched his first ranks raggedly work their way up. "'General, we can carry the ridge!'" he heard. Wood looked around and "said, 'Can you do it?' They said, 'We can.' 'Men, go ahead!'"[34]

Brig. Gen. August Willich, commanding one of Wood's brigades, may have been responsible for triggering this advance. "I understand since that the order was given to take only the rifle pits at the foot of the ridge," he reported, but at the time "I did not understand it so; I only understood the order to advance." When Maj. John McClenahan of the 15th Ohio, commanding Willich's skirmish line, asked the jovially gruff German where his skirmishers should halt, "he replied, 'I don't know, at Hades I expect.'" Since the other brigade commanders in Wood's division understood that the order was to reach the foot of the ridge and halt, Willich's movement likely sparked a more general advance. One of his soldiers, in a letter home to his German-language newspaper in Louisville, recalled: "We went at the double quick until we were at the first line of the Rebels' fortifications, which they had left in a hurry. . . . After we had rested some at the first fortifications the voice of our old Blucher [General Willich] resounded: 'Second line forward.' [We] rose as one man [and] stormed toward the mountain."[35]

Another foreign-born Union general, John B. Turchin, led a brigade in Baird's division, adjoining Wood's left. Turchin also ordered his men up the slope soon after taking the first line of works, abandoned by Manigault's Confederates. Baird, trying to organize his other two brigades to follow, was intercepted by a courier from Orchard Knob, informing him "not to permit my men to go farther, and not to permit them to become engaged." Baird was shocked since this meant leaving Turchin to race up the ridge alone, but it was contradicted within "three minutes"—disregard, go on up.[36]

Sheridan was also temporarily checked. Just before advancing, he sent Capt. J. S. Ransom back to Granger for clarification "whether it was the first line to be carried or the ridge." Before Ransom returned, Sheridan's men advanced and seized that first line, and many were already pushing up the slope. At this moment Captain Ransom returned, first encountering Brig.

Gen. George D. Wagner, leading Sheridan's Second Brigade. He "informed General Wagner that it was the first line to be carried [only]," triggering a retreat to the base of the ridge. Next Ransom found Sheridan, who was not inclined to stop. "Believing the attack had assumed a new phase, and that I could carry the ridge, I could not order those officers and men who were so gallantly ascending the hill . . . to return." Fortunately, within a few minutes, one of Granger's staff officers arrived to amplify the commander's intent: "If, in my judgment," Sheridan learned, "the ridge could be taken, to do so." Without hesitation he waved his three brigades forward.[37]

All four divisions surged up the ridge, much to the shock of the spectators on Orchard Knob. Meigs noted that the original order "was to form on our side of the [enemy] breast-works, and then send a regiment or two to the right and sweep the rebels out of their works and capture as many as possible." Instead, he noted now, "the colors of three Regiments pushed on and up the slopes of a projecting spur . . . , and the regiments swarmed up after them." At this sight, recalled Joseph Fullerton of Granger's staff, "Grant quickly turned to Thomas, who stood by his side, and I heard him say, angrily: 'Thomas, who ordered those men up the ridge?' Thomas replied, in his usual slow, quiet manner, 'I don't know: I did not.' Then, addressing General Granger, he said, 'did you order them up, Granger?' 'No,' said Granger, 'they started up without orders. When those fellows get started all hell can't stop them.'" Then, recalled Fullerton, "Grant said something to the effect that somebody would suffer if it did not turn out well."[38]

Newspaperman Shanks remembered Thomas as saying, "with a slight hesitation, which betrayed the emotions which raged within him, 'General, I—I'm afraid they won't get up.' Grant, continuing to look steadily at the column, hesitated half a minute before answering; then taking the cigar he was smoking from between his fingers, he said, as he brushed away the ashes, 'Oh, give 'em time, general.'" Grant biographer Albert Richardson had a slightly different take on that exchange. Thomas fretted that "those fellows will be all cut to pieces. They will never get to the top." Grant responded: "Let us see what the boys can do. They are not so badly scattered as you think. You see a good deal more bare ground between them on that hill-side than you would if it were level. We will see directly. The boys feel pretty good; just let them alone."[39]

In 1897 an anonymous author posited yet another variation of this exchange. In this version "Grant saw [the charge] with amazement and indignation. He turned to Gen. Thomas, and asked angrily: 'who ordered those men up the ridge?' Thomas, stroking his full, red beard, remarked, calmly, 'Nobody seems to have ordered them. They are just going themselves.' 'Well, it will be all right if it is all right,' said Grant. 'But if it is not, the stars will fall.'" Meigs merely recorded that Grant "said it was contrary to orders, it was not his plan—he meant to form the lines and then prepare and launch columns of assault, but, as the men, carried away by their enthusiasm had gone so far, he would not order them back." In a private letter to West Point professor Dennis Hart Mahan, "Baldy" Smith observed that "as the lines moved out forty guns opened on them with shell & canister, but they moved steadily forward, took the lower rifle pits & the soldiers insisted so strenuously on assaulting the Ridge, that the Division Commanders were powerless to stay them & they carried that range of hills . . . in six different places & almost simultaneously."[40]

What "the boys" could do was take the crest, and in spectacular fashion. The confusion infecting the Confederates holding the lower line did not abate once they reached the upper line of entrenchments. There, poorly sited breastworks meant that their artillery and infantry fire overshot the onrushing Federals on the slopes, with much of it wasted. In some cases the retreating Rebel first line also obstructed the next line of defenders, forcing them to hold fire or shoot into their own comrades. When the Union troops surged over the crest and flooded into the Rebel defenses, even though all their formation was long gone, the blue tide seemed unstoppable. In a letter home Capt. C. Irvine Walker of the 10th South Carolina, a member of Manigault's brigade staff, lamented: "We have met with one of the most severe and unaccountable defeats of the whole war. There are only two reasons I can assign: 1st. the necessarily great lengths of our lines, and the scarcity of troops, the number being entirely inadequate to its defence. 2nd. An unaccountable panic seizing the whole left of the army. . . . I feel very much mortified at the result of the battle. We ought never to have been driven away by a front attack."[41]

The Confederate command was further fractured by the fact that Breckinridge was absent at the time of the assault, having taken Col. James T. Holtzclaw's brigade of Stewart's Division south along the ridge toward Rossville, where Union activity threatened to turn the Confederate left. (That activity came from Hooker's force and will be described in the next chapter.) Breckinridge's absence left only General Bragg to personally direct what was becoming a fast-developing disaster in the center of the Confederate line.

The 24th Wisconsin reached the crest just south of Bragg's headquarters. The regiment's adjutant was Lt. Arthur MacArthur, the eighteen-year-old son of a Milwaukee judge. The 24th's color sergeant, John Borth, who at forty-four was one of the older men in the regiment, had become winded near the top. MacArthur took up the colors for the final push. Years later he described the moment to his son, Douglas: "While I was carrying the flag a whole dose of canister went through it tearing it in a frightful manner." That enemy fire was too high, however; the only damage MacArthur sustained was "one scratch . . . through the rim of my hat." The lieutenant and his flag were among the very first to top the ridge, followed by a seemingly unstoppable flood of men in blue. MacArthur was awarded the Medal of Honor for having "seized the colors of his regiment at a critical moment and planted them on the captured works on the crest of Missionary Ridge."[42]

Bragg was personally caught up in this melee. "A panic which I had never before witnessed," he fumed, "seemed to have seized upon officers and men, and each seemed to be struggling for his personal safety, regardless of his duty or his character." At one point the army commander took a personal hand in attempting to stop the rout. When the color bearer of the 3rd Florida was cut down, Bragg dismounted to seize the flag. Rehorsed, he rallied the regiment before another Floridian took up the colors. "General Bragg was a brave old soldier, even if he was a tyrant to his men," marveled Lt. Henry Reddick, who witnessed the incident.[43]

But Bragg could not personally rally every regiment. The Union flood pierced the ridgetop defenses simultaneously in as many as six different places across the entire front. Stewart was riding the length of his line south of Bragg's headquarters when he met an officer of the general's staff, informing him, "our line had been broken somewhere to the north of Bragg's headquarters, and he had been sent to me for troops to restore the line." Astounded, Stewart recalled, "so far from having a man to spare, it was but a brief space until my own troops were overwhelmed." Now it became a question of *sauve qui peut*. "I rode to the next ridge in our rear and . . . fell in with General Breckinridge." That officer, noted Stewart, "was in a great state of distress. . . . [H]e had fallen into Hooker's column that passed through the gap and turned our flank—that [Clayton's] brigade had been cut to pieces and captured and he had lost his son, who, it afterwards appeared, had been captured."[44]

Bragg fleetingly attempted to organize a counterattack with Bate's Division, but it was of no use. Bowing to the inevitable, he sent word to Hardee (whose defense of his part of the ridge, against Sherman, had been entirely successful) to fall back on Chickamauga Station and began his own retreat, working his way through the mobs of retiring Rebels. Pvt. Sam Watkins of the 1st Tennessee recounted that as Bragg rode by, "the soldiers would yell . . . 'Bully for Bragg, he's hell on retreat.'" Now even Watkins, a confirmed Bragg hater, admitted: "[I] felt sorry for him. Bragg looked so . . . hacked and whipped and mortified and chagrinned at defeat."[45]

Astounded and elated, Grant, Thomas, Granger, and Meigs all now went forward. "General Grant determined to go to the summit, and see that proper order was restored," wrote Meigs. "I rode with him, soon found three brass pieces, a limber and caisson; but no lanyard and no artillery-men—the cartridges near the piece piled at its wheel were round shot." Meigs soon improvised a crew out of nearby Federals and, with the help of an "ordnance officer [who] heard me asking for primers," managed to fire the cannon. Major Connolly of Baird's staff was there to witness this exploit. "One of the first officers I saw at these guns was old Quartermaster General Meigs, wild with excitement, trying himself to wheel one of these guns on the rebels flying down the opposite side of the mountain, and furious because he couldn't find a lanyard with which to fire the gun."[46]

At 4:30 P.M. Dana succinctly informed Washington of the success. "Glory to God," he wired Stanton. "The day is decisively ours. Missionary Ridge has just been carried by a magnificent charge of Thomas' troops, and rebels routed. Hooker has got in their rear."[47]

10
"A MOST IMPORTANT POSITION"

*J*oseph Hooker's role in the victory on November 25 has long been overshadowed by the startling triumph of Thomas's men and obscured by Hooker's subsequent difficult relationship with both Grant and Sherman. His success at Rossville, however, greatly destabilized the Confederate flank and significantly enhanced the scope of the victory atop Missionary Ridge.

Thomas ordered Hooker to move "on the Rossville Road toward Missionary Ridge" at 10:10 A.M., though Hooker's own order outlining this movement to his subordinates, found in the official records, is timed at 9:30 A.M. His order follows Thomas's wording closely, stating: "The commands will advance on the Rossville road toward Mission Ridge. General Osterhaus will take the advance, guarding well his right flank." Given that phrasing, either Thomas's order was issued earlier or Hooker's was issued an hour later. In any case, Hooker wasted little time in moving out.[1]

General Osterhaus reported receiving the order at 10:00 A.M. and setting off at 10:30, "descending by the Chattanooga road . . . into the valley." As his troops did so, they observed an impressive sight, as recorded in the 13th Illinois's regimental history: "Almost the whole of General Grant's army, then in the valley, [was now] moving out toward the ridge, to battle: mostly infantry, but with it much artillery and some cavalry. It was a fine sight, such as few men ever see in a lifetime." Osterhaus's Federals marched unopposed as far as Chattanooga Creek, where they found their first Rebels, "wounded [men] that had been carried so far, and then for some reason abandoned." Having spent much of the night lying out, "they were quite bitter in their denunciations of being left to freeze to death." The Rebels had also burned the all bridges over the creek, apparently before the last of their own wounded could be evacuated safely to the rear.[2]

At noon by the Army of the Cumberland's headquarters clock, Thomas sketched out what he intended Hooker to accomplish. "I wish you and General Palmer [XIV Corps] to move forward firmly and steadily upon the enemy's works in front of Missionary Ridge, using General Sheridan as a pivot." This simple order provides modern readers with some insight into Thomas's (and by extension Grant's) thinking. Both Baird's and Johnson's divisions belonged to Palmer's XIV Corps, so in naming Palmer, Thomas could have been referring to either command, though by the timing of this order he likely meant the latter. By this time Baird already had orders in hand sending him to join Sherman, and two brigades of Johnson's division were ordered to replace Baird on the right. Thomas was also still concerned about the strength of the Confederate defenses below the ridge and how they could enfilade Granger's advance, which is why he wanted Hooker and Johnson to take those positions from the flank.[3]

At 1:25 P.M. Hooker answered Thomas with some bad news: "I have been delayed preparing a crossing at Chattanooga Creek," he penned. "Bridges are destroyed. Shall be stopped perhaps an hour. The advance are skirmishing with the enemy across the creek, probably rear guard." Hooker closed this note by writing that "the bearer [of this message] will return with any dispatches." If either Grant or Thomas sent back an answer, it went unrecorded.[4]

In the meantime, Osterhaus crossed the 27th Missouri Infantry on "a hastily constructed footbridge" and ordered his divisional pioneers to begin work on a more substantial span. The Missourians pressed forward about a mile to within "easy range" of Missionary Ridge, specifically Rossville Gap, where, reported Col. Thomas Curley of the 27th, "the enemy was strongly posted . . . with four pieces of artillery and a strong support of infantry." The cannon belonged to Capt. Ruel Anderson's Georgia Battery, deployed on a small rise in the gap overlooking the Old Federal Road at a point where it turned southeast to cross Missionary Ridge. Another road led off to the northeast in the direction of Bird's Mill, curving northward around Missionary Ridge's eastern flank. Those Rebel infantry were the 42nd and 43rd Georgia from Brig. Gen. Marcellus A. Stovall's brigade, posted about "300 yards" west of the gap on another "slight eminence." The Confederates were commanded by Col. Robert J. Henderson of the 42nd. Captain Anderson estimated that the first Yankees appeared in front of him at about 10:30 A.M. (probably too early), "throwing out a heavy line of skirmishers, advancing within 400 yards of my battery."[5]

Both Henderson and Colonel Curley agreed that the skirmishing lasted about two hours, sometimes fierce, but with neither side suffering heavy losses. Then Henderson noted an alarming sight: "Long lines of [Union] infantry were discovered moving to the right and left, which I at once conceived to be a flank movement." His assessment was correct. Osterhaus continued to push his infantry across the stream on the footbridge until both of his brigades were across. Then he sent Brig. Gen. Charles R. Woods's brigade "to take the ridge on the right" of the gap, "while four regiments" of Col. James A. Williamson's Iowa brigade "ascended the steep (Missionary) ridge on the left." Anderson's Georgians opened "a very severe artillery fire" directed at Woods's men but failed to check them.[6]

Badly outnumbered, Henderson ordered a retreat. He fell back in stages, with Anderson's guns withdrawing first while the Georgian infantry provided cover, retiring to take up Anderson's now vacated battery position. Once the guns were extricated safely, Henderson did not linger. "A new position was ordered to be taken on the heights," reported Lt. Col. Henry C. Kellogg of the 43rd Georgia, "which was maintained until our skirmishers and artillery could join us. Line of march was taken as soon as the detachment was together and continued until our arrival at Ringgold." Henderson's retreat left the road toward Bird's Mill completely uncovered, probably because the colonel was already so outnumbered he did not feel safe in dividing his force to try and cover both routes. Doing so, however, opened up a route for the Federals leading directly into Bragg's rear area on the east side of the ridge.[7]

The 27th Missouri, observing the Georgians depart, pursued closely and managed to secure the gap before the rest of Osterhaus's movement was completed. Colonel Curley reported with evident pride, "we . . . planted our standard on the top of Missionary Ridge, and on the left and rear of Bragg's army, a most important position." Osterhaus moved the remainder of his division into and through the gap, halted, and reported his success to Hooker, who was already bringing up Cruft's men, with Geary's troops following behind them.

The time was now perhaps 2:30 P.M. Sherman's fight was ending, if not over. Grant, in conversation with Thomas Wood, was thinking of ordering Thomas to attack the Confederate center. Though Hooker's movement was not observable from Orchard Knob and thus invisible to Grant, Bragg could easily see it from the higher elevation of Missionary Ridge. Though as yet the Rebel commander had no word from Henderson at Rossville of any attack, this new threat could not be ignored. He notified Breckinridge, whose sector extended to Rossville and whose own headquarters was less than a mile away. After a short conference, Bragg sent him off south along the crest of the ridge to determine the extent of the developing crisis at

Rossville, with the army commander taking personal charge of the Confederate center. Breckinridge was accompanied by a few staff officers, included among them his son Cabell, as well as his cavalry escort and the army's chief of artillery, Col. James H. Hallonquist. Bragg also directed Col. James T. Holtzclaw's Alabama brigade of Stewart's Division to join Breckinridge, supported by Humphrey's Arkansas Battery, commanded by Lt. John W. Rivers. Stewart's divisional artillery chief, Capt. Thomas J. Stanford, joined Rivers's movement. Rossville was three and a half miles distant.[8]

Having secured Rossville Gap, Hooker now turned his attention northward. He ordered Osterhaus "to advance along the northern road (toward Chattanooga) after having passed the gap." Osterhaus was in the process of moving his men through the gap when Cruft reached the scene. "Upon request of General Osterhaus," he reported, "the head of my column was halted long enough to communicate with General Hooker, who was but a short distance to the rear. His answer came in a few moments, . . . borne by Major General Butterfield, chief of staff." Hooker wanted Cruft "to occupy the ridge immediately and engage the enemy vigorously . . . pressing the line rapidly along the ridge. . . . General Osterhaus would support [my movement] in the valley on the right and General Geary in the valley on the left." Cruft reported that he ascended the ridge from the gap at about 4:00 P.M.[9]

The first Confederate Hooker's men encountered was eighteen-year-old Cabell Breckinridge, sent ahead to try and find Colonel Henderson and his Georgians. The young officer rode into the ranks of the 9th Iowa, mistaking them for friendly troops, and was quickly captured. He was brought to Osterhaus, to whom the youthful firebrand asserted that the Confederates "were winning the battle to that point"—true enough at the time. After appropriating young Breckinridge's fine white mare for his own use, the general sent the prisoner to the rear.[10]

The next collision came when General Cruft, Col. William Grose (commanding one of Cruft's brigades), their staffs, and Cruft's escort bumped into three companies of skirmishers from the 36th Alabama leading Holtzclaw's advance southward. The Rebels opened fire, driving Cruft's scouting party back into the ranks of the 9th Indiana, still toiling up the slope. Col. Isaac Suman led his Hoosiers into a sharp counterattack, scattering the Confederate skirmishers and forcing Holtzclaw's leading regiments to deploy. Capt. Benjamin L. Posey of the 38th Alabama described the moment as one of extreme confusion. His regiment was only able to manage the

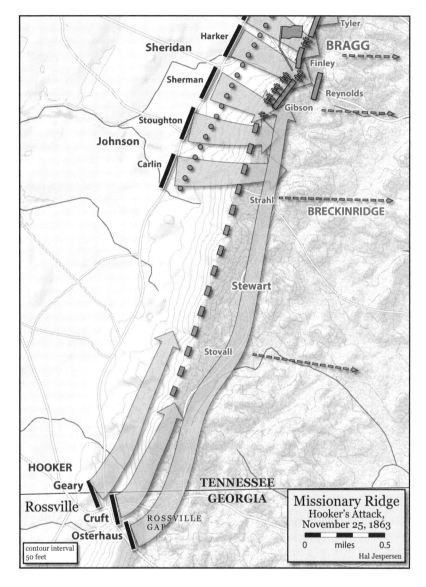

Sheridan
Harker
Tyler
BRAGG
Finley
Sherman
Reynolds
Gibson
Stoughton
Johnson
Carlin
Strahl
BRECKINRIDGE
Stewart
Stovall
HOOKER
Geary
TENNESSEE
Rossville
GEORGIA
Cruft
ROSSVILLE
GAP
Osterhaus

Missionary Ridge
Hooker's Attack,
November 25, 1863

contour interval
50 feet

0   miles   0.5
Hal Jespersen

deployment, noted Posey, "in some incomprehensible way." The Indianans pushed Posey and his comrades back 300 yards to some old abandoned earthworks, ironically constructed by some of Cruft's own men back in September just after the Battle of Chickamauga. Here the 38th and 36th Alabama attempted to make a stand.[11]

Holtzclaw's other two regiments, the 18th Alabama and the consolidated 32nd/58th Alabama, halted about 400 yards farther to the rear. "I scarcely got two regiments in line," reported Holtzclaw, "the Thirty-sixth and Thirty-eighth, which filled the position, when I discovered my flanks, right and left, were completely enveloped by the enemy, a column of which . . . passed around my left, capturing my ambulance train and medical stores in my rear." These were Osterhaus's men, flanking the Alabamans from a completely unexpected direction, to their east below Missionary Ridge. This movement triggered a near-rout in the 38th Alabama, which, according to Holtzclaw, was "getting into great confusion and reeling under the fire of the enemy."[12]

That "reeling" caught Lt. Col. John Inzer and his 32nd/58th Alabama by surprise when men of the 38th "came running out over us." Rushing to rally his own regiment lest it flee too, Inzer "ran down the line, placed the colors, and attempted to form the line here." He was only partially successful. Holtzclaw managed to eventually reform the 18th, 36th, and 32nd/58th into some semblance of a line. Breckinridge and the corps staff, "recklessly exposing themselves to the fire, did all that men could do in animating and encouraging the command." That accomplished, the colonel then informed Breckinridge that he "could hold the position in front" if the general could provide "support to check the column that enveloped my right flank. The message that I received [in return] was that the main line was broken in our rear and the ridge carried and that I must withdraw the command."[13]

It was now close to 5:00 P.M. Complete disaster had overtaken the Army of Tennessee. The storming of Missionary Ridge was complete. General Thomas, describing Granger's and Palmer's assault, reported that "our troops . . . carried the hill simultaneously at six different points." At the same time, Geary's line moved up along the western base, planting artillery to shell Holtzclaw's Rebels as they engaged Cruft. Eventually Geary's men ascended the ridge's western face about a mile and a half north of Rossville, aiming for a juncture with Carlin's brigade of Johnson's division, the rightmost command of the frontal assault. "The cheers from above," noted Geary, "were taken up and reechoed by our men below as they pressed forward, over ground strewn with arms and equipments of the enemy." Similarly, Osterhaus's troops worked their way northward along the eastern slope, pressing forward so quickly that, by the time he received the final orders to withdraw, Holtzclaw could only fall back along the crest, through a gap of no more than 400 yards between Geary's and Osterhaus's exuberant Federals. Here the Alabamans began "throwing away arms, blankets and everything to facilitate their escape. . . . [D]iscipline and courage alike were gone, and the greater portion of the command ran out like a mob, each endeavoring to be foremost." About half of them got away.[14]

The bulk of Holtzclaw's captured men were swept up by Osterhaus. "We . . . got into the rear of the rebel left," wrote Lt. Henry Kircher of the 12th Missouri. "This made them breake and run in confusion. [We] took some 900 prisoners and 1 piece of artillery. Night now closes all fun, and safed the rebs from a more thourough routing if it could be more so." In his brigade alone Holtzclaw reported a loss of not less than 36 officers and 591 enlisted men missing (nearly half of his engaged strength), suggesting that Kircher's figures were reasonably accurate. Osterhaus's division penetrated the farthest of any of Hooker's command that evening, reaching the vicinity of Bragg's former headquarters at the Moore House, where he found Sheridan's division of Granger's IV Corps on the same ground and Geary's men not far off. Like so many other Federal generals, Hooker followed his men up the ridge. "[We] marched to the rebel fighting ground on Missionary Ridge and bivouacked," Kircher continued. "Here one thundering hurrah after the other burst forth frome the 12th Army C. and our division as Genr. Hoocker approached. Still prisoners are brought in, in squads of 3 to 12. They all look healthy and gay and many of them have but little more fight in them, think their cause a lost one[.] So do I, and besides I hope thourough punishment awaits them."[15]

The one area where the Confederates were not driven from the ridge was at the north end. Not only did Cleburne's Division still hold Tunnel Hill, but Cheatham's, Walker's (commanded by Brig. Gen. States R. Gist), and Stevenson's Divisions all still held their positions. Baird's Federals scaled the ridge at the seam between Cheatham's and Anderson's Divisions, striking and forcing back the Tennessee brigade of newly promoted Brig. Gen. Alfred J. Vaughan. Capt. Arthur T. Fielder of the 12th Tennessee journaled that Vaughan's men were compelled to give way when Deas's Brigade on their left fell back. "There was an effort made to rally Deas['s] men," noted Fielder, "which was partially effected but they again soon run off in wild confusion." Fielder and his comrades, now outflanked, suffering "an enfolding fire," and nearly out of ammunition, "fell back a short distance and again rallied," whereupon Fielder fell wounded. Vaughan's resistance, however, bought time for General Cheatham to refuse his left flank, pivoting two of his own brigades backward to face south against Baird's men. With no threat from Sherman to the west or north, Cheatham held firm. Thus, Hardee's entire corps, half of the Army of Tennessee, remained intact.[16]

Grant understood the need to address the problem posed by Hardee's force, which was powerful and well positioned to launch a counterattack against the northern flank of the Union assault. He once again turned to Sherman. At 4:00 P.M. while on Orchard Knob and while the Federals were still scaling the ridge, Grant signaled him that "Thomas has engaged the enemy along his whole front & is driving him up." Shortly thereafter, he sent a much more emphatic directive: "Thomas has carried the hill and line in his immediate front. Now is your time to attack with vigor. DO SO!"[17]

Grant then left Orchard Knob to ride up the ridge and restore "proper order." If he assumed that Sherman would act promptly to join in and complete the victory, he was mistaken. None of the men under his friend's command bestirred any further that day, despite the large number of fresh, unengaged troops available—including Davis's division and Howard's XI Corps. As General Schurz noted, Sherman seemed more concerned with being attacked than doing any further attacking of his own.

Where Grant ascended the ridge, and to which sector of the assault he rode, has never been described in detail. Meigs's diary puts the quarter-master general on the northern shoulder of the assault amid Baird's men. Grant's description of his activities is, by contrast, vague. "The moment the troops were seen going over the last line of rebel defences, I ordered Granger to join his command, and mounting my horse I rode to the front. Thomas left about the same time." Here Grant noted that "Sheridan was already in pursuit of the enemy east of the ridge," but "Wood . . . , [who] accompanied his men on horseback in the charge . . . , did not join Sheridan in the pursuit. To the [Union] left, in Baird's front . . . the resistance was more stubborn and the contest lasted longer." Yet Grant must have been reasonably close to Granger during this time, close enough to observe the latter's demeanor. "I ordered Granger to follow the enemy with Wood's division, but he was so much excited, and kept up such a roar of musketry in the direction the enemy had taken, that by the time I could stop the firing the enemy had got well out of the way."[18]

If Grant followed the route of Wood's men, he ascended the ridge some-where a bit south of the Sutton House or perhaps one-half to three-quarters of a mile north of Bragg's headquarters. The most direct route from Orchard Knob to the crest of the ridge was via Bird's Mill Road, and if Grant followed it to the top, he crested the ridge almost directly in the center of Wood's line, with Hazen's brigade to the right and Willich's command to the left. He was definitely present with Willich at some point, for that officer reported "receiv[ing] orders from General Grant in person to reform the brigade on the crest for further eventualities, which I did."[19]

William Smith did not immediately accompany his cousin to the crest, though he did seem to have remarkably free access to the army's front lines. Smith watched the spectacular ascent and conquest of the ridge. Then, according to his diary entry:

> Expecting to have a long ride in pursuit I mount my horse and fly into town,—fill my flask and get back again . . . within a quarter of an hour— when I catch up to Maj. Rowley who is on his way out. We find the General and his party have just left for the Ridge. . . . We got to the ridge by a very rough road, impassable for anything but horses and men. On the top are several captured cannon, and a great many of our troops, resting, drawn up to repel any attempt to retake the heights. The farther we get to the north part of the Ridge the more loud and sharp is the musketry. It seems one continuous roll. Some poor fellows lying on the road, badly wounded—we stop and give some whiskey. We directly meet the General and his party, who are returning, as it is now near dark. . . . The enemy are routed on all hands, and to-morrow, we expect a big ride after them. The General calls to me and says I was very lucky to be here, as "it wasn't in half a dozen life times one could see so much of a battle with comparatively so little danger." He praised General Baird as a "*fine* officer."

Smith's passage suggests that Grant also rode north along the crest, perhaps as far as Baird's position, though neither Grant nor Baird mentioned any meeting. Given that that last organized Confederate resistance lay to the north, Grant's decision to head in that direction made sense.[20]

In any case, Grant certainly did not linger long atop the ridge. Before dark he returned to headquarters in Chattanooga. He had much to do. First, he informed Sherman of the "handsome manner in which Thomas' troops carried Missionary Ridge," thanks in part (as Grant and most others thought) to Sherman's own efforts to draw off Rebels from Bragg's center. He then laid out his future intentions: "The next thing now will be to relieve Burnside." Grant wanted Sherman's men to occupy "the railroad between Cleveland and Dalton," severing any chance of a rail connection between Bragg and Longstreet. "Granger will move up the south side of the Tennessee with . . . 20,000 men." Given the shortage of horses, Granger lacked wagons and instead would rely on "four days' rations" carried with the men as well as "the steamer *Chattanooga*, loaded with rations," for logistical support. Almost as an afterthought, Grant next wrote: "I take it for granted that Bragg's entire force has left. If not, of course the first thing to do is dispose of him." Then, in a postscript to this message, Grant made one final change to this plan, aimed at inflicting all the damage against the Rebels he could. "On reflection, I think we will push Bragg with all our strength to-morrow, and try if we cannot cut off a good portion his new troops and trains. His men have manifested a strong desire to desert for some time past, and we will now give them a chance. . . . Move the advance force early on the most easterly road taken by the enemy." This last directive placed Sherman in position to follow Bragg's line of retreat and support Thomas if the Army of the Cumberland managed to cut off a portion of the Rebel army. But it still left Sherman in position to quickly block the all-important Cleveland–Dalton rail connection.[21]

To accomplish that mission, next Grant informed Thomas to "start a strong reconnaissance in the morning at 7 A.M. to ascertain the position of the enemy. If . . . the enemy are in full retreat, follow them with all your force, except that which you intend Granger to take to Knoxville. . . . I have ordered Sherman to pursue also, he taking the most easterly road." Hooker proposed to move his men via Rossville toward Graysville (along the railroad at the Georgia-Tennessee line) and was authorized to do so, adding a third prong to the pursuit. Having put those affairs in motion, Grant then informed Halleck in Washington of the news. Dana had already sent a preliminary announcement, brief but to the point, at 4:30 P.M.: his "Glory to God" communique. At 7:30 P.M. Grant followed up with his own missive, detailing the planned movements by Sherman, Thomas, Granger, and Hooker as well as revealing his own confidence in the final outcome: "If Burnside holds out until . . . [Granger] gets beyond Kingston I think the Enemy [Longstreet] will fly. . . . I believe Bragg will lose much of his army by desertion in consequence of his defeat in the last three days fight."[22]

Union pursuit that night came from Sheridan's men and from Willich's brigade, the latter's men mounted at Granger's direction. Despite whatever excitability Grant thought he observed in the man, Granger was still trying to orchestrate the fighting. At 6:00 P.M. the IV Corps commander reported to Thomas, "I think we have them, but I want a battery." At 7:15 P.M. he elaborated: "It is probable that we can cut off a large number of the enemy by making a bold dash upon the Chickamauga, either upon the

Rossville road or the one north of it, or upon all the roads leading from our present front.... The enemy are evidently badly demoralized. Our men are in great courage and in spirits.... We have captured about forty pieces of artillery and about 2,000 prisoners ... besides 50 wagon loads of forage."[23]

Shortly after gaining the crest, Sheridan reported that "the enemy was retiring, but had a well-organized line covering his retreat." Beyond that thin gray-clad bulwark, however, the Federal noted that Bragg's "disorganized troops, a large wagon train and several pieces of artillery could be distinctly seen fleeing ... within a distance of half a mile. I at once directed [Brig. Gen. George D.] Wagner and [Col. Charles D.] Harker to press their rear guard." That rear guard was a cobbled-together force improvised by Brigadier General Bate, commanding Breckinridge's old division. Sheridan's men pressed, and Bate gave ground, falling back to "a high, formidable ridge" about "1 mile from Missionary Ridge." There, his men made another stand, until Wagner sent the 15th Indiana and 26th Ohio to threaten Bate's flank, forcing another retreat. Here, Sheridan halted his advance while he went to look for support.[24]

In his 1888 memoir Sheridan crafted a scene where he discovered Granger at Bragg's newly captured headquarters, already abed and seemingly content to rest on his laurels. It took some pushing, claimed Sheridan, before Granger grudgingly "told me finally to push on to the crossing of Chickamauga Creek." Only partially satisfied, he returned to his division "about midnight" and headed for the creek. But Sheridan's account seems both self-serving and erroneous.

As evidenced by Granger's 7:15 dispatch, the corps commander was already urging a move toward Chickamauga Creek. Additionally, both Granger's and Sheridan's official reports seem to correlate better with the senior general's version of the night's events. Granger reported that "it was my design, as soon as the troops were sufficiently rested, to move, and, as soon as I could procure guides, to push Sheridan's division, supported by Wood's, down Moore's road, and, if possible, get possession of the crossings of Chickamauga Creek; then, swinging my column around, to move toward the north end of Mission Ridge." A lack of guides, noted Granger, meant that he "was not able to commence the movement until midnight." The drama found in Sheridan's memoir is absent in his official report, which stated only that "about 12 o'clock at night, being ordered with my division to press the enemy, I drove him over Chickamauga Creek.... I reached the creek at about 2 o'clock in the morning."[25]

At the time, Granger was acting in the absence of orders from any higher authority. Thomas made no written reply to his 7:15 note until midnight, and it is unclear when he received that reply. Granger's ideas for the next day's pursuit modeled Grant's in pushing forward on all roads and sending Hooker to Rossville, but Granger himself would play no part in that operation. As discussed, he was assigned a different mission. Thomas wrote, "I have just seen General Grant, who desires that you make preparations to move up the river as soon as possible." But Thomas's answer seems to have gone first to Sheridan, who returned it with the following addendum: "This message was sent to Missionary Ridge, but as messages came from there, I concluded he [Granger] is in town." Had that message been sent sooner, or received more quickly, Granger might have been saved a bit of trouble with Grant a couple of days later.[26]

Missionary Ridge was a thrilling moment for all who witnessed it, not the least for the various reporters gathered in Chattanooga. Sensing that he was on the cusp of momentous events, Sylvanus Cadwallader made elaborate plans to get his story out to the public as rapidly as possible. In the past his influence with Grant had been strong enough to get his stories sent over the wires from Chattanooga. This time, however, urgent military traffic would take precedence. Thus, when he left Orchard Knob on the afternoon of November 25, it was not to go to the top of Missionary Ridge. Instead he hurried into town, where a fresh horse was waiting for him, and rode all night to Bridgeport, catching an early morning train to Nashville. All that haste availed him little, however, since two train wrecks delayed him a further twenty hours. He wrote his story on the train, and upon reaching his destination—and after approval by the post commander—he had it wired to the *Chicago Times*. Shortly thereafter he met both William Shanks, correspondent for the *New York Herald*, and another reporter named Woodward, who wrote for the *Cincinnati Times*. Both men had also hurried from Chattanooga to file their stories, but Cadwallader beat them both. Over the coming days, all three men's reportage electrified the North as they described aspects of the battle.[27]

11

"A VERY DANGEROUS DEFILE"

*A*s the sun rose on November 26, conflicting military necessities pulled Grant's attention in two directions. Bragg's demoralized army was almost certainly headed south into Georgia, and every dictum of the military art demanded an aggressive pursuit. Conversely, with Burnside besieged in Knoxville, and who knew how close to disaster, East Tennessee remained a priority. Moreover, even if Longstreet abandoned his siege, the last thing Grant wanted was for any of his troops to rejoin the Army of Tennessee. Fortunately for Federal fortunes (though Grant did not yet know it), there was little chance of that happening quickly, if at all.

Col. Eli Long's cavalry brigade was largely responsible for preventing Longstreet from rejoining Bragg. Long's troopers, it will be recalled, crossed the Tennessee on the afternoon of November 24, following Sherman's infantry, and headed in the direction of Cleveland, Tennessee. Grant had never wholly abandoned the idea of a cavalry raid. Since a deep strike toward Dalton was out of the question, Long's much more limited operation was substituted instead. Once beyond Sherman's lines, however, his troopers were effectively incommunicado and would remain so for several days.

Long struck out for Tyner's Station on the Chattanooga & Cleveland Railroad, just east of Missionary Ridge. There he paused just long enough to tear down the telegraph wires and capture the civilian operator before pushing on. Long's men rode thirteen miles that evening, stopping repeatedly to rip down the telegraph wires and to damage the railroad "by burning and tearing up the track." The column halted to rest at midnight, "with orders not to unsaddle our horses, as we were in the immediate rear of the rebel army." Proof of that fact came when Brig. Gen. Marcus Wright's brigade trains blundered into the Federal column and were captured in toto.[1]

Setting out on the morning of November 25, Long's men rode the remaining sixteen miles to Cleveland, inflicting what damage they could along the way. After driving off the 2nd Kentucky Cavalry (CS) defending the town, Long dispatched a force north to Charleston, Tennessee, where the Confederates were struggling to rebuild the rail bridge over the Hiwassee. Bushrod Johnson was at Loudon, about forty miles northeast of Charleston. By 5:00 P.M. the brigade commander passed on disturbing news to Longstreet: "The enemy's cavalry," Johnson wired, "are in sight of Charleston and moving on the bridge. . . . We have but one regiment at Charleston." To Longstreet, it now appeared that Union troops were between himself and Bragg.[2]

On November 26 Colonel Long concentrated on inflicting maximum damage. Dividing his forces, he ordered detachments down the rail lines south toward Dalton, back east toward Tyner's, and north toward Charleston. Each column concentrated on ripping up track and bending the iron rails by heating them over bonfires of crossties. Scouring Cleveland, Long reported that he destroyed "a considerable lot of rockets and shells, large quantities of corn, several bales of new grain sacks, . . . several railroad cars . . . , [and] the large copper rolling mill—the only one of the kind in the Confederacy." The 1st Ohio Cavalry also "destroyed ten miles of the Dalton track."[3]

On the twenty-seventh, menaced by gathering Confederate cavalry, Long abandoned Cleveland and headed for the banks of the Tennessee River north of Chattanooga, where he reestablished contact with the rest of the Union army, reporting his own successes and learning for the first time of the tremendous victory achieved on Missionary Ridge in their absence.

Sherman's pursuit effort began "about midnight, the 25th," when, reported Jefferson C. Davis, "I received orders to cross the South Chickamauga Creek, and move up the north bank in the direction of Chickamauga Station." Davis marched as far as Boyce's Station (where the road to Harrison branched off) until halted by a thick fog, making it "impossible to proceed farther without great risk." His men were boiling coffee and cooking breakfast when, "shortly after daylight," General Howard arrived, leading his XI Corps toward the same destination. At 8:00 A.M., the fog having begun to dissipate, Davis resumed his march, skirmishing with Rebel cavalry. From prisoners the Federals learned "of the general retreat of Bragg's army." Shortly thereafter, "after a sharp skirmish," the 21st Kentucky (US) captured Chickamauga Station.[4]

Large quantities of Rebel supplies, painstakingly accumulated there for Bragg's army, could not be moved and were put to the torch. General Lewis's Orphan Brigade drew this unpleasant duty. Men who had been on short rations for two months due to Bragg's transportation issues now watched in frustration as many thousands of those rations went up in smoke. The job was far from complete even at 11:00 A.M., when Davis's Yankees appeared; many stores fell into Union hands undamaged.

Those supplies might have been taken much earlier by Sheridan's men, but the general halted his men on the west bank of South Chickamauga Creek. His troops reached its banks a little south of Chickamauga Station as early as 2:00 A.M. Col. Francis T. Sherman of the 88th Illinois, commanding one of Sheridan's brigades, reported that his troops were also roused at midnight and "marched on the road to Bird's Mill about 1 ½ miles in pursuit, and halted until 11 A.M." At 2:00 A.M. much of Bragg's army—especially those parts of Hardee's Corps defending the Tunnel Hill area—were still filing southward through Chickamauga Station toward Ringgold. A more aggressive move by both Sheridan and Thomas Wood of Granger's IV Corps might have caught many of these Confederates on the move, dividing Bragg's forces still further. But with Knoxville still uppermost in his mind, Grant had already directed Granger to return to Chattanooga and prepare to march north.[5]

Granger's departure left Thomas with only Palmer's XIV Corps and Hooker's polyglot command to pursue Bragg. At 10:00 A.M. that morning, Hooker asked Thomas for permission to "move to Graysville via Rossville." Hooker believed that if he were "not prevented from making this movement rapidly," he could intercept "a portion of the . . . retreating column." He also asked for support from Palmer and at least some help from Sheridan, whom Hooker thought should "be instructed to destroy the railroad bridge across Chickamauga River" north of Chickamauga Station.[6]

At 1:00 P.M. Thomas approved all of Hooker's ideas except for aid from Sheridan, ordering Palmer to "report to General Hooker, and co-operate with him in his movement on Graysville." At 1:45 P.M. he again informed Granger "that it is General Grant's order that you complete your preparations for the Knoxville expedition as soon as possible," perhaps because the order of the previous evening went astray. Granger's men were soon headed back to Chattanooga. Hooker's idea—Sheridan's proposed bridge-destruction mission—was now superfluous; Davis's men had already captured both the bridge in question and Chickamauga Station. Accordingly, Col. Francis Sherman of Sheridan's command reported that his brigade received orders at 4:00 P.M. "to return to our old camp . . . , at which place we arrived at 6 P.M."[7]

Much to Grant's subsequent irritation, Granger's midnight-pursuit order, coupled with the failure of Thomas's 7:00 P.M. directive to reach Granger in a timely fashion, meant that the IV Corps's departure for East Tennessee was delayed at least a day. Had Granger's troops returned to Chattanooga on the evening of the twenty-fifth or even in the early hours of the twenty-sixth, they could have started up the Tennessee for Knoxville either late in the day on the twenty-sixth or early on the twenty-seventh, had Grant so desired. The lack of an immediate order for Granger to do so, however, suggested that at the time, Grant was not nearly so concerned with the supposed delay.

By 1:30 P.M. on the twenty-sixth, Charles Dana reported that there was little doubt "Bragg is in full retreat, burning his depots and bridges. The Chickamauga Valley, for a distance of 10 miles, is full of the fires lighted in his flight." Hooker's trek toward Graysville was plagued by this destruction, especially of the bridges. Palmer's corps—minus Davis's men, still under Sherman's control—took the lead, with Richard Johnson's division in the van. On reaching the crossing over West Chickamauga Creek, General Carlin, commanding Johnson's First Brigade noted, "we found that the bridge had been destroyed by the retreating enemy." After improvising "a temporary structure," his troops moved on to the next obstacle, Peavine Creek, "which we were also compelled to bridge." These efforts, said Carlin, "delayed our march several hours and [were] very unfortunate, for otherwise we would have had an opportunity to strike the enemy in a favorable position and could have accomplished results worth having." By the time the Federals were able to cross Peavine, night was falling; by the time they neared Graysville, it was full dark. There were troops moving on the Graysville road, but Carlin was unable to determine if they were Rebels or fellow Federals, perhaps of Sherman's command. After some limited stumbling around in the woods, Palmer halted for the night. In his report Carlin noted that the day's haul was "a fine Napoleon gun," abandoned during the retreat, "about 40 Georgia militia . . . , [and] three commissioned officers of the Sixteenth South Carolina."[8]

Grant was not pleased. Instead of catching Bragg on the move and inflicting an even more devastating defeat of the Army of Tennessee, November 26 produced only skirmishing. Earlier he had reiterated Sherman's orders to follow Bragg's army "on the most easterly road . . . , [t]he object being to bring him to battle again, if possible." In a second dispatch, after explaining Sherman's movements of that morning, Grant directed Thomas to "please move in the direction of the enemy all the force indicated for the pursuit . . . with all possible dispatch." But at 6:00 P.M. Grant wrote to Thomas: "Sherman is now with his advance about 2 miles North of Graysville. Had some skirmishing all day with the rear guard of the enemy which seems to be protecting a large wagon train. If Sheridan had been where his advance at 12 O'clock indicated he would be at this time the enemy rear would have been cut off. Sherman will push forward to Graysville in the morning. Direct your troops to push forward to the same point as early in the morning as possible." Of course, the order that pulled Sheridan off Missionary Ridge that morning and sent his command back to Chattanooga came from Grant himself. He was attempting to orchestrate movements in two opposite directions simultaneously: pushing Hooker and Sherman south to strike Bragg before he fell back into a defensible position in North Georgia while also demanding that Granger hustle northward up the Tennessee toward Knoxville. On November 26 neither effort was working particularly well.[9]

Meanwhile, Bragg established his headquarters at Catoosa Station, two miles south of Ringgold, sometime on the morning of the twenty-sixth. At 11:30 A.M. he informed Longstreet of the disaster and urged him "to fall back . . . upon Dalton, if possible." If that was "impracticable . . . you will have to fall back towards Virginia." Bragg also ordered Longstreet to dispatch all of the Army of Tennessee's remaining cavalry to Dalton. This message, sent via Major General Wheeler, would be three days in transit.[10]

Bragg next laid out his plans for the twenty-seventh. The army would continue to Dalton, though not without a rear guard. That task fell upon Major General Cleburne and his division, whose stalwart defense of Tunnel Hill was the single redeeming aspect of November 25's otherwise unmitigated disaster. That afternoon Cleburne sent his aide Captain Buck to army headquarters for additional instructions. There, Buck was greeted by an unusually emotional Bragg. Clasping Buck's right hand in both of his own, the general instructed the captain to "tell General Cleburne to hold his position at all hazards, and keep back the enemy, until the artillery and transportation of the army is secure, the salvation of which depends on him." Buck was shocked. Bragg, he thought, "exhibited more excitement than I supposed possible for him. He had evidently not rested during the [previous] night."[11]

Hooker resumed the march at 6:00 A.M. on the twenty-seventh. According to the 13th Illinois's regimental history, Hooker turned to that "glorious soldier," General Osterhaus, to again lead the pursuit. Osterhaus's column marched past Palmer's troops to take up the advance, followed by Geary's division of the XII Corps. The Federals pressed on without artillery, which was still far behind due to the bridging problems.[12]

The once-prosperous town of Ringgold lay at the western foot of a steep ridge. Ringgold Gap was a break in that ridge, through which flowed East Chickamauga Creek and, alongside the stream, ran the tracks of the

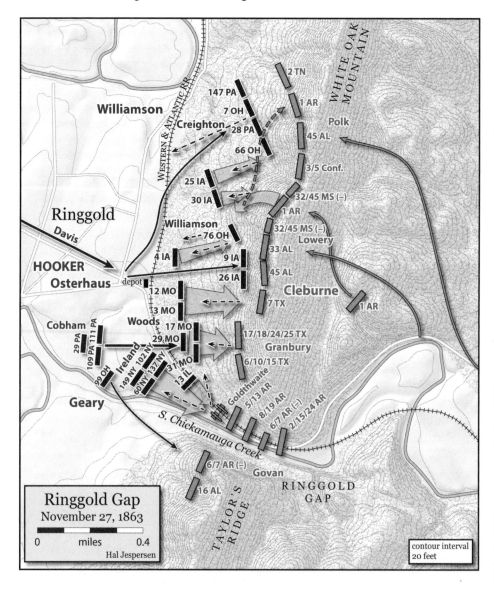

Western & Atlantic Railroad. That portion of the ridge north of the creek was called White Oak Mountain; to the south, Taylor's Ridge. Cleburne placed two regiments of Govan's Brigade on Taylor's Ridge, with the rest of the brigade and two artillery pieces in the gap. Granbury's Texans took up positions atop White Oak Mountain. Cleburne's other two brigades were held in reserve on the far side of the ridge. It was yet another formidable defensive position.

Both Hooker and Osterhaus had just spent the past two days driving Confederate troops from equally formidable positions, however, and they were not deterred. Osterhaus reached Ringgold at about 7:00 A.M. The town, at one time a thriving stop on the Western & Atlantic, was now a nearly deserted shambles, having been fought over several times since September. In his diary Pvt. Jacob Early of the 99th Ohio described the place as "a stinking Secesh hole, but it was [once] a rich place [with] good buildings." Osterhaus rode through the empty streets to halt at the stone depot, from where he saw the last of a line of Confederate wagons slipping through the gap. Cleburne's infantry and artillery, artfully concealed, were not in view. Next, General Hooker arrived, informed by a local that the Rebels were in full retreat and in "disarray." Osterhaus thought he could capture the wagons, just visible in the gap, with little effort. Hooker agreed and ordered him to "attack immediately." If necessary, other troops would be sent up the face of White Oak Mountain on a flanking move as they came up.[13]

Brig. Gen. Charles Woods's brigade led the fight. Woods sent his three regiments of Missourians up the shoulder of White Oak, while the 13th Illinois headed straight into the gap. The 76th Ohio also began climbing White Oak farther to the north. Granbury's concealed line of Texans opened fire on the Missourians, inflicting heavy loss and driving them back to the valley floor, where they sought shelter behind the curving railroad embankment. The 13th Illinois, facing similarly intense musketry and the fire of Cleburne's artillery, became pinned down around the buildings of the Isaac Jobe farm, three hundred yards south of the stone depot and one hundred yards short of the gap. Of his Missourians, Woods reported, they were so disrupted that "they were not again entirely rallied until after the enemy retired."[14]

Undaunted, Osterhaus reinforced Woods with Col. James Williamson's brigade, six veteran regiments of Iowans. He directed Williamson's men to climb the ridge nearer the 76th Ohio, apparently beyond the right flank of

Granbury's Rebels. In response, Cleburne dispatched both of his reserve brigades, those of Lowery and Polk, scrambling up the eastern face while the Federals toiled up the other side. The Ohioans found the western face of White Oak extremely steep "and covered for a great part with small, loose stones, or 'shale' which made the ascent slow and exceedingly toilsome." At the crest they were met by the first of Cleburne's defenders.[15]

Brigadier General Polk reported that his leading regiment reached the crest to discover the enemy "within 20 steps of the top." A furious firefight ensued, which cost the Ohioans 40 percent of their two hundred men, cutting down eight of the regimental color guard, and leaving the 76th pinned just short of the summit. Next came the 4th Iowa, of Williamson's brigade, which slammed into the consolidated 32nd/45th Mississippi from Lowrey's command. Rebel losses were much lighter thanks to their gaining the crest first. The Mississippians reported only one man killed and seventeen wounded.[16]

With Osterhaus blunted, Hooker reinforced the assault with Geary's easterners of the XII Corps, now just coming up. But they met only more of the same. These Rebels were clearly not routed, broken, or dispirited. With Geary's failure to make any headway, Hooker and Osterhaus abandoned any idea of a quick infantry victory and waited for artillery support. When the column's guns arrived shortly after noon, Hooker ordered them to shell the ridge and gap but to little effect. Next, Grant arrived, and after sizing up the situation, he ordered Hooker to break off the action. Shortly thereafter, his mission fulfilled and the army trains safely away, Cleburne retreated to the next ridgeline at Tunnel Hill. His stand at Ringgold earned him army-wide accolades and the thanks of the Confederate Congress.[17]

At 12:30 P.M. Grant informed Sherman that "Hooker has engaged the enemy here, strongly posted on the hills. It looks as if it will be hard to dislodge them." He next proposed an alternate strategy: "If you can move down with a force east of the ridge on the east side of the railroad it will effectually turn the enemy's position." Grant also explained his current thinking: "I do not care about the pursuit being continued farther south. I am anxious, however, to have the Cleveland and Dalton Railroad effectually destroyed. I think one brigade will be sufficient to do this." His next dispatch was to Thomas, written at 1:00 P.M., informing that officer that "Hooker has just driven the enemy from this place, capturing three pieces of artillery and some prisoners. Sherman is nearby. It is reported by citizens that Longstreet is expected tomorrow, and that the enemy will make a stand near Dalton." But Grant hedged: "I think it best not to rely on the statements of citizens altogether. You will direct Granger, therefore, to start at once. . . . Should he obtain satisfactory evidence that Longstreet has abandoned the siege . . . he will return at once." Here was the first postbattle order actually sending Granger northward.[18]

Dana's dispatches of November 27 and 28 provide some additional insight into how the senior Union officers were interpreting events. At 10:00 A.M. on the twenty-seventh, for example, while recounting the latest statistics of victory and describing Sherman's and Hooker's movements, he also reported that "Wood's and Sheridan's divisions, Fourth Corps, returned to Chattanooga last evening, preparatory to marching up the Tennessee, but doubtful whether the movement will be made, [since] Sherman's occupation of the railroad being most probably sufficient to compel Longstreet's retreat." As for Hooker's performance at Ringgold, Dana proved scathing: "Yesterday the first great fault in this admirable campaign occurred. . . . General Hooker arrived here about 9 A.M. . . . The enemy were drawn up in the narrow gorge. . . . It was a very dangerous defile to attack in front, and common sense plainly dictated that it should be turned. . . . However, Hooker attacked in front, . . . [and lost] 500 killed and wounded, where there was no necessity of losing 50."[19]

When Cleburne evacuated Ringgold Gap, Union troops followed, pushing as far as Tunnel Hill but no farther. Grant was now focused on Burnside. Lincoln, of course, had never forgotten East Tennessee, even for a minute. On the morning of November 26, while congratulating Grant for the successes achieved so far, the president closed with two words: "Remember Burnside."[20]

Granger's men departed Chattanooga just after midday on November 28, headed up the Tennessee. Grant, as was becoming customary, was impatient, a sentiment exacerbated by his annoyance with the IV Corps commander. In his memoir Grant stated that Granger "was to start the moment Missionary Ridge was carried, and under no circumstances were the troops to return to their old camps." But then he reversed that directive in a verbal communication with Thomas, telling him "not to start Granger until he received further orders from me." As seen in the written dispatch quoted above, Grant did not issue those orders until 1:00 P.M. on the twenty-seventh. He then remained at Ringgold overnight, returning to Chattanooga on the evening of November 28, where in his memoir he erroneously complained, "I then found that Thomas had not yet started Granger, thus having lost a full day."[21]

Here, Grant's memory failed him in several ways. Granger clearly needed and was ordered to march back to his camps on November 26; the idea of marching straight from the battlefield with no time to resupply ammunition, cook the needed four days' rations the men would carry with them, or even get a night's sleep was preposterous. There was also no need to march straight from the battlefield since, as Dana acknowledged at the time, no one was even sure Granger would be required at Knoxville until midday of November 27, when Grant halted the pursuit of Bragg at Ringgold. All of Grant's communications at the time acknowledged the conditional, rather than the absolute, nature of Granger's mission. In a dispatch to Maj. Gen. John G. Foster of the IX Corps, commanding at Cumberland Gap, Grant outlined his plans after the victory on Missionary Ridge, which clearly did not require Granger's immediate departure: "I shall pursue Bragg tomorrow [November 26], and start a heavy column up the Tennessee Valley, the day after." Even in his 1:00 P.M. missive to Halleck on the twenty-seventh, he wrote that "Granger will be all ready to start for Knoxville this evening and will go unless it is positively learned that Longstreet has fled."[22]

Finally, Granger's troops unquestionably departed at midday on November 28, not November 29. In addition to the official records, numerous contemporary diaries and various postwar memoirs of the troops involved all make that fact clear. Colonel Sherman's diary for Saturday, November 28, is unequivocal: "Marched at 1 o'c P.M. up the Tennessee (so[uth] side). Went into camp at dark across [South] Chickamauga [Creek]." Thomas Cantwell of the 26th Ohio, one of Sheridan's men, noted that the regiment "marched 6 miles" amid a cold rain. Maurice Marcoot of the 15th Missouri, another of Sheridan's veterans, recalled, "on the 28th of November, only three days after the great battle of Mission Ridge, we were supplied with three days' rations and ordered out on a forced march . . . to Knoxville."[23]

Grant would later attribute all this perceived delay to Granger's mulishness, asserting that the corps commander "was very reluctant to go, having convinced himself it was a very bad move to make." That might well have been, but Granger also had valid concerns. The men of the IV Corps, according to Tom Wood, were largely dressed in rags. They "had had no clothing issued to them since leaving Middle Tennessee in the preceding summer. The troops were in poor condition indeed for a forced march. . . .

The clothes on their backs were much worn, and their shoes were about worn out; in fact, not a few of the men were as good as barefooted." Despite these shortcomings, Wood insisted that "as soon, however, as a very slight, absolutely necessary preparation could be made, Granger was ready to proceed." After the war Maj. Gen. David S. Stanley, a former Cavalry Corps commander in the Army of the Cumberland who later served in the IV Corps, summarized the disagreement. "The whole thing amounts to this: General Granger wanted to tarry two days, to get shoes for his men; General Grant wanted him to march without shoes." Given the winter weather, Granger's objections seem less like foot-dragging and more like reasonable concerns. To be sure, the general was quarrelsome, outspoken, and periodically thoughtless; all factors that doubtless grated on Grant (and Sherman as well), but the difficulty stemmed from far more than, as James Wilson later wrote, "Granger having a swelled head" from Chickamauga.[24]

On November 29 Granger's column reached Harrison, thirteen miles upstream from Chattanooga, and the next day crossed the Hiwassee River at Charleston. This second leg was a much more grueling march of twenty-three miles, with the weather "very cold and freezing." From the ranks of the 9th Kentucky, Lt. Marcus Woodcock concurred, finding the temperature "exceedingly cold." Offsetting the air's frigidity, he noted the warmth of the locals, "prominent subjects of rebel tyranny—Loyal East Tennesseans. All along the road they seemed to welcome us as deliverers and received us with all possible demonstrations of joy."[25]

Nonetheless, Grant was dissatisfied and had already decided to supersede Granger. Once again he turned to his most trusted subordinate. On the twenty-ninth he wrote Sherman: "Granger is on the way to Burnsides relief but I have lost all faith in his energy or capacity to manage an expedition of the importance of this one. I am inclined to think therefore I shall have to send you." Grant then explained about the arrangements for rations; the existence of another column, numbering "from 3500 to 5000" under General Foster, coming from Cumberland Gap; and finally warning that the latest messages from Burnside (as of the morning of the twenty-seventh) stated that Knoxville could only hold out "to about the 3rd of December." Grant's note, including Burnside's news, was entrusted to Wilson and Dana, who reached Sherman at Charleston on December 1.[26]

At 8:00 P.M. on the twenty-ninth, Grant informed Halleck of this decision, explaining that "Sherman was sent to the Hiawassie [sic], and I have sent orders to him to take command of the whole. . . . I made this change knowing Sherman's promptness and ability—If Burnside holds out [a] short time he will be relieved." That same day Grant informed Burnside that no less than "three columns [were] in motion for your relief." These included the Sherman-Granger force, a cavalry division under Brig. Gen. Washington Elliott from Middle Tennessee, and Foster's command from Cumberland Gap. All three elements, according to the note, should be at Knoxville by December 2. In order to ensure its safe delivery into the right hands, Grant directed his staff to send multiple copies by separate couriers.[27]

The right hands, as it turned out, were those of both Burnside and Longstreet. In fact, it was intended as a deception. Chief of Staff Rawlins instructed Col. Robert Byrd to send a copy of the note, penned in Grant's own hand (Longstreet knew Grant from the prewar years and would recognize his handwriting) "by someone whom you can trust with instructions to let it fall into the hands of the enemy without fail." Five more copies were sent direct to Burnside, one of which arrived on December 2. Longstreet reported the capture of his copy of the dispatch on December 1.[28]

Sherman's column did not reach Knoxville by the second and was still a good five days' march away. But the ruse worked, not in the least because Longstreet was already growing desperate by the time this message fell into his hands. On November 26 and 27, he reported hearing "various rumors of a battle being fought at Chattanooga," but nothing definitive; Bragg's note of the twenty-sixth, sent via Wheeler, had yet to reach him. Nonetheless, the rumors were enough to convince Longstreet that he must act, and he ordered an assault on Burnside's defenses for November 28. That attack, launched against Fort Sanders (on the northeast corner of Burnside's line) on November 29, proved a bloody failure, costing the assault force 813 casualties out of about 3,000 men, contrasted with just 13 Federal losses. Lacking enough troops to fully envelop Burnside, who was still getting supplies hauled in from Cumberland Gap and from the south side of the Tennessee, and unable to take the town by storm, Longstreet elected to retreat. His troops began heading north toward the Virginia line on December 2.[29]

On December 5 Sherman halted his own force at Maysville, fifteen miles from Knoxville, and ordered Granger's men to keep moving. When Sherman and Granger arrived at Knoxville the next day, they found Longstreet gone and, far from starving, Burnside's command to be well situated. The three generals conferred, and Burnside indicated that he was already thinking of pursuit. In a letter to his brother, John, on December 29, Sherman bragged a bit: "Granger was ordered to push for Knoxville, but his movements were so slow that Grant impatient called on me, and my move was the most rapid of the war & perfectly successful. I could have gone after Longstreet," he added, "but Burnside Ranked me and it was his business not mine." Sherman amplified this conversation a bit in his memoir: "I offered to join in the pursuit, though in fact my men were worn out, and suffering in that cold season. . . . Burnside explained to me that, reinforced by Granger's two divisions, he would be able to push Longstreet out of East Tennessee." Thus, Sherman and his own force were not needed, which suited him just fine.[30]

But it did not suit Granger. As he saw it, his men were now marooned in East Tennessee and destined for yet more time living on short rations. Sherman dismissed these objections: "Granger . . . most unreasonably, I thought, remonstrated against being left; complaining bitterly of what he thought was hard treatment to his men and himself. I know that his language and manner at that time produced on my mind a bad impression, and it was one of the causes which led me to relieve him as a corps commander in the campaign of the next spring." Granger probably had a point. His men were so badly fixed for equipment and supplies that Burnside decided to leave them in Knoxville while his own troops, the putatively besieged garrison, pursued Longstreet. But Granger's manner was counterproductive. On December 11 Dana informed Stanton: "Grant is very angry with Granger for misconduct in the Chattanooga battle, and now for unwillingness to march after Longstreet. Granger will probably be removed and Sheridan assigned to succeed him, subject to approval of [the] Government. Granger is certainly unfit to command." This was a staggeringly abrupt reversal. Just two months previously, Dana had likened this same officer to the French marshal Michael Ney, "the bravest of the brave" of Napoleon's generals.[31]

Bragg's defeat and Knoxville's relief, all accomplished in a little less than two months' time, seemed astounding achievements to both the long suffering Lincoln administration and a war-weary Northern populace. Perhaps, at long last, victory might be in sight after all. Grant's star, already on the rise, now rocketed to unprecedented heights.

12
THE BEST-PLANNED BATTLE?

Collectively, the battles for Chattanooga—Orchard Knob, Lookout Mountain, Missionary Ridge, and "operations following as far as Ringgold Gap"—cost the Union army 753 killed, 4,722 wounded, and 349 missing, an aggregate loss of 5,824 officers and men. Against that figure the Army of Tennessee suffered 361 killed, 2,160 wounded, and a staggering 4,146 missing or captured, a total loss of 6,667 officers and men. But General Thomas's provost marshal noted that the number of Confederate prisoners and deserters received for the period of October 20 to December 1 was actually much higher: 573 deserters and 5,569 prisoners, a total of 6,142 troops falling into enemy hands. Moreover, Confederate records from the campaign are by no means complete. Many regimental and brigade reports were lost or never filed. In sum, Bragg lost close to 9,000 men (two-thirds of them to capture) during those six weeks. By December 3, the Army of Tennessee was reduced to a total of 36,064 men present (including noncombatants) and had only 30,127 "effectives." The Confederates also suffered in materiel. Forty pieces of artillery, numerous gun carriages and caissons, and 6,175 "small arms, mostly Enfield," were among the Federal spoils.[1]

Breaking out the Union losses by engagement, Sherman's column suffered approximately 1,600 casualties in his fight for Tunnel Hill, Thomas's four divisions in the Army of the Cumberland lost 3,300 troops in the fight for Orchard Knob and in the charge up Missionary Ridge, while Hooker's force, even given the bloody repulse at Ringgold, incurred about 900 losses. With control of the battlefield and the restoration of rapid communications with the North, this time the Union wounded, unlike those who fell at Chickamauga, could expect more timely and effective care. Chattanooga was a resounding Federal victory, made all the more astonishing by the amazing feat of arms on Missionary Ridge.

With Longstreet's retreat, Grant was satisfied that he had accomplished all that was needed in Tennessee. He wasted no time in contemplating his next move. "It may now safely be assumed that the enemy are driven from this front, or at least that they no longer threaten it in any formidable numbers," he informed General Halleck on December 7. The terrain and the season, he continued, meant "that an extensive campaign from here this Winter may be looked upon as impossible." But not wishing to keep upward of 100,000 troops "idle for months," Grant proposed stripping Chattanooga and Knoxville of excess forces and pursuing his preferred objective, "to move by way of New Orleans and Pascagoula on Mobile." From there, he thought, a "campaign into the interior of Alabama, and possibly, Georgia" would outflank the Army of Tennessee and possibly even "force Lee to abandon Virginia & North Carolina."[2]

Though Grant's proposal makes for tantalizing speculation, it was not meant to be. There was considerably less enthusiasm for the idea in Washington. Halleck was ten days even in replying, and then he only acknowledged receipt of Grant's December 7 wire without commenting on the idea's merits. As a reinforcement, Charles Dana left Chattanooga for the capital on December 12, arriving there on the eighteenth, where he presented Grant's concept personally. In the days that followed, despite Dana's personal lobbying and the seeming concurrence of Lincoln, Stanton, and Halleck, the idea foundered over one sticking point. "You would be authorized to proceed immediately with its execution," wrote Dana, "but for the anxiety . . . respecting East Tennessee. If Longstreet were expelled from that country, you could start for Mobile at once."[3]

This was because Longstreet's small army had retreated only as far as Rogersville, Tennessee, sixty-five miles from Knoxville, and gained strength, drawing reinforcements from southwest Virginia. By mid-December, the Confederate general estimated his force at nearly 20,000 men. Lincoln and Stanton were unwilling to accept the risk of losing Knoxville again if Grant stripped the region for his expedition to the Gulf. They thought his plan sound in theory but practicable only if Longstreet were safely and semipermanently out of the picture—driven back into southwest Virginia or moved to rejoin Lee. To be sure, Halleck listed other potential roadblocks that might trip up Grant's plan: ensuring Bragg's army was pushed deeper into Georgia, clearing out West Tennessee (where Brig. Gen. Nathan Bedford Forrest was starting to make trouble), and Maj. Gen. Nathaniel Banks's intended movement up the Red River toward Texas. The threat posed by Longstreet, however, remained uppermost.[4]

Thus, Grant spent a quiet December in Chattanooga, relaxing with his staff, handling routine matters, and basking in his recent successes. To

Congressman Elihu Washburne on December 2, he described the battle in glowing terms: "Last week was a stiring time with us and a magnificent victory was won. The spectacle was grand beyond anything . . . on this Continent. . . . Our troops behaved most magnificently and have inflicted on the enemy the heavyest blow they have yet received during the war." On December 7 President Lincoln declared a day of national prayer and thanksgiving. To Grant he wrote: "I wish to tender you, and all under your command, my more than thanks—my profoundest gratitude—for the skill, courage, and perseverance, with which you and they, over so great difficulties, have effected that important object. May God bless you all." Other plaudits followed. Washburne introduced a joint resolution in Congress thanking Grant for his deeds, and in some circles newspapers began to suggest that the general might make a good candidate for president.[5]

Grant also played tourist. In a letter home on December 14, Maj. Michael Fitch wrote: "I was out on the Chickamauga battlefield a few days ago in the escort of Grant and Thomas." Fitch, serving on Brigadier General Johnson's divisional staff, was a member of the 21st Wisconsin, a regiment heavily engaged in that earlier battle. "Grant . . . was anxious to ride over the battlefield. . . . We rendezvoused at General Thomas' headquarters, and rode via Rossville and through the gap, then down the Lafayette Road. The route brought us first to the left of our lines [Kelly Field] where our division lay on that memorable Sunday. As Grant gazed at the bullet riddled trees . . . [Fitch heard him remark], [t]hese trees would make a good lead mine." The field's condition was gruesome. Riding into the woods where the 21st Wisconsin was engaged on Saturday, Fitch "saw six or seven skeletons of our brave boys unburied. . . . General Thomas cut a hickory cane close by them, and so did I. I was just wondering how much it would bring in the great Sanitary Fair, as a relic from the battlefield?"[6]

Despite his dismissal of Hooker's battle as mere mythology, Grant also ventured up to the crest of Lookout Mountain, which was both a prewar tourist attraction and now the scene of the Union success of November 24. His trip is documented in one of the most familiar photographs to emerge from the war: An iconic picture of the general, cigar clamped between his teeth, turned profile and facing several members of his staff. Many soldiers would follow suit in the months to come, including several other generals, but few images would become as memorable as that taken of Grant.

On December 22 Grant departed for Nashville, transferring his headquarters to a place where he could better control all the elements of his new command. One important reason was railroad access: Chattanooga would lack a direct rail connection until January 1864, when the bridges over the Tennessee River and Running Water Creek were completed.

Grant briefly returned to Chattanooga around Christmas before traveling to Knoxville, partly by steamboat and then by taking the short stretch of functioning rail line into the East Tennessee city itself. His purpose was to evaluate whether General Foster, the man who had replaced Burnside when that officer returned to Virginia, could successfully wage a winter offensive against Longstreet. The weather was awful, and Grant quickly decided that any further offensive action in the region was impossible, a decision confirmed when the general elected to return to Nashville via the Army of the Ohio's attenuated supply line through the Cumberland Gap. He had to travel by horseback from Knoxville to Lexington, Kentucky, approximately 170 miles. "The road over the Cumberland Gap and back of it," Grant noted, "was strewn with debris of broken wagons and dead animals, much as I had found it on my first trip to Chattanooga over Waldron's Ridge."[7]

* * *

Thus ended the military campaign for Chattanooga, a decisive stroke in the American Civil War. This did not end the fighting over Chattanooga, however, as battles now waged with words instead of swords, cannon, and musketry.

The literature of the war provides the interested reader with no shortage of controversy. This is especially true for that material published in the five decades following its end, as soldiers from both armies, from generals to privates, weighed in with their opinions and recollections. Every battle and campaign seemingly produced its share of disputes. Certainly, Chattanooga generated a vast amount of such debate. Sorting out fact from fiction and trying to lay bare what really happened can be a thankless task and, often, impossible.

On December 29, 1863, General Sherman wrote to his brother, John, back home in Lancaster Ohio, enclosing a copy of his report of the campaign. In his letter Sherman opened: "I invite attention to the part referring to the Assault on Tunnel Hill. I know Grant in his report will dwell on this same part." Then he fumed: "I was provoked that [Montgomery] Meigs, looking at us from [Orchard Knob] should report me repulsed, and that Mr.

Stanton should publish his letter. . . . The whole philosophy of the battle was that I should get by a dash a position on the Extremity of Missionary Ridge from which the enemy would be forced to drive me, or allow his Depot at Chickamauga Station to be in danger. I expected Bragg to attack me at daylight, but he did not and to bring matters to a crisis quick . . . , Grant ordered me to assume the offensive." Here, Sherman's description of his orders bears little resemblance to those Grant issued him at the time. Of particular note was his declaration that he expected to be attacked, not to do the attacking.[8]

In his 1875 memoir Sherman insisted that the view Meigs had from Orchard Knob allowed him to observe only the later attacks launched by Matthies, Raum, and Buschbeck. "These two [sic, three] brigades," Sherman claimed, "were in the nature of supports, and did not constitute a part of the real attack." When Meigs reported Sherman repulsed, "it was *not so.*" Sherman based this claim on the fact that Corse's men clung to the north end of Tunnel Hill all day, "persistently, stubbornly, and well." He failed to note, however, that he never drove Cleburne's men from their positions or captured Tunnel Hill.[9]

Sherman added that he was never properly supported, looking for Thomas's attack early in the day, but it did not come. He also claimed that his assault on Tunnel Hill "had drawn vast masses of the enemy to our flank," thus making Thomas's own charge successful when it was finally made late in the day. Here, Sherman was echoing what had become by 1875 a standard, Grant-friendly view of the battle. In 1868 Richardson penned: "Sherman was to capture the north end of the ridge. Though fighting stubbornly for hours he was unable to carry it. But he threatened Bragg's depot . . . so seriously that the Rebel commander weakened his center to save his right flank and rear." Also appearing in 1868, former Grant aide Adam Badeau wrote: "Grant's real object was completely gained, for Bragg was forced to weaken his centre to support the rebel right. Column after column of the rebels was soon streaming towards Sherman."[10]

Of course, as Confederate reports became more widely available, it became obvious that those "columns streaming towards Sherman" came from Bragg's abandoned left, not his center, and that only one small brigade was sent to the right. Army of the Cumberland writers made much of this fact in later years. Chaplain Van Horne, in his biography of Thomas, labeled Sherman's assertion "an untenable assumption—contradicted by Grant's orders and official report, though assumed to be true by many historians,—that Sherman's attack was designed as a feint to cause Bragg to weaken his center."[11]

The similar controversy that sprang up over Grant's orders to charge Missionary Ridge has been fully explored in chapter 9, and there is no need to discuss them again here. Most of the contemporary evidence strongly suggests that Grant never intended a full-scale attack on the ridge, or at least not until both of Bragg's flanks were fully turned. Only in later accounts did the idea of pausing at the first line to reform and then launch "columns of assault" to storm the crest gain traction. Grant might well have intended to launch just such an assault if the opportunity beckoned—he told Meigs as much that evening—but the idea never went beyond supposition. Both Meigs's and Dana's first reports clearly describe the charge up the ridge as a spontaneous effort.

Grant found serious fault with at least two officers during the campaign: Gordon Granger and Joseph Hooker. His problem with Granger stemmed from the corps commander's reluctance and supposed foot-dragging during the relief of Knoxville as well as his usual cantankerousness and argumentative nature. Grant's denigration of Hooker arose from a distrust of that officer's ego and ambition. Provoked by Hooker's oft-bombastic attitude in claiming honors for his command, Grant in response dismissed or belittled Hooker's real accomplishments and accused him of excessive delays on November 25.

Granger found himself sidelined in the spring of 1864, replaced by General Howard. Having developed a similarly strong distaste for Granger based on their mutual service in East Tennessee, with Grant's permission, Sherman ordered Howard to assume command of the IV Corps. Curiously, earlier in his memoir, when discussing their joint expedition to Knoxville, Sherman made no bones about his decision to relieve Granger. But later in that same book, when discussing Granger's actual replacement, Sherman told a different tale: "Granger, as usual, was full of complaints . . . , and he stated to me personally that he had a leave of absence in his pocket, of which he intended to take advantage very soon." Normally, a corps commander was not replaced for taking leave; a junior officer might rise to temporary command while he was away, but this was not a permanent replacement. That was not what happened to Granger. On April 6, 1864, the War Department issued a formal order stating unequivocally that "Major General Gordon Granger is relieved from command of the 4th Army Corps, and Major General O. O. Howard is assigned thereto, in his stead." There seems to be no contemporary evidence that Granger took any leave.[12]

Whatever the circumstances of it, this change certainly suited Grant, who insisted that Granger "must never be put in command of troops" again. Eventually, he found a way around that proscription thanks to political connections. Granger returned to the field via New Orleans, where he commanded a corps in the operations directed against Mobile in 1865. Andrew Johnson, the military governor of Tennessee, and James A. Garfield, formerly Rosecrans's chief of staff and now a sitting Republican congressman, both helped Granger attain that command, where he performed competently. Granger was certainly quarrelsome, and his odd fascination with artillery proved distracting, but he paid an unjust price for those quirks when he irritated Grant and Sherman.[13]

Hooker's actions at Lookout Mountain and especially at Rossville were crucial to the ultimate victory on November 25. Grant seemed of two minds about the famed "Battle above the Clouds." In his memoirs Grant bestowed real praise, labelling Hooker's "achievement in bringing his command around the point of Lookout Mountain . . . brilliant." But he also found Hooker to be "a dangerous man. He was not subordinate to his superiors." Further, in a widely reprinted interview, newspaperman John Russell Young asked Grant about the battle: "The battle of Lookout Mountain is one of the romances of the war," the general replied. "There was no such battle, and no action even worthy to be called a battle on Lookout Mountain. It is all poetry."[14]

On November 25 Grant remembered Hooker's role poorly. He recalled that Hooker was off "bright and early" that day, "with no obstructions in his front but distance" and the burned bridge over Chattanooga Creek. Then he claimed that Hooker "was detained four hours crossing Chattanooga Creek, and thus was lost the immediate advantage I expected from his forces." Though Hooker's flanking movement via Rossville collapsed Bragg's southern flank, Grant instead attributed "the bulk of the capture of prisoners, artillery, and small arms" to "Sheridan's prompt movement" on the night of the twenty-fifth.[15]

In fact, Hooker was not off "bright and early" simply because, at first light, his orders still called for him to isolate any Rebels remaining atop Lookout Mountain; the effort against Rossville was more of an afterthought. Contrary to another Grant claim, it was midmorning before the Federals determined that Bragg had abandoned Lookout Mountain. Thomas did not even order Hooker to move on Rossville until then; once so ordered, he began his march promptly at around 10:00 A.M. Hooker reached Chattanooga Creek around noon, where he was indeed delayed due to a lack of pontoons. His pioneers had to fashion a field-expedient bridge with the materials at hand before his artillery and ammunition wagons could cross. But Hooker did not merely sit idle while the bridge was constructed. He aggressively pushed his skirmishers across the creek to press the Confederates guarding Rossville and had the gap in hand at about the time Thomas's main body was beginning their advance against Missionary Ridge. Osterhaus's movement northward along the back (eastern) side of the ridge, reaching Bragg's headquarters that same evening, resulted in thousands of captured Rebels. "Baldy" Smith later asserted that "the movement of Hooker from Rossville, ordered by Thomas—not Grant—won the battle of the 25th of November."[16]

Grant was further annoyed by Hooker's attempt to claim a lion's share of the glory over captures. When Hooker finally submitted his official report of the campaign in February 1864, wherein he claimed the capture of "6,547 prisoners" and "not less than 10,000 stand of small arms," Grant appended an acerbic addendum: "Attention is called to that part of the report giving, from the reports of his subordinate commanders, the number of prisoners and small-arms captured, which is greater than the number really captured by the whole army."[17]

Hooker remained in the Army of the Cumberland until the summer of 1864, heading up the XX Corps through much of the Atlanta Campaign. Though he and his troops did good service and saw hard fighting, friction with Thomas (at least as Sherman related it) and especially Sherman led him to resign after the death of Maj. Gen. James B. McPherson on July 22, 1864, creating a vacancy to command the Army of the Tennessee. Though Hooker was the senior man, Sherman bypassed him to appoint the same officer who earlier supplanted Granger: Oliver O. Howard. The affront was compounded by the fact that Sherman chose not just any junior officer, but Howard, whom Hooker blamed for the Chancellorsville debacle. With that resignation, his military career was over.

Unsurprisingly, Hooker returned Grant's dislike in kind. Regarding Missionary Ridge, he later claimed, at least as reported by Sherman biographer Lloyd Lewis, that "Grant had said, at the day's end, 'Damn the battle! I had nothing to do with it.'" In the 1870s sculptor James E. Kelly recalled a telling incident. When someone asked Hooker about Grant's dismissal of

Lookout Mountain as "poetry" and "that there was no battle at Lookout Mountain, or words to that effect," Hooker sarcastically replied: "General Grant? Who is General Grant? I never heard of General Grant." Hooker's denials continued in like vein for several exchanges. "I asked him," stated Kelly, "if this interview were true. Gen. Hooker replied, 'The only way to fight the devil is to use his own weapons.'"[18]

The relationship between Grant and his senior subordinate, George Thomas, was damaged by their mutual service at Chattanooga, largely because Grant's restless, impatient nature clashed with Thomas's deliberate, calculating style. Grant was under intense pressure from Washington—from Lincoln, Stanton, and Halleck—not only to resolve the Army of the Cumberland's situation but also to do something to help Burnside in East Tennessee. He translated that pressure downward, ordering Thomas to attack Bragg on November 7. Much to Grant's frustration, Thomas demurred. The fact then was that the Army of the Cumberland was crippled by the lack of horseflesh. With so many of its animals dead or near death from starvation, Grant's plan for an early, rapid offensive had little hope of success. When presented with that reality, he acquiesced, but his frustration with Thomas's inaction never really subsided, as evidenced by Sherman's recollection of his friend's comment about the Army of the Cumberland being "demoralized" on November 15.

Thomas, an intensely private man, kept his feelings concerning his fellow officers largely to himself. When the general died in 1870, his personal correspondence was destroyed, leaving a void that has never really been filled. Yet Thomas's taciturnity did not stop others in the Army of the Cumberland from criticizing Grant openly after the war, fanning a rivalry between Army of the Cumberland men and Army of the Tennessee men, with the former vigorously defending their own officers—Rosecrans and Thomas in particular—against what they perceived as character attacks found in Grant's and Sherman's own postwar writings.

Of all the senior officers involved, Sherman performed least well during the Chattanooga fighting. He never received a word of criticism or blame for his multiple missteps, at least not from Grant. The war of words that sprang up between Sherman and the many Army of the Cumberland veterans, who viewed him as the slanderer of their accomplishments and reputation, was both unseemly and long lasting. Overheated passions led to misstatements and inflated accusations on both sides. But unquestionably, Sherman stumbled badly at Chattanooga. His approach to that place was slowed unnecessarily by poor planning and march discipline, all at a time when Grant fretted about every hour. His crossing of the Tennessee was executed well, but frittering away the most of the day on November 24 after that successful crossing negated nearly all the surprise thus gained. His failure to occupy the terrain Grant intended him to take was compounded by Sherman's very careless report of that same night stating that he had indeed seized Missionary Ridge as far as the railroad tunnel, which was in no way true. The dawn attack Grant expected never materialized and eventually turned into a series of feeble, piecemeal jabs against a prepared enemy position that produced serious losses for no gain. When Grant forcefully demanded that Sherman renew his attack to support Thomas's surprisingly successful ascent of the ridge, nothing came of that order either. Nor did that failure draw any reprimand—or even mention in Grant's report.

When Grant arrived in Chattanooga that October, he was unfamiliar both with the tactical situation and the Army of the Cumberland. Though he had some acquaintance with many of its officers from earlier in the war or from prewar service, he had not commanded those men in camp, campaign, and battle, had not come to trust them as he had Sherman and his soldiers in the Army of the Tennessee. It was only natural that he called on the familiar troops and their leaders to join him, or for him to rely first on their combat skills in the coming test of arms. It was also in keeping with his character, to whom loyalty counted for so much, to excuse Sherman's stumbles. Grant, however, never lost confidence in Sherman, naming that general to replace him as overall commander in the West after deciding to direct the war in 1864–65 as general in chief of Union armies from Virginia, accompanying the Army of the Potomac. Grant might have blundered here had he retained confidence in Sherman only to have his friend repeat those failings at Chattanooga on a larger scale while moving against Atlanta, but that did not happen. Sherman proved himself by repeatedly outflanking Gen. Joseph Johnston across North Georgia to eventually capture Atlanta that September. In the afterglow of that triumph, the stumbles of Chattanooga were largely forgotten.

Given the criticisms listed above, the question might be: Was Grant essential to the success at Chattanooga, or was he just lucky? While Grant did benefit from good fortune, especially given all the blunders Braxton Bragg committed during the campaign, he also provided real command strengths that tended to be very rare in Civil War generals.

Grant demonstrated a doggedness in his maintenance of the overall objective, tactical flexibility, and perseverance in the face of setbacks. His initial charge was to rescue the Army of the Cumberland at Chattanooga and Burnside's Army of the Ohio in East Tennessee, while remaining in control of both critical geographic objectives. Military history is replete with generals who lose their larger perspective to focus on an immediate objective: Grant never did. And though his patience frayed during the campaign's seemingly interminable delays, he never suffered from that failure of nerve that has also gripped other commanders. Grant postponed and revised his plans as needed to fit circumstances.

As just one example of Grant's grasp of the overall strategic picture, we have Eli Long's cavalry raid on Cleveland, which historically is perhaps the least commonly noted element of Grant's plan. It should not be overlooked. Long's objective was not tactical but operational; he was directed not to strike at Bragg's immediate flank but instead sent to interrupt any move by Longstreet back into Georgia. The mission worked perfectly. Longstreet became aware within hours that Union horsemen had cut him off from a quick rendezvous with Bragg, which greatly influenced his retreat northward toward Virginia.

In his memoirs Grant stated, "my recollection is that my first orders for the battle of Chattanooga were as fought," suggesting that his original plan won the day with little or no modification. He did himself a disservice. The Battle of Chattanooga was not fought according to an unchanged master plan set in stone and bereft of deviation; instead, that victory required a great deal of adaptation and improvisation. As Count Helmut von Moltke observed, no plan survives contact with the enemy. Ergo, those qualities do not detract from the skills of a great commander—they are the critical hallmarks of a great commander.[19]

When Osterhaus could not join Sherman due to the collapse of the bridge at Brown's Ferry, Grant gave the last-minute authorization for Hooker's attack on Lookout Mountain, which, aside from the skirmish at Orchard Knob, proved to be the first successful blow of the battle. And even though Grant originally wanted Bragg to hold on to Lookout, thus keeping the smaller Rebel army overextended, when on the morning of the twenty-fifth he and Thomas sent Hooker to Rossville, they put in motion one of the decisive strokes of the whole engagement. Similarly, when Sherman failed to achieve his objectives at the north end of Missionary Ridge, Grant was willing to make what by conventional military wisdom was a foolhardy attack, a frontal assault against the Confederate lines at the foot of Missionary Ridge. That gamble paid dividends far in excess of what any of the watching commanders expected: the complete collapse of Bragg's center.

And therein lies one of the essential differences between Grant and the man who was perhaps his closest military peer on that field: George H. Thomas. Thomas opposed that assault, and had he been in command, it seems unlikely to have ever occurred. But as Thomas biographer Francis F. McKinney wrote, Missionary Ridge highlighted "the basic differences between these two leaders—how to save time and how to calculate military risks.... Grant brought to the Union armies something that no other western commander had brought them and the results pleased Lincoln. This was his energetic attempt to do the things that Washington wanted done in the way that Washington wanted them done and with the tools that he had at hand." By contrast, noted McKinney, "Thomas had refused consistently and stubbornly to work this way. [Thomas] . . . specified his needs for any job . . . and refused to move until his specifications were met. . . . [T]his seemed like procrastination to his superiors." Though McKinney did not include Rosecrans in this assessment, he might as well have, since this was also the way that commander worked.

Grant also displayed a facility for communication with Washington that his predecessors lacked. Rosecrans had a long history of hectoring quarrelsomeness with his superiors, so much so that even before his defeat at Chickamauga, his days in command were likely numbered. Thomas proved less argumentative, but his innately reticent nature often left Washington unsure about his intentions. Grant communicated daily, reported his circumstances optimistically, and explained his plans clearly. Most importantly, he followed through quickly. During the long months of the Vicksburg Campaign, Grant enjoyed the luxury of limited communications with Washington, since the telegraph ended at Memphis, and from there dispatches had to be carried via riverboat, often resulting in several days between transmission and receipt. This gave Grant time to compose his replies and frame his answers. At Chattanooga he had no such luxury; he was in direct contact with the War Department, and transmission times were measured in hours, not days. Nevertheless, he displayed that same facility at reassurance and optimism.

Of course, Grant displayed his own frustrations with the circumstances and the personalities of officers he commanded at both Chattanooga and

Knoxville: Burnside, Willcox, and Thomas were all targets of that frustration. And yet, after each setback, Grant focused on revising his plans and preparing anew for the effort to come. The only commander to escape criticism was Sherman, for whom Grant proved especially understanding, making allowances and even assuming personal blame over the delays en route to Chattanooga and for his failed effort at Tunnel Hill.

Finally, Grant held the initiative throughout the six weeks that mark the campaign for Chattanooga. The Rebels did little to try and counterattack or forestall his moves, even when they were, by necessity, given the time to do so. In this, fortune again favored Grant. He was aided greatly by two men, both of whom he acknowledged in his memoirs: Braxton Bragg and Confederate president Jefferson Davis. "The victory at Chattanooga was won against great odds, considering the advantage the enemy had of position, and was accomplished more easily than expected by reason of Bragg's . . . several grave mistakes," namely sending Longstreet to Knoxville, sending yet more troops to Longstreet on "the eve of battle," and in placing his defenses in front of Missionary Ridge rather than at the crest. As for Davis, wrote Grant, "on several occasions during the war he came to the relief of the Union army by means of his *superior military genius*."[20]

Fort Donelson first brought Grant to national attention and, more importantly, caught Lincoln's eye. Shiloh was a stumble, but one that Grant survived. The surrender of the Confederate army at Vicksburg erased any lingering blemish and probably earned Grant a place among the war's best generals. But it took Chattanooga, where Lincoln turned to him in a moment of crisis and he delivered yet another resounding victory, to unquestionably elevate Grant to the next level as overall commander of the Union war effort and secure his place in American military history.

APPENDIX

NOTES

BIBLIOGRAPHY

INDEX

APPENDIX: ORDER OF BATTLE, CHATTANOOGA CAMPAIGN

Units and commands on detached duty are not listed.

Overall Union forces: Maj. Gen. Ulysses S. Grant

Army of the Cumberland: Maj. Gen. George H. Thomas

General Headquarters

1st Ohio Sharpshooters, 10th Ohio Infantry

IV Corps: Maj. Gen. Gordon Granger

FIRST DIVISION: BRIG. GEN. CHARLES CRUFT

Escort: Co. E, 92nd Illinois Mounted Infantry

Second Brigade: Brig. Gen. Walter C. Whitaker

96th Illinois, 35th Indiana, 8th Kentucky, 40th Ohio, 51st Ohio, 99th Ohio

Third Brigade: Col. William Grose

59th Illinois, 75th Illinois, 84th Illinois, 9th Indiana, 36th Indiana, 24th Ohio

SECOND DIVISION: MAJ. GEN. PHILIP H. SHERIDAN

First Brigade: Col. Francis T. Sherman

36th Illinois, 44th Illinois, 73rd Illinois, 74th Illinois, 88th Illinois, 22nd Indiana, 2nd Missouri, 15th Missouri, 24th Wisconsin

Second Brigade: Brig. Gen. George D. Wagner

100th Illinois, 15th Indiana, 40th Indiana, 51st Indiana, 57th Indiana, 58th Indiana, 26th Ohio, 97th Ohio

Third Brigade: Col. Charles G. Harker

22nd Illinois, 27th Illinois, 42nd Illinois, 51st Illinois, 79th Illinois, 3rd Kentucky, 64th Ohio, 65th Ohio, 125th Ohio

Artillery: Capt. Warren P. Edgarton

Battery M, 1st Illinois Lt.; 10th Indiana Battery; Battery G, 1st Missouri Light; Battery I, 1st Ohio Light; Battery G, 4th U.S.; Battery M, 4th U.S.

THIRD DIVISION: BRIG. GEN. THOMAS J. WOOD

First Brigade: Brig. Gen. August Willich

25th Illinois, 35th Illinois, 89th Illinois, 32nd Indiana, 68th Indiana, 8th Kansas, 15th Ohio, 49th Ohio, 15th Wisconsin

Second Brigade: Brig. Gen. William B. Hazen

6th Indiana, 5th Kentucky, 6th Kentucky, 23rd Kentucky, 1st Ohio, 6th Ohio, 41st Ohio, 93rd Ohio, 124th Ohio

Third Brigade: Brig. Gen. Samuel Beatty

79th Indiana, 86th Indiana, 9th Kentucky, 17th Kentucky, 13th Ohio, 19th Ohio, 59th Ohio

Artillery: Capt. Cullen Bradley

Bridges's Battery, Illinois Light; 6th Ohio Battery; 20th Ohio Battery; Battery B, Pennsylvania Light

XI Corps: Maj. Gen. Oliver O. Howard

Independent Company, 8th New York Infantry

SECOND DIVISION: BRIG. GEN. ADOLPH VON STEINWEHR

First Brigade: Col. Adolphus Buschbeck

33rd New Jersey, 134th New York, 154th New York, 27th Pennsylvania, 73rd Pennsylvania

Second Brigade: Col. Orland Smith

33rd Massachusetts, 136th New York, 55th Ohio, 73rd Ohio

THIRD DIVISION: MAJ. GEN. CARL SCHURZ

First Brigade: Brig. Gen. Hector Tyndale

101st Illinois, 45th New York, 143rd New York, 61st Ohio, 82nd Ohio

Second Brigade: Col. Wladimir Krzyzanowski

58th New York, 119th New York, 141st New York, 26th Wisconsin

Third Brigade: Col. Frederick Hecker

80th Illinois, 82nd Illinois, 68th New York, 75th Pennsylvania

Artillery: Maj. Thomas W. Osborn

Battery I, 1st New York Light; 13th New York Light; Battery I, 1st Ohio Light: Battery K, 1st Ohio Light; Battery G, 4th U.S.

XII Corps (only one division present)

SECOND DIVISION: BRIG. GEN. JOHN W. GEARY

First Brigade: Col. Charles Candy

5th Ohio, 7th Ohio, 29th Ohio, 66th Ohio, 28th Pennsylvania, 147th Pennsylvania

Second Brigade: Col. George A. Cobham Jr.

29th Pennsylvania, 109th Pennsylvania, 111th Pennsylvania

Third Brigade: Brig. Gen. George Sears Greene

60th New York, 78th New York, 102nd New York, 137th New York, 149th New York

Artillery: Maj. John A. Reynolds
Battery E, Pennsylvania Light.; Battery K, 5th U.S.

XIV Corps: Maj. Gen. John M. Palmer
Co. L, 1st Ohio Cavalry

FIRST DIVISION: BRIG. GEN. RICHARD W. JOHNSON
First Brigade: Brig. Gen. William P. Carlin
104th Illinois, 38th Indiana, 42nd Indiana, 88th Indiana, 2nd Ohio, 33rd Ohio, 94th Ohio, 10th Wisconsin
Second Brigade: Col. Marshall F. Moore
19th Illinois, 11th Michigan, 69th Ohio, 15th U.S. (1st, 2nd Battalions), 16th U.S. (1st Battalion), 18th U.S. (1st, 2nd Battalions), 19th U.S. (1st Battalion)
Third Brigade: Brig. Gen. John C. Starkweather
24th Illinois, 37th Indiana, 21st Ohio, 74th Ohio, 78th Pennsylvania, 79th Pennsylvania, 1st Wisconsin, 21st Wisconsin
Artillery: Commander unknown
Battery C, 1st Illinois Light; Battery A, 1st Michigan Light; Battery H, 5th U.S. (temporarily attached to Sheridan's division, IV Corps)

SECOND DIVISION: BRIG. GEN. JEFFERSON C. DAVIS
First Brigade: Brig. Gen. James D. Morgan
10th Illinois, 16th Illinois, 60th Illinois, 21st Kentucky, 10th Michigan
Second Brigade: Brig. Gen. John Beatty
34th Illinois, 78th Illinois, 98th Ohio, 108th Ohio, 113th Ohio, 121st Ohio
Third Brigade: Col. Daniel McCook
85th Illinois, 86th Illinois, 110th Illinois, 125th Illinois, 52nd Ohio
Artillery: Capt. William A. Hotchkiss
Battery I, 2nd Illinois Light; 2nd Minnesota Light Battery; 5th Wisconsin Light Battery

THIRD DIVISION: BRIG. GEN. ABSALOM BAIRD
First Brigade: Brig. Gen. John B. Turchin
82nd Indiana, 11th Ohio, 17th Ohio, 31st Ohio, 36th Ohio, 89th Ohio, 92nd Ohio
Second Brigade: Col. Ferdinand Van Derveer
75th Indiana, 87th Indiana, 101st Indiana, 2nd Minnesota, 9th Ohio, 35th Ohio, 105th Ohio
Third Brigade: Col. Edward H. Phelps
10th Indiana, 74th Indiana, 4th Kentucky, 10th Kentucky, 18th Kentucky, 14th Ohio, 38th Ohio

Artillery: Capt. George R. Swallow
7th Indiana Light Battery; 19th Indiana Light Battery; Battery I, 4th U.S.

ENGINEER TROOPS: BRIG. GEN. WILLIAM F. SMITH
Engineers: 1st Michigan Engineers (detachment), 13th Michigan, 21st Michigan, 22nd Michigan, 18th Ohio

PIONEERS: COL. GEORGE P. BUELL
1st Battalion, 2nd Battalion, 3rd Battalion

Artillery Reserve: Brig. Gen. John M. Brannan

FIRST DIVISION: COL. JAMES BARNETT
First Brigade: Maj. Charles S. Cotter
Battery B, 1st Ohio Light; Battery C, 1st Ohio Light; Battery E, 1st Ohio Light; Battery F, 1st Ohio Light
Second Brigade: Commander unknown
Battery G, 1st Ohio Light; Battery M, 1st Ohio Light; 18th Ohio Battery; 20th Ohio Battery

SECOND DIVISION: COMMANDER UNKNOWN
First Brigade: Capt. Josiah W. Church
Battery D, 1st Michigan Light; Battery A, 1st Tennessee Light; 3rd Wisconsin Light Battery; 8th Wisconsin Light Battery; 10th Wisconsin Light Battery
Second Brigade: Capt. Arnold Sutermeister
4th Indiana Light Battery; 8th Indiana Light Battery; 11th Indiana Light Battery; 21st Indiana Light Battery; Co. C, 1st Wisconsin Heavy Artillery

Cavalry Corps (mostly not present)

Second Brigade, Second Division: Col. Eli Long
98th Illinois Mounted Infantry, 17th Indiana Mounted Infantry, 2nd Kentucky Cavalry, 4th Michigan Cavalry, 1st Ohio Cavalry, 3rd Ohio Cavalry, 4th Ohio Cavalry (1 battalion), 10th Ohio Cavalry

Post of Chattanooga: Col. John G. Parkhurst

44th Indiana, 15th Kentucky, 9th Michigan

Army of the Tennessee: Maj. Gen. William T. Sherman

XV Corps: Maj. Gen. Frank P. Blair

FIRST DIVISION: BRIG, GEN. PETER J. OSTERHAUS
First Brigade: Brig, Gen. Charles R. Woods
13th Illinois, 3rd Missouri, 12th Missouri, 17th Missouri, 27th Missouri, 29th Missouri, 31st Missouri, 32nd Missouri, 76th Ohio

Second Brigade: Col. James A. Williamson
4th Iowa, 9th Iowa, 25th Iowa, 26th Iowa, 30th Iowa, 31st Iowa
Artillery: Capt. Henry H. Griffiths
1st Iowa Light Battery; Battery F, 2nd Missouri Light; 4th Ohio Light Battery

SECOND DIVISION: BRIG. GEN. MORGAN L. SMITH
First Brigade: Brig. Gen. Giles A. Smith
55th Illinois, 116th Illinois, 127th Illinois, 6th Missouri, 8th Missouri, 57th Ohio, 13th U.S. (1st Battalion)
Second Brigade: Brig. Gen. Joseph A. J. Lightburn
83rd Indiana, 30th Ohio, 37th Ohio, 47th Ohio, 54th Ohio, 4th West Virginia
Artillery: Commander unknown
Battery A, 1st Illinois Light; Battery B, 1st Illinois Light; Battery H, 1st Illinois Light

FOURTH DIVISION: BRIG. GEN. HUGH EWING
First Brigade: Col. John M. Loomis
26th Illinois, 90th Illinois, 12th Indiana, 100th Indiana
Second Brigade: Brig. Gen. John M. Corse
40th Illinois, 103rd Illinois, 6th Iowa, 46th Ohio
Third Brigade: Col. Joseph R. Cockerill
48th Illinois, 97th Indiana, 99th Indiana, 53rd Ohio, 70th Ohio
Artillery: Capt. Henry Richardson
Battery F, 1st Illinois Light; Battery I, 1st Illinois Light; Battery D, 1st Missouri Light

XVII Corps: Commander unknown

SECOND DIVISION: BRIG. GEN. JOHN E. SMITH
First Brigade: Col. Jesse I. Alexander
63rd Illinois, 48th Indiana, 59th Indiana, 4th Minnesota, 18th Wisconsin
Second Brigade: Col. Green B. Raum
56th Illinois, 17th Iowa, 10th Missouri, 24th Missouri, 80th Ohio
Third Brigade: Brig. Gen. Charles L. Matthies
93rd Illinois, 5th Iowa, 10th Iowa, 26th Missouri
Artillery: Capt. Henry Dillon
Cogswell's Illinois Battery, 6th Wisconsin Light Battery, 12th Wisconsin Light Battery

Army of Tennessee: Gen. Braxton Bragg
>   *Organization shown from November 12, 1863.*

General Headquarters

>   *1st Louisiana (regulars), 1st Louisiana Cavalry*

Longstreet's Corps: Lt. Gen. James Longstreet

(from the Army of Northern Virginia, detached to East Tennessee in early November)

MCLAWS'S DIVISION: MAJ. GEN. LAFAYETTE MCLAWS

Kershaw's Brigade: Brig. Gen. Joseph B. Kershaw

2nd South Carolina, 3rd South Carolina, 7th South Carolina, 8th South Carolina, 15th South Carolina, 3rd South Carolina Battalion

Humphreys's Brigade: Brig. Gen. Benjamin C. Humphreys

13th Mississippi, 17th Mississippi, 18th Mississippi, 21st Mississippi

Wofford's Brigade: Col. S. Z. Ruff

16th Georgia, 18th Georgia, 24th Georgia, Cobb's Legion, 3rd Georgia Battalion Sharpshooters

Bryan's Brigade: Brig. Gen. Goode Bryan

10th Georgia, 50th Georgia, 51st Georgia, 53rd Georgia

Artillery: Maj. Austin Leyden

Peeples's Georgia Battery, Wolihin's Georgia Battery, York's Georgia Battery

HOOD'S DIVISION: BRIG. GEN. MICAH JENKINS

Jenkins's Brigade: Col. John Bratton

1st South Carolina, 2nd South Carolina Rifles, 5th South Carolina, 6th South Carolina, Hampton Legion, Palmetto Sharpshooters

Law's Brigade: Brig. Gen. Evander M. Law

4th Alabama, 15th Alabama, 44th Alabama, 47th Alabama, 48th Alabama

Robertson's Brigade: Brig. Gen. Jerome B. Robertson

3rd Arkansas, 1st Texas, 4th Texas, 5th Texas

Anderson's Brigade: Brig. Gen. George T. Anderson

7th Georgia, 8th Georgia, 9th Georgia, 11th Georgia, 59th Georgia

Benning's Brigade: Brig. Gen. Henry L. Benning

2nd Georgia, 15th Georgia, 17th Georgia, 20th Georgia

Artillery: Col. E. Porter Alexander

Fickling's South Carolina Battery, Jordan's Virginia Battery, Moody's Louisiana Battery, Parker's Virginia Battery, Taylor's Virginia Battery, Woolfolk's Virginia Battery

Hardee's Corps: Lt. Gen. William J. Hardee

CHEATHAM'S DIVISION: BRIG. GEN. JOHN K. JACKSON
Jackson's Brigade: Col. C. J. Wilkinson
1st Georgia, 5th Georgia, 47th Georgia, 65th Georgia, 2nd Battalion Georgia Sharpshooters, 5th Mississippi, 8th Mississippi
Moore's Brigade: Brig. Gen. John C. Moore
37th Alabama, 40th Alabama, 42nd Alabama
Walthall's Brigade: Brig. Gen. Edward C. Walthall
24th Mississippi, 27th Mississippi, 29th Mississippi, 30th Mississippi, 34th Mississippi
Wright's Brigade: Brig. Gen. Marcus J. Wright
8th Tennessee, 16th Tennessee, 28th Tennessee, 38th Tennessee, 51st/52nd Tennessee, Murray's Tennessee Battalion
Artillery: Maj. Melancton Smith
Fowler's Alabama Battery, McCants's Florida Battery, Scogin's Georgia Battery, Turner's (Smith's) Mississippi Battery

HINDMAN'S DIVISION: BRIG. GEN. J. PATTON ANDERSON
Anderson's Brigade: Col. William F. Tucker
7th Mississippi, 9th Mississippi, 10th Mississippi, 41st Mississippi, 44th Mississippi, 9th Mississippi Battalion Sharpshooters
Manigault's Brigade: Brig. Gen. Arthur M. Manigault
24th Alabama, 28th Alabama, 34th Alabama, 10th/19th South Carolina
Deas's Brigade: Brig. Gen. Zachariah C. Deas
19th Alabama, 22nd Alabama, 25th Alabama, 39th Alabama, 50th Alabama, 17th Alabama Battalion Sharpshooters
Vaughan's Brigade: Brig. Gen. Alfred J. Vaughan Jr.
11th Tennessee, 12th/47th Tennessee, 13th/154th Tennessee, 29th Tennessee
Artillery: Maj. Alfred R. Courtney
Dent's Alabama Battery, Garrity's Alabama Battery, Doscher's (Scott's) Tennessee Battery, Hamilton's (Water's) Alabama Battery

BUCKNER'S DIVISION: BRIG. GEN. BUSHROD R. JOHNSTON
(except for Reynolds's Brigade and the artillery, was sent to East Tennessee on November 22)
Johnson's Brigade: Col. John S. Fulton
17th/23rd Tennessee, 25th/44th Tennessee, 63rd Tennessee
Gracie's Brigade: Brig. Gen. Archibald Gracie Jr.
41st Alabama, 43rd Alabama, Hilliard's (Alabama) Legion (1st, 2nd, 3rd, 4th Battalions)

Reynolds's Brigade: Brig. Gen. A. W. Reynolds
(attached to Stevenson's Division after November 22)
58th North Carolina, 60th North Carolina, 54th Virginia, 63rd Virginia
Artillery: Maj. Samuel C. Williams
Bullen's (Darden's) Mississippi Battery, Jeffress's Virginia Battery, Kolb's Alabama Battery

WALKER'S DIVISION: BRIG. GEN. STATES RIGHTS GIST
Maney's Brigade: Brig. Gen. George W. Maney
1st/27th Tennessee, 4th Tennessee (Provisional Army), 6th/9th Tennessee, 41st Tennessee, 50th Tennessee, 24th Tennessee Battalion Sharpshooters
Gist's Brigade: Col. James McCullough
46th Georgia, 8th Georgia Battalion, 16th South Carolina, 24th South Carolina
Wilson's Brigade: Col. Claudius C. Wilson
25th Georgia, 29th Georgia, 30th Georgia, 26th Georgia Battalion, 1st Georgia Battalion Sharpshooters
Artillery: Maj. Robert Martin
Bledsoe's Missouri Battery, Ferguson's South Carolina Battery, Howell's Georgia Battery

Breckinridge's Corps: Maj. Gen. John C. Breckinridge

CLEBURNE'S DIVISION: MAJ. GEN. PATRICK R. CLEBURNE
Liddell's Brigade: Col. Daniel C. Govan
2nd/15th Arkansas, 5th/13th Arkansas, 6th/7th Arkansas, 8th Arkansas, 19th/24th Arkansas
Smith's Brigade: Col. Hiram B. Granbury
6th/10th Texas Infantry/15th Texas Dismounted Cavalry, 7th Texas, 17th/18th/24th/25th Texas Dismounted Cavalry
Polk's Brigade: Brig. Gen. Lucius Polk
1st Arkansas, 3rd/5th Confederate, 2nd Tennessee, 35th/48th Tennessee
Lowrey's Brigade: Brig. Gen. Mark P. Lowrey
16th Alabama, 33rd Alabama, 45th Alabama, 32nd/45th Mississippi, 15th Mississippi Battalion Sharpshooters
Artillery: Capt. John Good
Key's (Calvert's) Arkansas Battery, Douglas's Texas Battery, Goldthwaite's (Semple's) Alabama Battery, Shannon's (Swett's) Mississippi Battery

STEWART'S DIVISION: MAJ. GEN. ALEXANDER P. STEWART
Adam's Brigade: Col. Randall L. Gibson
13th/20th Louisiana, 16th/25th Louisiana, 19th Louisiana, 4th Louisiana Battalion, 14th Louisiana Battalion Sharpshooters

Strahl's Brigade: Brig. Gen. Otho F. Strahl
4th/5th Tennessee, 19th Tennessee, 24th Tennessee, 31st Tennessee, 33rd
Tennessee

Clayton's Brigade: Col. J. T. Holtzclaw
18th Alabama, 32nd/58th Alabama, 36th Alabama, 38th Alabama

Stovall's Brigade: Brig. Gen. Marcellus A. Stovall
40th Georgia, 41st Georgia, 42nd Georgia, 43rd Georgia, 52nd Georgia

Artillery: Capt. Henry C. Semple
Anderson's (Dawson's) Georgia Battery, Rivers's (Humphreys's) Arkansas
Battery, Oliver's Alabama Battery, Stanford's Mississippi Battery

BRECKINRIDGE'S DIVISION: MAJ. GEN. WILLIAM B. BATE

Lewis's Brigade: Brig. Gen. Joseph H. Lewis
2nd Kentucky, 4th Kentucky, 5th Kentucky, 6th Kentucky, 9th Kentucky,
Morgan's Dismounted Cavalry

Bate's Brigade: Col. R. C. Tyler
37th Georgia, 4th Georgia Battalion Sharpshooters, 10th Tennessee, 15th/37th
Tennessee, 20th Tennessee, 30th Tennessee, 1st Tennessee Battalion

Florida Brigade: Col. Jesse J. Finley
1st/3rd Florida, 4th Florida, 6th Florida, 7th Florida, 1st Florida Dismounted
Cavalry

Artillery: Capt. C. H. Slocomb
Gracey's (Cobb's) Kentucky Battery, Mebane's Tennessee Battery, Vaught's
(Slocomb's) Louisiana Battery

STEVENSON'S DIVISION: MAJ. GEN. CARTER L. STEVENSON

Brown's Brigade: Brig. Gen. John C. Brown
3rd Tennessee, 18th/20th Tennessee, 32nd Tennessee, 45th Tennessee, 23rd
Tennessee Battalion

Cumming's Brigade: Brig. Gen. Alfred Cumming
34th Georgia, 36th Georgia, 39th Georgia, 56th Georgia

Pettus's Brigade: Brig. Gen. Edmund W. Pettus
20th Alabama, 23rd Alabama, 30th Alabama, 31st Alabama, 46th Alabama

Artillery: Capt. William W. Carnes
Baxter's Tennessee Battery, Marshall's Tennessee Battery, Van Den Corput's
Georgia Battery, Rowan's Georgia Battery

Cavalry

The bulk of Maj. Gen. Joseph Wheeler's Cavalry Corps was operating in East
Tennessee, first with Stevenson, then with Longstreet. Only Kelly's Division

remained with Bragg. Of that force, General Kelly and Wade's brigade were operating around Cleveland, Tennessee.

KELLY'S DIVISION: BRIG. GEN. JOHN H. KELLY

First Brigade: Col. William B. Wade

1st Confederate, 3rd Confederate, 8th Confederate, 10th Confederate

Second Brigade: Col. J. Warren Grigsby

2nd Kentucky, 3rd Kentucky, 9th Kentucky, Allison's Tennessee Squadron, Hamilton's Tennessee Battalion, Rucker's Legion

Artillery: Commander unknown

Huggins's Tennessee Battery, Huwald's Tennessee Battery, White's Tennessee Battery, Wiggins's Arkansas Battery

NOTES

CCNMP   Chickamauga-Chattanooga National Military Park, Fort
Oglethorpe, GA

OR   U.S. War Department. *The War of the Rebellion: A
Compilation of the Official Records of the Union and
Confederate Armies.* 128 vols. Washington, DC: U.S.
Government Printing Office, 1880–1901. All references are to
series 1 unless otherwise noted.

PUSG   John Y. Simon and John F. Marszalek, eds. *The Papers of
Ulysses S. Grant,* 32 vols. Carbondale: Southern Illinois
University Press, 1967–2012.

Prologue

1. *OR*, 30(1):161.

2. Brooks D. Simpson, *Ulysses S. Grant: Triumph over Adversity, 1822–1865* (New York: Houghton Mifflin, 2000), 222.

3. *PUSG*, 9:197.

4. For contrasting views of this incident, see Simpson, *Ulysses S. Grant,* 222–23; and Joseph A. Rose, *Grant under Fire: An Exposé of Generalship and Character in the American Civil War* (New York: Alderhanna, 2015), 254–56.

5. *PUSG*, 9:233–34.

6. *PUSG*, 9:235.

7. *OR*, 30(3):841.

8. *OR*, 30(3):888, 923.

9. *OR*, 30(3):945.

1. "Some Western General of High Rank"

1. William Marvel, *Burnside* (Chapel Hill: University of North Carolina Press, 1991), 280–81.

2. *OR*, 30(3):718; David Homer Bates, *Lincoln in the Telegraph Office* (New York: Century, 1907), 202.

3. *OR*, 30(1):142–43, 192.

4. *OR*, 30(1):146, 149; John Hay, *Inside Lincoln's White House: The Complete*

Civil War Diary of John Hay, ed. Martin Burlingame and John R. Turner Ettlinger (Carbondale: Southern Illinois University Press, 1997), 85.

5. Marvel, *Burnside*, 288–89.

6. *OR*, 30(4):25.

7. Gideon Welles, *Diary of Gideon Welles, Secretary of the Navy under Lincoln and Johnson*, 2 vols. (Boston, Houghton Mifflin, 1909), 1:444, 447–48.

8. Hay, *Inside Lincoln's White House*, 86.

9. Hay, *Inside Lincoln's White House*, 86; Roger Pickenpaugh, *Rescue by Rail: Troop Transfer and the Civil War in the West, 1863* (Lincoln: University of Nebraska Press, 1998), 4–5.

10. Pickenpaugh, *Rescue by Rail*, 6. The XI and XII Corps were selected for this move, nearly 20,000 men in all.

11. Edwin B. Coddington, *The Gettysburg Campaign: A Study in Command*, 2 vols. (Norwalk, CT: Easton, 1997), 1:130–33.

12. Frank P. Varney, *General Grant and the Rewriting of History: How the Destruction of General William S. Rosecrans Influenced Our Understanding of the Civil War* (El Dorado Hills, CA: Savas-Beatie, 2013), 36. Hartsuff was a prewar friend of Rosecrans's.

13. William M. Lamers, *The Edge of Glory: A Biography of General William S. Rosecrans, U.S.A.* (Baton Rouge: Louisiana State University Press, 1999), 103–30.

14. Hay, *Inside Lincoln's White House*, 87.

15. Charles A. Dana, *Recollections of the Civil War, with the Leaders at Washington and in the Field in the Sixties* (New York: D. Appleton, 1902), 21.

16. Dana, *Recollections*, 107.

17. Henry Villard, *Memoirs of Henry Villard, Journalist and Financier, 1835–1900*, 2 vols. (Boston: Houghton, Mifflin, 1904), 2:185; Gordon Granger to William S. Rosecrans, June 6, 1864, William S. Rosecrans Papers, University of California, Los Angeles.

18. *OR*, 30(1):202.

19. *OR*, 30(1):215.

20. Peter Cozzens, *The Shipwreck of Their Hopes: The Battles for Chattanooga* (Urbana: University of Illinois Press, 1994), 17–18.

21. *OR*, 30(1): 218–19, 221.

22. John Hay, *Lincoln and the Civil War: In the Diaries and Letters of John Hay*, selected and with an introduction by Tyler Dennett (1939; repr., Westport, CT: Negro Universities Press, 1972), 106; *OR*, 30(3):946.

23. Grant, *Personal Memoirs*, 1:583–84, 2:17; *PUSG*, 9:292.

24. "Rosecrans's Removal," *Indianapolis Times*, Mar. 13, 1882.

25. Lamers, *Edge of Glory*, 379.

26. Grant, *Personal Memoirs*, 2:18–19.

27. *PUSG*, 9:298.

28. John Hay, *Lincoln and the Civil War*, 115; James A. Garfield to William S. Rosecrans, Dec. 16, 1863, Rosecrans Papers.

29. *OR*, 30(1):221.

30. Grant, *Personal Memoirs*, 2:26.

31. Lamers, *Edge of Glory*, 391–92.

32. *OR*, 30(4):479; Lamers, *Edge of Glory*, 393. Rosecrans was correct about malice but not its source: the malice came from Dana.

33. Dana, *Recollections*, 130–31.

34. Grant, *Personal Memoirs*, 2:28.

35. Oliver O. Howard, *Autobiography of Oliver Otis Howard, Major General United States Army*, 2 vols. (New York: Baker & Taylor, 1907), 1:457; K. Jack Bauer, ed., *Soldiering: The Civil War Diary of Rice C. Bull, 123rd New York Volunteer Infantry* (Novato, CA: Presidio, 1977), 96.

36. O. O. Howard to Elizabeth, Oct. 24, 1863, Oliver Otis Howard Papers, Hawthorne-Longfellow Library, Bowdoin College, Brunswick, ME; Oliver O. Howard, "Grant at Chattanooga," *Personal Recollections of the War of the Rebellion, Addresses Delivered before the New York Commandery of the Loyal Legion of the United States, 1861–1865* (New York: Published by the Commandery, 1891), 246.

37. Howard, "Grant at Chattanooga," 246.

38. Howard, "Grant at Chattanooga," 246.

39. James H. Wilson, *Under the Old Flag: Recollections of Military Operations in the War for the Union, the Spanish War, the Boxer Rebellion, etc.*, 2 vols. (New York: D. Appleton, 1912), 1:264–65. Grant was still suffering from his leg injury.

40. Grant, *Personal Memoirs*, 2:121; Simpson, *Ulysses S. Grant*, 228.

41. Howard, "Grant at Chattanooga," 247.

42. Grant, *Personal Memoirs*, 2:28; Wilson, *Under the Old Flag*, 268–69.

2. "Wet, Dirty, and Well"

1. Bruce Catton, *Grant Takes Command* (Boston: Little, Brown, 1968), 37; *PUSG*, 9:317–18.

2. Mary Nicely, *Chattanooga Walking Tour & Historic Guide* (Chattanooga, 2002), 29. The house no longer survives; it was torn down in the 1920s.

3. Wilson, *Under the Old Flag*, 273–74. Wilson provided an earlier version of this encounter to Hamlin Garland, which appeared in 1898. See Hamlin Garland, *Ulysses S. Grant: His Life and Character* (New York: Doubleday and McClure, 1898), 242.

4. Simpson, *Ulysses S. Grant*, 228; Catton, *Grant Takes Command*, 38; Ron Chernow, *Grant* (New York: Penguin, 2017), 312.

5. James R. Gilmore, "The Relief of Rosecrans," *Burial of General Rosecrans, Arlington National Cemetery, May 17, 1902* (Cincinnati, 1903), 85.

6. Dana, *Recollections*, 133; James H. Wilson Diary, Oct. 23, 1863, Delaware Historical Society; *PUSG*, 9:317–18. It is worth noting that Wilson's diary described Hooker's snub at Stevenson in some detail, in a passage very similar to the description found in Wilson's memoir. It is curious that he would record that incident in his contemporary diary but not the one at Thomas's headquarters.

7. Horace Porter, *Campaigning with Grant* (New York: Century, 1897), 4.

8. "Transcript of J. J. Reynolds Interview," Hamlin Garland Papers, University of Southern California, Los Angeles.

9. Porter, *Campaigning with Grant*, 5.

10. James W. Livingood, *The Chattanooga Country: Gateway to History. The Nashville to Atlanta Rail Corridor of the 1860s* (Chattanooga, TN: Chattanooga Area Historical Association, 1995), 4–13.

11. Livingood, *Chattanooga Country*, 19.

12. Robert C. Black III, *The Railroads of the Confederacy* (Chapel Hill: University of North Carolina Press, 1952), 195–96.

13. John R. Brooke et al., *Report of a Board of Army Officers upon the Claim of Maj. Gen. William Ferrar Smith, U.S.V., Major, U.S. Army (Retired) That He, and Not General Rosecrans, Originated the Plan for the Relief of Chattanooga in October, 1863* (Washington, D.C.: U.S. Government Printing Office, 1901), 8–9.

14. Quoted in David A. Powell, *Battle above the Clouds: Lifting the Siege of Chattanooga and the Battle of Lookout Mountain, October 16–November 24, 1863* (El Dorado Hills, CA: Savas Beatie, 2017), 38–39; Samuel H. Sprott, *Cush: A Civil War Memoir*, ed. Louis R. Smith Jr. and Andrew Quist (Livingston, AL: Livingston Press at the University of West Alabama, 1999), 67.

15. Alexander Mendoza, *Confederate Struggle for Command: General James Longstreet and the First Corps at Chattanooga* (College Station: Texas A&M University Press, 2008), 92.

16. William F. Smith, *Autobiography of Maj. Gen. William F. Smith, 1861–1864*, ed. Herbert M. Schiller (Dayton, OH: Morningside House, 1990), 72.

17. Smith, *Autobiography*, 66–67.

18. *OR*, 30(3): 890; William G. LeDuc, "The Little Steamboat That Opened the 'Cracker Line,'" in *Battles and Leaders of the Civil War*, ed. Robert Underwood Johnson and Clarence Clough Buel, 4 vols. (New York: Thomas Yoseloff, 1956), 4:676–77.

19. For the details of Rosecrans's plan, see Brooke, *Report of a Board of Army Officers*, 14–16.

20. Grant, *Personal Memoirs*, 2:28.

21. Frank to "Dear William," Nov. 4, 1863, 136th New York File, CCNMP; *OR*, 30(2):723.

22. *OR*, 30(2):723–24.

23. Russell M. Tuttle, *The Civil War Journal of Lt. Russell M. Tuttle, New York Volunteer Infantry*, ed. George H. Tappan (Jefferson, NC: McFarland, 2006), 96.

24. *OR*, 30(2):713; Tuttle, *Civil War Journal*, 96.

25. Alexander Summers, *Gone to Glory at Farmington: A Profile of Col. James Monroe of Mattoon, Hero of Two Regiments in the Civil War* (Mattoon, IL: Mattoon Historical Society, 1963), 26. Conversely, Wheeler recorded the Union losses at 29 killed and 159 wounded, stating that his own casualties amounted to "less than a quarter" of the Federal loss.

26. William G. LeDuc, *Recollections of a Civil War Quartermaster: The Auto-biography of William G. LeDuc* (St. Paul, MN: North Central, 1963), 101.

27. *OR*, 31(1):43–44.

3. "They Looked upon the Garrison as Prisoners of War"

1. Porter, *Campaigning with Grant*, 6.

2. Grant, *Personal Memoirs*, 2:31; William Farrar Smith and Henry M. Cist, "Comments on General Grant's 'Chattanooga,'" in Johnson and Buel, *Battles and Leaders*, 3:714. Smith's bid for sole credit of the plan that opened the "Cracker Line" hinged on his claim to have personally selected Brown's Ferry as the landing site for a surprise amphibious movement, a point refuted by an army review board that was finally created to settle the matter in 1901.

3. *OR*, 31(1):713. Bear Creek flows into the Tennessee at the Alabama-Mississippi state line.

4. *OR*, 31(1):712, 718.

5. *OR*, 31(1):739. As noted earlier, the true father of this operation was probably Rosecrans.

6. *OR*, 31(1):43–44.

7. Arnold Gates, ed., *The Rough Side of War: The Civil War Journal of Chelsey A. Mosman, 1st Lieutenant, Company D, 59th Illinois Infantry Regiment* (Garden City, NY: Basin, 1987), 105.

8. Gates, *Rough Side of War*, 106–9.

9. *OR*, 31(1):92. Both regiments were recruited from local loyalists.

10. Brian C. Melton, *Sherman's Forgotten General: Henry W. Slocum* (Columbia: University of Missouri Press, 2007), 147.

11. *PUSG*, 9:323.

12. Howard, *Autobiography*, 1:459; OR, 31(1):72. Howard had a clear interest in diminishing Hooker's reputation and took every opportunity to do so in his

memoirs. But as Dana's telegrams demonstrate, Grant and Thomas were also less than pleased with Hooker's excuses.

13. Hartwell Osborn, *Trials and Triumphs: The Record of the Fifty-Fifth Ohio Volunteer Infantry* (Chicago: A. C. McClurg, 1904), 118–19. As will be seen, Bragg failed to occupy the gorge because he lacked both the troops and the means to supply them for any length of time west of Lookout Mountain.

14. *OR*, 31(1):77–80.

15. Albert G. Hart, "The Surgeon and the Hospital in the Civil War," *Papers of the Military Historical Society of Massachusetts*, 15 vols. (Boston: Military Historical Society of Massachusetts, 1913), 13:279–80.

16. William C. Jordan, *Some Events and Incidents during the Civil War* (Montgomery, AL: Paragon, 1909), 55–56.

17. J. Gary Laine and Morris M. Penny, *Law's Alabama Brigade in the War between the Union and the Confederacy* (Shippensburg, PA: White Mane, 1996), 178–79.

18. Laine and Penny, *Law's Alabama Brigade*, 182.

19. *OR*, 31(1):78–79; Grant, *Personal Memoirs*, 2:37.

20. Adin B. Underwood, *The Three Years' Service of the Thirty-Third Mass. Infantry Regiment, 1862–1865. And the Campaigns and Battles of Chancellorsville, Beverly's Ford, Gettysburg, Wauhatchie, Chattanooga, Atlanta, the March to the Sea and through the Carolinas in Which It Took Part* (Boston: A. Williams, 1881), 154–55.

21. *OR*, 31(1):221–22.

22. *OR*, 31(1):217.

23. *OR*, 31(1):53–54, 60.

24. *OR*, 31(1):56, 72.

25. Smith, *Autobiography*, 77; *OR*, 31(1):72.

26. *OR*, 31(1):225–26.

27. For an excellent description of the Wauhatchie fight, see Douglas R. Cubbison, "Midnight Engagement: John Geary's White Star Division at Wauhatchie," *Civil War Regiments* 3, no. 2 (1993): 70–104.

28. Wiley Sword, *Mountains Touched with Fire: Chattanooga Besieged, 1863* (New York: St. Martin's, 1995), 141.

29. For the full transcripts of the court, which convened in January 1864, see *OR*, 31(1):137–216.

30. *OR*, 31(1):218.

4. "Recollect That East Tennessee Is My Horror"

1. See "Virginia & Tennessee Tonnage, Eastbound Food," Confederate Railroads, http://www.csa-railroads.com/Virginia_and_Tennessee_Tonnage,_Eastbound_Food.htm, accessed Aug. 5, 2018.

2. For a detailed look at this episode, see David Madden, "Unionist Resistance to Confederate Occupation: The Bridge Burners of East Tennessee," *East Tennessee Historical Society Publications* 52–53 (1980–81): 22–40.

3. James Lee McDonough, *William Tecumseh Sherman: In the Service of My Country, a Life* (New York: W. W. Norton, 2016), 289; *OR*, 31(3):297.

4. Earl J. Hess, *The Knoxville Campaign: Burnside and Longstreet in East Tennessee* (Knoxville: University of Tennessee Press, 2012), 14.

5. *PUSG*, 9:337–38, 340.

6. Hess, *Knoxville Campaign*, 26.

7. Grant, *Personal Memoirs*, 2:49.

8. *PUSG*, 9:342–43; *OR*, 31(3):16.

9. *PUSG*, 9:354–55.

10. Thomas L. Connelly, *Autumn of Glory: The Army of Tennessee, 1862–1865* (Baton Rouge: Louisiana State University Press, 1971), 245–55.

11. Lynda Lasswell Crist, Kenneth H. Williams, and Peggy L. Dillard, eds. *The Papers of Jefferson Davis*, vol. 10, *October 1863–August 1864* (Baton Rouge: Louisiana State University Press, 1999), 36–37.

12. *OR*, 31(1):218.

13. Richard M. McMurry, ed., *An Uncompromising Secessionist: The Civil War of George Knox Miller, Eighth (Wade's) Confederate Cavalry* (Tuscaloosa: University of Alabama Press, 2007), 154.

14. *OR*, 31(1):455.

15. *OR*, 31(3):634–35.

16. *OR*, 31(3):637.

17. Grant, *Personal Memoirs*, 2:42–43. Just prior to their move west in September, most of Longstreet's men drew new uniforms, with coats made of British wool and identified as steel gray in color. Federal accounts described these coats as dark blue. At Chickamauga many Federals believed Longstreet's men were fellow Yankees, at least until they opened fire.

18. Grant, *Personal Memoirs*, 2:49–50.

19. *OR*, 31(2):57.

20. *OR*, 31(3):73; Smith and Cist, "Comments on General Grant's 'Chattanooga,'" 715.

21. Smith and Cist, "Comments on General Grant's 'Chattanooga,'" 716.

22. William F. Smith, "An Historical Sketch of the Military Operations around Chattanooga, Tennessee, September 22 to November 27, 1863," In *The Mississippi Valley, Tennessee, Georgia, Alabama, 1861–1864*, vol. 8 of *Papers of the Military Historical Society of Massachusetts* (Boston: Military Historical Society of Massachusetts, 1910), 193–94. Though Smith's account of this incident is self-serving, aimed at both casting doubt on Grant's abilities (with whom he had a major

falling-out in Virginia in 1864) and at taking credit for all the notable actions of the campaign, the core facts are corroborated by contemporary evidence.

23. *OR*, 31(2):58–59.

24. *OR*, 31(2):58–59.

25. Francis F. McKinney, *Education in Violence: The Life of George H. Thomas and the History of the Army of the Cumberland* (Detroit: Wayne State University Press, 1961), 275.

26. *OR*, 31(2):29.

27. Grant, *Personal Memoirs*, 2:50; John G. Nicolay and John Hay, *Abraham Lincoln: A History*, 10 vols. (New York: Century, 1904), 8:130.

28. Grant, *Personal Memoirs*, 2:52; George Brent Journal, Nov. 10, 1863, Braxton Bragg Papers, William Palmer Collection, Western Reserve Historical Society, Cleveland, OH.

29. G. Moxley Sorrel, *At the Right Hand of Longstreet: Recollections of a Confederate Staff Officer* (Lincoln,: University of Nebraska Press, 1999), 211.

30. Hess, *Knoxville Campaign*, 39–49, 49–52, 56–62, 95.

31. *OR*, 31(2):3.

32. *OR*, 31 (3):207.

33. *OR*, 31 (3):216.

34. *OR*, 31 (3):215–16.

35. *OR*, 31 (3):226.

36. *OR*, 31 (3):233.

37. *OR*, 31 (3):239; Robert Garth Scott, ed., *Forgotten Valor: The Memoirs, Journals, & Civil War Letters of Orlando B. Willcox* (Kent, OH: Kent State University Press, 1999), 471–72. There is no mention of this criticism of Willcox in Grant's memoirs.

38. Donn Piatt and Henry V. Boynton, *George H. Thomas: A Critical Biography* (Cincinnati: Robert Clarke, 1893), 475.

39. *OR*, 31(3):181–82.

40. *OR*, 31(1):269.

5. "We Went in a Zigzag"

1. John F. Marszalek, *Sherman: A Soldier's Passion for Order* (New York: Free Press, 1993), 238.

2. Brooks D. Simpson and Jean W. Berlin, eds., *Sherman's Civil War: Selected Correspondence of William T. Sherman, 1860–1865* (Chapel Hill,: University of North Carolina Press, 1999), 552, 556.

3. P. J. Carmody, "The Battle of Collierville," *Journal of the American Irish Historical Society* 9 (1910): 467.

4. James B. Swan, *Chicago's Irish Legion: The 90th Illinois Volunteers in the Civil War* (Carbondale: Southern Illinois University Press, 2009), 18; E. O. Hurd, "The Battle of Collierville," *Sketches of War History, 1861–1865*, vol. 5 (Cincinnati: Robert Clarke, 1903), 244.

5. *OR*, 30(2):760; Carmody, "Battle of Collierville," 468.

6. *OR*, 30(2):760; Hurd, "Battle of Collierville," 245; Carmody, "Battle of Collierville," 470.

7. *OR*, 30(1):713. Bear Creek flows into the Tennessee River at the state line between Mississippi and Alabama. Soldiers referred to it as being in either state.

8. *OR*, 30(1):817–24.

9. Mary Bobbitt Townsend, *Yankee Warhorse: A Biography of Major General Peter Osterhaus* (Colombia: University of Missouri Press, 2010), 122–23.

10. Tamara A. Smith, "A Matter of Trust: Grant and James B. McPherson," in *Grant's Lieutenants: From Cairo to Vicksburg*, ed. Steven E. Woodworth (Lawrence: University Press of Kansas, 2001), 155–56, 160.

11. Edwin C. Bearss, "Misfire in Mississippi: McPherson's Canton Expedition," *Civil War History* 8, no. 4 (Dec. 1962): 401–16.

12. For an excellent modern biography of Logan, see Gary Ecelbarger, *Black Jack Logan: An Extraordinary Life in Peace and War* (Guilford, CT: Lyons, 2005).

13. *OR*, 31(1):759.

14. Grant, *Personal Memoirs*, 1:574. Here Grant exaggerated, but only slightly, since Blair had entered service as a colonel in July 1862, was promoted to brigadier general a month later, and received his second star in November.

15. Grant, *Personal Memoirs*, 1:497–98.

16. Ecelbarger, *Black Jack Logan*, 159.

17. Charles W. Wills, *Army Life of an Illinois Soldier, Including a Day-by-Day Record of Sherman's March to the Sea: Letters and Diary of Charles W. Wills* (Carbondale: Southern Illinois University Press, 1996), 199; Earl J. Hess, ed., *A German in the Yankee Fatherland: The Civil War Letters of Henry A. Kircher* (Kent, OH: Kent State University Press, 1983), 137.

18. Hess, *A German in the Yankee Fatherland*, 140. Though Kircher now served in a Missouri regiment, he lived across the Mississippi River in Illinois before the war and first enlisted in the 9th Illinois.

19. Hess, *A German in the Yankee Fatherland*, 140; William T. Sherman, *Memoirs of General William T. Sherman*. 2 vols. (New York: D. Appleton, 1875), 1:372.

20. Sherman, *Memoirs*, 1:360; *OR*, 31(3):80.

21. *PUSG*, 9:360.

22. Ely S. Parker to Nicholson Parker, Nov. 18, 1863, Ely S. Parker Papers, American Philosophical Society Library, Philadelphia.

23. *PUSG*, 9:330–31; Livingood, *Chattanooga Country*, 498–99.

24. *PUSG*, 9:352.

25. *PUSG*, 9:339, 350–51.

26. *PUSG*, 9:379.

27. *PUSG*, 9:378.

28. *PUSG*, 9:378. All of the following describe Grant as refusing to grant Emilie a pass: R. Gerald McMurtry, *Confederate General Ben Hardin Helm: Kentucky Brother In-Law of Abraham Lincoln* (Fort Wayne, IN: Lincoln National Life Foundation, 1959), 12; Katherine Helm, *The True Story of Mary, Wife of Lincoln, Containing the Recollections of Mary Lincoln's Sister Emilie (Mrs. Ben Hardin Helm), Extracts from Her War-Time Diary Numerous Letters and other Documents Now First Published* (New York: Harper & Brothers, 1928), 220; Doris Kerns Goodwin, *Team of Rivals: The Political Genius of Abraham Lincoln* (New York: Simon and Schuster, 2005), 590.

29. Goodwin, *Team of Rivals*, 590–91; *PUSG*, 9:379.

30. Howard, "Grant at Chattanooga," 248.

31. Howard, "Grant at Chattanooga," 248–49.

32. Grant, *Personal Memoirs*, 2:52–53.

33. Sherman, *Memoirs*, 1:361.

34. Sherman to James A. Garfield, July 28, 1870, William T. Sherman Papers, Library of Congress, Washington, D.C. Sherman related this incident to show that his friend Thomas was not "as imperturbable" as he was so often described.

35. Sherman, *Memoirs*, 1:362; William Wrenshall Smith, "Holocaust Holiday: The Journal of a Strange Vacation to the War-torn South and a Visit with U. S. Grant," *Civil War Times Illustrated* 18, no. 6 (Oct. 1979): 28–30.

36. Sherman, *Memoirs*, 1:362.

37. Sherman, *Memoirs*, 1:363.

38. Smith, "Holocaust Holiday," 32.

39. *PUSG*, 9:396–97; Dana, *Recollections*, 132; *OR*, 31(3):145.

40. *PUSG*, 9:400.

41. *OR*, 31(3):163.

42. *OR*, 31(3):167.

43. *OR*, 31(2):31, 127.

6. "The Elements Were against Us"

1. Walter H. Hebert, *Fighting Joe Hooker* (Indianapolis: Bobbs-Merrill, 1944), 262.

2. Sherman, *Memoirs*, 1:388–89; Cozzens, *Shipwreck of their Hopes*, 121.

3. *OR*, 31(2):583–84; H. H. Orendorff et al. *Reminiscences of the Civil War from Diaries of Members of the 103rd Illinois Volunteer Infantry, 1904* (Chicago: Press of J. F. Leaming, 1904), 23–24.

4. *OR*, 31(2):667.

5. *OR*, 31(2):642; Green B. Raum, "With the Western Army: Sherman's March to Chattanooga," *National Tribune*, Apr. 3, 1902; Committee of the Regiment, *The Story of the Fifty-Fifth Regiment Illinois Volunteer Infantry in the Civil War, 1861–1865* (Clinton, MA: W. J. Coulter, 1887), 279.

6. Gates, *Rough Side of War*, 123; *OR*, 31(2):63.

7. *OR*, 31(2):39.

8. Alonzo L. Brown, *History of the Fourth Regiment of Minnesota Volunteers during the Great Rebellion, 1861–1865* (St. Paul, MN: Pioneer, 1892), 266.

9. *OR*, 31(2):63–64.

10. Simpson and Berlin, *Sherman's Civil War*, 572.

11. *PUSG*, 9:428.

12. *OR*, 31(2):32, 572; Sherman, *Memoirs*, 1:389.

13. Grant, *Personal Memoirs*, 1:432.

14. Committee of the Regiment, *Fifty-Fifth Regiment Illinois Volunteer Infantry*, 281; Joseph A. Saunier, ed., *A History of the Forty-Seventh Regiment Ohio Veteran Volunteer Infantry, Second Brigade, Second Division, Fifteenth Army Corps, Army of the Tennessee* (Hillsboro, OH: Lyle Printing, 1903), 197.

15. *OR*, 31(2):314, 346–67; Hebert, *Fighting Joe Hooker*, 262.

16. Orendorff, *Reminiscences of . . . 103rd Illinois Volunteer Infantry*, 24.

17. *OR*, 31(2):32.

18. *PUSG*, 9:430–31.

19. *OR*, 31(2):32.

20. *OR*, 31(3):732, 736.

21. George Brent Journal, Nov. 12, 1863, Braxton Bragg Papers, William Palmer Collection, Western Reserve Historical Society, Cleveland, OH; Nathaniel Cheairs Hughes Jr., ed., *Liddell's Record: St. John Richardson Liddell. Brigadier General, CSA. Staff Officer and Brigade Commander, Army of Tennessee* (Baton Rouge: Louisiana State University Press, 1985), 158.

22. Simon B. Buckner to Victor Von Sheliha, Nov. 5, 1863, Simon B. Buckner Papers, Huntington Library, San Marino, CA; Brent Journal, Nov. 21, 1863, Bragg Papers.

23. *OR*, 31(2):32, 128.

24. R. Lockwood Tower, ed., *A Carolinian Goes to War: The Civil War Narrative of Arthur Middleton Manigault, Brigadier General, C.S.A.* (Columbia: University of South Carolina Press, 1983), 131.

25. *Chicago Evening Journal*, Dec. 5, 1863.

26. Christopher Chancellor, ed., *An Englishman in the American Civil War: The Diaries of Henry Yates Thompson, 1863* (London: Sidgwick & Jackson, 1971), 150.

27. Philip J. Reyburn, *Clear the Track:. A History of the Eighty-Ninth Illinois Volunteer Infantry, the Railroad Regiment* (Bloomington, IN: Authorhouse, 2012), 315.

28. Tower, *A Carolinian Goes to War*, 130–31.

29. Tower, *A Carolinian Goes to War*, 131; *OR*, 31(2):282–83; Reyburn, *Clear the Track*, 315.

30. *OR*, 31(2):66, 251, 253; John M. Hoffmann, ed., "First Impressions of Three Days' Fighting: Quartermaster General Meigs's 'Journal of the Battle of Chattanooga,'" in *Ulysses S. Grant: Essays and Documents*, ed. David L. Wilson and John Y. Simon (Carbondale: Southern Illinois University Press, 1981), 71.

31. *OR*, 31(2):674, 753–54; Tower, *A Carolinian Goes to War*, 134.

32. Grant, *Personal Memoirs*, 1:436.

7. "It Is All Poetry"

1. *OR*, 31(2):106–7, 31(3):231.

2. Townsend, *Yankee Warhorse*, 124–25.

3. *OR*, 31(2):315.

4. *OR*, 31(2):315.

5. Sword, *Mountains Touched with Fire*, 205.

6. *OR*, 31(2):490; Allan L. Fahnestock Diary, Nov. 23, 1863, Abraham Lincoln Presidential Library, Springfield, IL.

7. Carl Schurz, *The Reminiscences of Carl Schurz*, 3 vols. (New York: McClure, 1908), 1:71–72. The XI Corps suffered a loss of four killed and thirty-two wounded on November 23. *OR*, 31(2):348.

8. Committee of the Regiment, *Fifty-Fifth Regiment Illinois Volunteer Infantry*, 283; *OR*, 31(2):641.

9. *OR*, 31(2):107, 572–73; Nathaniel Cheairs Hughes Jr. and Gordon D. Whitney, *Jefferson Davis in Blue: The Life of Sherman's Relentless Warrior* (Baton Rouge: Louisiana State University Press, 2002), 204.

10. *OR*, 31(2):348; Howard, *Autobiography*, 1:481–82.

11. Livingood, *Chattanooga Country*, 433.

12. *PUSG*, 9:440–41.

13. *OR*, 31(2):148.

14. Cozzens, *Shipwreck of Their Hopes*, 160–61.

15. *OR*, 31(2):692–94, 703.

16. *OR*, 31(2):170.

17. Edward F. Hopkins, "Reminiscences of the Late War," undated clipping, 149th New York Infantry File, CCNMP; Charles A. Partridge, *History of the Ninety-Sixth Regiment Illinois Volunteer Infantry* (Chicago: Brown, Pettibone, 1887), 268.

18. *OR*, 31(2):694–96.

19. *OR*, 31(2):600.

20. Sprott, *Cush*, 68; Partridge, *Ninety-Sixth Regiment Illinois Volunteer Infantry*, 270; War Department Tablet for Howell's Battery on Lookout Mountain, CCNMP.

21. Carlin Brigade Tablet on Lookout Mountain, CCNMP.

22. Chancellor, *An Englishman*, 153–57.

23. Partridge, *Ninety-Sixth Regiment Illinois Volunteer Infantry*, 269; "Grant. Correspondence of the New York *Herald*," *Chicago Tribune*, July 27, 1878.

24. *OR*, 31(2):573.

25. Wilson, *Under the Old Flag*, 1:294–95.

26. Cozzens, *Shipwreck of Their Hopes*, 149–50.

27. J. E. Walton, "Mission Ridge," *National Tribune*, Nov. 1, 1888.

28. Cozzens, *Shipwreck of Their Hopes*, 151–54.

29. Cozzens, *Shipwreck of Their Hopes*, 155–57.

30. *OR*, 31(2):573.

31. Boynton is quoted in Cozzens, *Shipwreck of Their Hopes*, 155. Boynton was a veteran of the battle, having served as the lieutenant colonel of the 35th Ohio, and received the Medal of Honor for his actions on November 25. As a member of the Army of the Cumberland, his criticism of Grant and the Army of Tennessee sometimes took on a partisan tone, but his assessment of Sherman's failure on November 24 is sound.

32. *PUSG*, 9:443; *OR*, 31(2):67.

33. *OR*, 31(2):561.

8. "We Shall Have a Battle on Mission Ridge"

1. *OR*, 31(2):48.

2. Smith, "Holocaust Holiday," 35; Hoffmann, "First Impressions of Three Days' Fighting," 72.

3. *OR*, 31(2):721–22.

4. T. J. Wright, *History of the Eighth Regiment Kentucky Vol. Inf. during Its Three Years Campaigns, embracing Organization, Marches, Skirmishes and Battles of the Command, with Much of the History of the Old Reliable Third Brigade, Commanded by Hon. Stanley Matthews, and Containing Many Interesting and Amusing Incidents of Army Life* (St. Joseph, MO: St. Joseph Steam Printing., 1880), 213–14; *OR*, 31(2):113.

5. *OR*, 31(2):67.

6. Connelly, *Autumn of Glory*, 273. For Bragg's allegation about Breckinridge, see *OR*, 52(2):745.

7. Irving A. Buck, *Cleburne and His Command*, with a foreword by Bell I. Wiley (Dayton, OH: Press of Morningside Bookshop, 1982), 164–67.

8. *OR*, 31(2):574.

9. *OR*, 31(2):629, 636.

10. *OR*, 31(2):633. They were, however, quite possibly reflective of Sherman's own strongly defensive mindset that morning.

11. Roger Boedecker, *The Civil War Service of the 127th Illinois Volunteer Infantry* (N.p., 2007), 52–53.

12. Boedecker, *127th Illinois Volunteer Infantry*, 52–53.

13. Jesse H. Bennett to Ezra A. Carman, Dec. 18, 1907, 46th Ohio File, CCNMP.

14. Theodore Jones to Ezra A. Carman, Jan. 2, 1908, 30th Ohio File, CCNMP.

15. John R. Lundberg, *Granbury's Texas Brigade: Diehard Western Confederates* (Baton Rouge: Louisiana State University Press, 2012), 117–18. The Warren Light Artillery was also known as Swett's Battery for its first commander.

16. Jones to Carman, Jan. 2, 1908, 30th Ohio File, CCNMP.

17. James B. Smith to Ezra A. Carman, Dec. 17, 1907, 40th Illinois File, CCNMP.

18. Jones to Carman, Jan. 2, 1908, 30th Ohio File, CCNMP.

19. Jones to Carman, Jan. 2, 1908, 30th Ohio File, CCNMP.

20. *OR*, 31(2):636; Lundberg, *Granbury's Texas Brigade*, 120.

21. *OR*, 31(2):726, 735.

22. *OR*, 31(2):739; William C. Davis, *The Orphan Brigade: The Kentucky Confederates Who Couldn't Go Home* (Garden City, NY: Doubleday, 1980), 198.

23. Swan, *Chicago's Irish Legion*, 101; Eli J. Sherlock, *Memorabilia of the Marches and Battles in which the One Hundredth Regiment of Indiana Infantry Volunteers Took an Active Part. War of the Rebellion, 1861–1865* (Kansas City, MO: Gerald-Woody Printing, 1896), 54; *OR*, 31(2):633, 735.

24. Swan, *Chicago's Irish Legion*, 104–5, 112; *OR*, 31(2):633. According to Swan's narrative, when O'Meara's body was shipped back to Chicago, "General Grant ordered the coffin to be opened that he might look upon the face of the gallant hero."

25. *OR*, 31(2):44, 68.

26. Cozzens, *Shipwreck of Their Hopes*, 220–22.

27. *OR*, 31(2):643–44.

28. *OR*, 31(2):652.

29. *OR*, 31(2):652.

30. Green B. Raum, "With the Western Army: Fight on Tunnel Hill," *National Tribune*, May 1, 1902.

31. Buck, *Cleburne and His Command*, 170; Cozzens, *Shipwreck of Their Hopes*, 235–36; Robert M. Collins, *Chapters from the Unwritten History of the War between the States; or, The Incidents in the Life of a Confederate Soldier in Camp, on the March, in the Great Battles, and in Prison* (St. Louis: Nixon-Jones Printing, 1893), 180. Collins made no further explanation of his decision to abandon his sword for a rock in the subsequent hand-to-hand fight.

32. Raum, "With the Western Army: Fight on Tunnel Hill."

33. Schurz, *Reminiscences*, 3:75.

34. Thomas B. Van Horne, *The Life of Major General George H. Thomas* (New York: Charles Scribner's Sons, 1882), 189; Henry J. Aten, *History of the Eighty-Fifth Regiment, Illinois Volunteer Infantry* (Hiawatha, KS, 1901), 136.

35. Emerson Opdycke, "Suggestions on Chattanooga, Box 131, *Century* Papers, New York Public Library.

9. "Inspired by the Impulse of Victory"

1. *OR*, 31(2):67.

2. Smith, "Holocaust Holiday," 35. Brig. Gen. Robert Anderson, who commanded Fort Sumter in April 1861, was later the commander of the Department of the Cumberland. Maj. Gen. Don Carlos Buell followed Anderson in that post. Maj. Gen. John C. Frémont, "the Pathfinder" of prewar fame based on his western explorations, briefly commanded the Department of the Missouri, in which Grant served. Frémont recruited a flashily dressed European-style troop of cavalry to serve as his headquarters guard, which soon became the object of much ridicule by more down-to-earth officers.

3. Smith, "Holocaust Holiday," 35. "Lagow" was Capt. Clark B. Lagow of Grant's staff, who, despite joining Rawlins in a temperance pledge in 1862, was soon to resign from Grant's service due to an especially egregious drinking incident on November 15, 1863.

4. Hoffman, "First Impressions of Three Days' Fighting," 73; Thomas J. Wood, "The Battle of Missionary Ridge," in *Sketches of War History, 1861–1865*, ed. W. H. Chamberlin, vol. 4 (Cincinnati: Robert Clarke, 1896), 33.

5. Smith, *Autobiography*, 80. Smith probably did not realize that during the morning, very little of Bragg's artillery was in position to fire. Most of the guns were withdrawn overnight from the base of the ridge, and now they hurriedly took up new positions atop it.

6. The two most useful analyses of all these competing accounts are Brooks D. Simpson, "What Happened on Orchard Knob? Ordering the Attack on Missionary Ridge," in *The Chattanooga Campaign*, ed. Steven E. Woodworth and Charles D. Grear (Carbondale: Southern Illinois University Press, 2012), 84–105; and Rose, *Grant under Fire*, 289–98. Simpson is largely favorable to Grant, while Rose offers a strongly contrasting view.

7. *OR*, 31(2):112–13. Grant later wrote something considerably different. "Hooker was ordered to move at the same hour [as Sherman], and endeavor to intercept the enemy's retreat if he still remained; if he had gone, then to move directly to Rossville and operate against the left and rear of the force on Missionary Ridge. Thomas was not to move until Hooker had reached Missionary Ridge." Grant, *Personal Memoirs*, 2:443.

8. Joseph S. Fullerton, "The Army of the Cumberland at Chattanooga," in Johnson and Buel, *Battles and Leaders*, 3:723.

9. *OR*, 31(2):14–15.

10. *OR*, 31(2):67.

11. *OR*, 31(2):113–14. The timing of these various communiques might seem odd—Dana reporting that Hooker controlled Lookout Mountain at 9:00 A.M., seemingly prior to Hooker's own report of that news sent at 9:20, for example—but without proper synchronization of watches, different headquarters and observers relied on their own watches for timing, which could be inconsistent.

12. *OR*, 31(2):508; Adam Badeau, *Military History of Ulysses S. Grant, from April, 1861, to April, 1865*, 2 vols. (New York: D. Appleton, 1885), 1:506–7.

13. *OR*, 31(2):68; Theodore Jones to Ezra A. Carman, Jan. 2, 1908, CCNMP. See also chapter 8.

14. Hoffman, "First Impressions of Three Days' Fighting," 73–74.

15. William F. G. Shanks, *Personal Recollections of Distinguished Generals* (New York: Harper & Brothers, 1866), 118; Smith, "Holocaust Holiday," 36.

16. Albert D. Richardson, *A Personal History of Ulysses S. Grant* (Hartford, CT: American Publishing, 1868), 365. Writing in the years after Grant's death, journalist Sylvanus Cadwallader described a very similar scene, inserting himself as Grant's addressee. See Sylvanus Cadwallader, *Three Years with Grant* (Lincoln: University of Nebraska Press, 1996), 152.

17. Wood, "Missionary Ridge," 34; and "A Thrilling War Chapter: The Battle of Missionary Ridge," *New York Times*, July 15, 1876. Wood and Grant had been at West Point together, with Grant two years ahead; this was one reason why Wood thought Grant sought him out as a sounding board.

18. *OR*, 31(2):96, 132.

19. *OR*, 31(2):34.

20. Hoffman, "First Impressions of Three Days' Fighting," 72–73; McKinney, *Education in Violence*, 293.

21. Wood, "Thrilling War Chapter."

22. Richardson, *Personal History of Ulysses S. Grant*, 365–66.

23. Wilson, *Under the Old Flag*, 2:297–98.

24. Absalom Baird to William F. Smith, Feb. 27, 1888, "Correspondence Relating to Chickamauga and Chattanooga," in *The Mississippi Valley Tennessee, Georgia, Alabama 1861–1864*, vol. 8 of *Papers of the Military Historical Society of Massachusetts* (Boston: 1910), 249–50.

25. Alexander P. Stewart, "The Army of Tennessee: A Sketch," in *The Military Annals of Tennessee: Confederate*, 2 vols., ed. John Berrian Lindsley (1886; repr., Wilmington, NC: Broadfoot, 1995) 1:83; Sam Davis Elliott, "This Grand and Imposing Array of Brave Men: The Capture of Rossville Gap and the Defeat

of the Confederate Left," in *The Chattanooga Campaign*, ed. Steven E. Woodworth and Charles D. Grear (Carbondale: Southern Illinois University Press, 2012), 110.

26. Larry J. Daniel, *Cannoneers in Gray: The Field Artillery of the Army of Tennessee, 1861–1865* (Tuscaloosa: University of Alabama Press, 1989), 111–12.

27. Tower, *A Carolinian Goes to War*, 136; John Hoffmann, *The Confederate Collapse at the Battle of Missionary Ridge: The Reports of James Patton Anderson and His Brigade Commanders* (Dayton, OH: Morningside House, 1985), 70.

28. *OR*, 31(2):257, 459, 508; Baird to Smith, Feb. 27, 1888, "Correspondence Relating to Chickamauga and Chattanooga," 250.

29. *OR*, 31(2):189. In that report Baird did not identify Wilson by name, stating merely that it was an officer on Thomas's staff. But in his postwar letter to Smith, he did name Wilson, who was actually on Grant's staff.

30. Philip H. Sheridan, *Personal Memoirs of P. H. Sheridan, General United States Army, in Two Volumes*, 2 vols. (New York: Charles L. Webster, 1888), 1:308–10.

31. Paul M. Angle, ed., *Three Years in the Army of the Cumberland: The Letters and Diary of Major James A. Connolly* (Bloomington: Indiana University Press, 1959), 150; Kenneth W. Noe, ed., *A Southern Boy in Blue: The Memoir of Marcus Woodcock, 9th Kentucky Infantry (U.S.A.)* (Knoxville: University of Tennessee Press, 1996), 236.

32. Tower, *A Carolinian Goes to War*, 138.

33. Ron Skellie, ed., *Lest We Forget: The Immortal Seventh Mississippi*, vol. 2, *A Regimental History Told by and for the Men of the 7th Mississippi Volunteers, Later the 7th Regiment Mississippi Infantry and Their Comrades in Arms of the Mississippi "High Pressure Brigade" of the "Army of Tennessee"* (Birmingham, AL, 2012), 608–10.

34. Robert L. Kimberly and Ephraim S. Holloway, *The Forty-First Ohio Veteran Volunteer Infantry in the War of the Rebellion, 1861–1865* (Cleveland: W. R. Smellie, 1897), 70; Edwin W. High, *History of the Sixty-Eighth Regiment Indiana Volunteer Infantry, 1862–1865, with a Sketch of E. A. King's Brigade, Reynolds' Division, Thomas' Corps, in the Battle of Chickamauga* (Metamora, IN, 1902), 150.

35. *OR*, 31(2):264; Alexis Cope, *The 15th Ohio Volunteers and Its Campaigns, War of 1861–5* (Columbus, OH, 1916), 381; Joseph R. Reinhardt, ed., *August Willich's Gallant Dutchmen: Civil War Letters from the 32nd Indiana Infantry* (Kent, OH: Kent State University Press, 2006), 162.

36. *OR*, 31(2):509.

37. *OR*, 31(2):190–91.

38. Hoffman, "First Impressions of Three Days' Fighting," 74; Fullerton, "Army of the Cumberland at Chattanooga," 725.

39. Shanks, *Personal Recollections of Distinguished Generals*, 118; Richardson, *Personal History of Ulysses S. Grant*, 367.

40. "The Fight for Chattanooga," *National Tribune*, Nov. 18, 1897, Hoffman, "First Impressions of Three Days' Fighting," 74; William Farrar Smith to Dennis Hart Mahan, Dec. 7, 1863, William F. Smith Papers, Library of Congress, Washington, D.C.

41. William Lee White and Charles Denny Runion, eds., *Great Things Are Expected of Us: The Letters of Colonel C. Irvine Walker, 10th South Carolina Infantry, C.S.A.* (Knoxville: University of Tennessee Press, 2009), 83.

42. William J. K. Beaudot, *The 24th Wisconsin Infantry in the Civil War: The Biography of a Regiment* (Mechanicsburg, PA: Stackpole, 2003), 265–66.

43. *OR*, 31(2):665; Henry W. Reddick, *Seventy-Seven Years in Dixie: The Boys in Gray of 61–65* (Santa Rosa, FL, 1910), 44.

44. Alexander P. Stewart to General Smith, Feb. 15, 1894, "Correspondence Relating to Chickamauga and Chattanooga," 252–53.

45. Sam R. Watkins, *Co. "Aytch" Maury Grays, First Tennessee Regiment; or, A Side Show of the Big Show*, ed. Ruth Hill Fulton McCallister (Franklin, TN: Providence House, 2007), 128–29.

46. Hoffman, "First Impressions of Three Days' Fighting," 75; Angle, *Three Years in the Army of the Cumberland*, 150.

47. *OR*, 31(2):68.

10. "A Most Important Position"

1. *OR*, 31(2):336. Inconsistencies of timing between various commands are common on Civil War battlefields, and Thomas's own headquarters had a long history of assigning later times to events. At the Battle of Chickamauga, his orders and dispatches, as well as the times given in his report, are consistently at least one hour later than most other Federal reports and correspondence.

2. *OR*, 31(2):600; Committee of the Regiment, *Military History and Reminiscences of the Thirteenth Regiment of Illinois Volunteer Infantry in the Civil War of the United States, 1861–1865* (Chicago: Women's Temperance Publishing, 1892), 378.

3. *OR*, 31(2):116.

4. *OR*, 31(2):116.

5. Elliott, "This Grand and Imposing Array," 110; Janet B. Hewett, Noah Andre Trudeau, and Bryce A. Suderow, eds., *Supplement to the Official Records of the Union and Confederate Armies* (Wilmington, NC: Broadfoot, 1994–2004), ser. 1, 6:176 (hereafter cited as *ORS*).

6. *ORS*, 6:171; *OR*, 31(2):601.

7. *ORS*, 6:174.

8. William C. Davis, *Breckinridge: Statesman, Soldier, Symbol* (Baton Rouge: Louisiana State University Press, 1974), 388–89; Elliott, "This Grand and Imposing Array," 114. Holtzclaw commanded the brigade in Brig. Gen. Henry D. Clayton's absence.

9. *OR*, 31(2):147, 601.

10. Elliott, "This Grand and Imposing Array," 115. Cabell Breckinridge was exchanged in the spring of 1864 and rejoined his father in Virginia.

11. Ben Lane, "Captain Posey's Narrative," *Mobile Register and Advertiser*, Dec. 27, 1863.

12. *ORS*, 6:157.

13. Mattie Lou Teague Crow, ed., *The Diary of a Confederate Soldier: John Washington Inzer, 1834–1928* (Huntsville, AL, 1977), 44; *ORS*, 6:157.

14. *OR*, 31(2):401; *ORS*, 6:159.

15. Hess, *A German in the Yankee Fatherland*, 144; *ORS*, 6:159.

16. M. Todd Cathey, ed., *Captain A. T. Fielder's Civil War Diary, Company B, 12th Tennessee Infantry, C.S.A., July, 1861–June, 1865* (Nashville: Tennessee Historical Society, 2012), 286.

17. *PUSG*, 9:447.

18. Grant, *Personal Memoirs*, 2:82.

19. *OR*, 31(2):265. This Bird's Mill Road, leading from Chattanooga eastward over Missionary Ridge, should not be confused with the similarly named road leading northeast from Rossville to Bird's Mill, used by Osterhaus.

20. Hoffman, "Holocaust Holiday," 36.

21. *OR*, 31(2):45–46.

22. *OR*, 31(2):45, 68; *PUSG*, 9:449. In subsequent dispatches, dated 8:00 P.M. on November 25 and 10:00 A.M. on November 26, Dana detailed the results of the fighting, tallying losses, noting captures, and describing the action, especially Thomas's charge.

23. *OR*, 31(2):117.

24. *OR*, 31(2):191; Cozzens, *Shipwreck of Their Hopes*, 339–40.

25. Sheridan, *Personal Memoirs*, 1:316; *OR*, 31(2):134.

26. *OR*, 31(2):117.

27. Sylvanus Cadwallader, *Three Years with Grant* (Lincoln: University of Nebraska Press, 1996), 156–61.

11. "A Very Dangerous Defile"

1. W. H. H. Benefiel, *Souvenir the Seventeenth Indiana Regiment. A History from Its Organization to the End of the War, Giving Description of Battles, etc. Also, List of the Survivors; Their Names, Ages, Company, and P. O. Address; and Interesting Letters from Comrades Who Were Not Present at the Regimental Reunions* (Elwood, IN: Model Printing & Litho, 1913), 70–71; *OR*, 31(2):708–9.

2. *OR*, 31(3):750.

3. *OR*, 31(2):561. The loss of the rolling mill, vital in creating sheet copper needed for the manufacture of bronze cannon as well as rifle and pistol caps, created a supply crisis within the Confederate armaments industry.

4. *OR*, 31(2):491.

5. *OR*, 31(2):196.

6. *OR*, 31(2):118–19.

7. *OR*, 31(2):119, 196.

8. Robert I. Girardi and Nathaniel Cheairs Hughes Jr., eds., *The Memoirs of Brigadier General William Passmore Carlin, U.S.A.* (Lincoln: University of Nebraska Press, 1999), 118; *OR*, 31(2):70, 464. South Chickamauga Creek forks into east and west branches about two miles south of Chickamauga Station at Mission Mills. Peavine Creek is a tributary of East Chickamauga Creek.

9. *OR*, 31(2):46; *PUSG*, 9:453.

10. *OR*, 31(3):760.

11. Buck, *Cleburne and His Command*, 177.

12. Committee, *Thirteenth Regiment of Illinois Volunteer Infantry*, 383.

13. Kevin B. McCray, *A Shouting of Orders: A History of the 99th Ohio Volunteer Infantry Regiment* (Xlibris, 2003), 310; Townsend, *Yankee Warhorse*, 138.

14. *OR*, 31(2):608.

15. Charles H. Kibler, *76th Ohio at Ringgold or Taylor's Ridge, a Little History*, Harrisburg Civil War Roundtable Collection, Army Historical and Education Center, Carlisle, PA.

16. *OR*, 31(2):760.

17. There are two significant terrain features named Tunnel Hill in the Chattanooga Campaign: Tunnel Hill on Missionary Ridge in Tennessee, and Tunnel Hill, Georgia, where the Western & Atlantic Railroad passes through Chetoogeta Mountain.

18. *OR*, 31(2):46–47.

19. *OR*, 31(2):70.

20. *OR*, 31(2):25.

21. Grant, *Personal Memoirs*, 2:89–90, 92. As has been seen, this delay stemmed from Grant, not Thomas, in not ordering Granger to move sooner than November 27.

22. *PUSG*, 9:450.

23. C. Knight Aldrich, ed., *Quest for a Star: The Civil War Letters and Diaries of Colonel Francis T. Sherman of the 88th Illinois* (Knoxville: University of Tennessee Press, 1999), 92; Jeffrey A. Hill, *The 26th Ohio Veteran Volunteer Infantry: The Groundhog Regiment* (Bloomington, IN: Authorhouse, 2010), 349; Donald Allendorf, *Long Road to Liberty: The Odyssey of a German Regiment in the Yankee*

Army, the 15th Missouri Volunteer Infantry (Kent, OH: Kent University Press, 2006), 161.

24. Grant, *Personal Memoirs*, 2:92; Wood and Stanley quoted in Robert C. Conner, *General Gordon Granger: The Savior of Chickamauga and the Man behind Juneteenth* (Philadelphia: Casemate, 2013), 135; Wilson, *Under the Old Flag*, 1:304.

25. Aldrich, *Quest for a Star*, 92; Noe, *Southern Boy in Blue*, 243–44.

26. *PUSG*, 9:474. In fact, Grant had already made up his mind to send Sherman by at least November 28. He informed General Foster of that fact in a dispatch of that date. See *OR*, 31(3):266.

27. *PUSG*, 9:464–65.

28. *PUSG*, 9:466; *OR*, 31(1):462.

29. *OR*, 31(1):460–62.

30. Simpson and Berlin, *Sherman's Civil War*, 577; Sherman, *Memoirs*, 1:367–68.

31. Sherman, *Memoirs*, 1:368; *OR*, 31(1):264–65.

12. The Best-Planned Battle?

1. *OR*, 31(2):88, 99, 684, 783. "Effectives" meant enlisted men, with arms, ready for action. Officers were not counted in that category.

2. *PUSG*, 9:500–501.

3. *PUSG*, 9:502.

4. *OR*, 31(3):817; *PUSG*, 9:501–2. In response to this fear, Dana argued that "the surest means of getting the rebels altogether out of East Tennessee is to be found in the Army of the Potomac" but was told "from that army nothing is to be hoped under its present commander."

5. *PUSG*, 9:491; Lincoln quoted in Simpson, *Ulysses S. Grant*, 243.

6. Michael H. Fitch, *Echoes of the Civil War as I Hear Them* (New York: R. F. Fenno, 1905), 183, 187. Fitch remembered that Grant, Thomas, Johnson, and Baldy Smith were among those accompanying the excursion. As for relics, in his 1863 letter Fitch was prescient. Today, "War Logs" from Chickamauga can be found in museums and former G.A.R. Halls all over the country.

7. Grant, *Personal Memoirs*, 2:101–2.

8. Simpson and Berlin, *Sherman's Civil War*, 576–77. Edwin Stanton arranged to have Meigs's letter published in the November 30 edition of the *New York Tribune*.

9. Sherman, *Memoirs*, 1:403.

10. Sherman, *Memoirs*, 1:404; Richardson, *Personal History of Ulysses S. Grant*, 364; Badeau, *Military History of Ulysses S. Grant*, 1:505.

11. Van Horne, *Life of Major General George H. Thomas*, 186.

12. Sherman, *Memoirs*, 2:465; "Important War Department Order," *Wisconsin State Journal*, Apr. 7, 1864.

13. Conner, *General Gordon Granger*, 150–51.

14. Grant, *Personal Memoirs*, 2:78, 81, 539; "Grant. Correspondence of the New York *Herald*," *Chicago Tribune*, July 27, 1878.

15. Grant, *Personal Memoirs*, 2:78, 81.

16. Smith, "Military Operations around Chattanooga," 245.

17. *OR*, 31(2):324–25.

18. Lloyd Lewis, *Sherman, Fighting Prophet* (New York: Harcourt Brace, 1932), 323; William B. Styple, ed., *Generals in Bronze: Interviewing the Commanders of the Civil War* (Kearny, NJ: Belle Grove, 2005), 44. For Hooker's complete rebuttal, see "Gen. Hooker," *Chicago Daily Tribune*, Aug. 8, 1878.

19. Grant, *Personal Memoirs*, 2:88.

20. Grant, *Personal Memoirs*, 2:85, 87.

BIBLIOGRAPHY

Internet Sources

Bright, David L. "Virginia & Tennessee Tonnage, Eastbound Food," Confederate Railroads Website, http://www.csa-railroads.com/Virginia_and_Tennessee _Tonnage,_Eastbound_Food.htm, accessed on 8/5/2018.

Unpublished Sources

Abraham Lincoln Presidential Library, Springfield, IL
    Allan L. Fahnestock Diary
American Philosophical Society Library, Philadelphia
    Ely S. Parker Papers
Army Heritage and Education Center, Carlisle, PA
    Harrisburg Civil War Round Table Collection
        Charles H. Kibler, *76th Ohio at Ringgold or Taylor's Ridge, a Little History*
Bowdoin College, Hawthorne-Longfellow Library, Brunswick, ME
    Oliver Otis Howard Papers
Chickamauga-Chattanooga National Military Park, Fort Oglethorpe, GA
    40th Illinois Infantry File
    136th New York Infantry File
    Edward F. Hopkins, "Reminiscences of the Late War," 149th New York Infantry File
    30th Ohio Infantry File
    46th Ohio Infantry File
Delaware Historical Society, Wilmington
    James H. Wilson Diary
Huntington Library, San Marino, CA
    Simon B. Buckner Papers
Library of Congress, Washington, D.C.
    William T. Sherman Papers
    William F. Smith Papers
New York Public Library
    Emerson Opdycke, "Suggestions on Chattanooga." Box 131, *Century* Papers

University of California, Los Angeles
 William S. Rosecrans Papers
University of Southern California, Los Angeles
 "Transcript of Joseph J. Reynolds Interview," Hamlin Garland Papers
Western Reserve Historical Society, Cleveland, OH
 Braxton Bragg Papers, William Palmer Collection

Government Documents

Brooke, John R., et al. *Report of a Board of Army Officers upon the Claim of Maj. Gen. William Ferrar Smith, U.S.V., Major, U.S. Army (Retired) That He, and Not General Rosecrans, Originated the Plan for the Relief of Chattanooga in October, 1863*. Washington, D.C.: U.S. Government Printing Office, 1901.

U.S. War Department. *The War of the Rebellion: A Compilation of the Official Records of the Union and Confederate Armies*. 128 vols. Washington, D.C.: U.S. Government Printing Office, 1880–1901.

Articles and Essays

Bearss, Edwin C. "Misfire in Mississippi: McPherson's Canton Expedition." *Civil War History* 8, no. 4 (December 1962): 401–16.

Byers, S. H. M. "Sherman's Attack at the Tunnel." In Johnson and Buel, *Battles and Leaders*, 3:712–13.

Carmody, P. J. "The Battle of Collierville." *Journal of the American Irish Historical Society* 9 (1910): 466–70.

"Chattanooga." *Chicago Evening Journal*, December 5, 1863.

"Correspondence Relating to Chickamauga and Chattanooga." In *The Mississippi Valley Tennessee, Georgia, Alabama 1861–1864*, vol. 8 of *Papers of the Military Historical Society of Massachusetts*, 247–71. Boston: Military Historical Society of Massachusetts, 1910.

Cubbison, Douglas R. "Midnight Engagement: John Geary's White Star Division at Wauhatchie." *Civil War Regiments* 3, no. 2 (1993): 70–104.

Elliott, Sam Davis. "This Grand and Imposing Array of Brave Men: The Capture of Rossville Gap and the Defeat of the Confederate Left." In *The Chattanooga Campaign*, edited by Steven E. Woodworth and Charles D. Grear, 106–31. Carbondale: Southern Illinois University Press, 2012.

"The Fight for Chattanooga." *National Tribune*, November 18, 1897.

Fullerton, Joseph S. "The Army of the Cumberland at Chattanooga." In Johnson and Buel, eds., *Battles and Leaders*, 3:719–26.

"Gen. Hooker." *Chicago Daily Tribune*, August 8, 1878.

Gilmore, James R. "The Relief of Rosecrans." *Burial of General Rosecrans, Arlington National Cemetery, May 17, 1902*. Cincinnati, 1903.

"Grant. Correspondence of the New York *Herald*." *Chicago Tribune*, July 27, 1878.

Grant, Ulysses S. "Chattanooga." In Johnson and Buel, *Battles and Leaders*, 3:679–711.

Hart, Albert G. "The Surgeon and the Hospital in the Civil War." In *Civil and Mexican Wars*, vol. 13 of *Papers of the Military Historical Society of Massachusetts*, 229–85. Boston: Military Historical Society of Massachusetts, 1913.

Hoffmann, John M., ed. "First Impressions of Three Days' Fighting: Quartermaster General Meigs's 'Journal of the Battle of Chattanooga.'" In *Ulysses S. Grant: Essays and Documents*, edited by David L. Wilson and John Y. Simon, 59–76. Carbondale: Southern Illinois University Press, 1981.

Howard, Oliver O. "Grant at Chattanooga." *Personal Recollections of the War of the Rebellion, Addresses Delivered before the New York Commandery of the Loyal Legion of the United States, 1861–1865*. New York: Published by the Commandery, 1891.

Hurd, E. O. "The Battle of Collierville." *Sketches of War History, 1861–1865*. Vol. 5, 243–54. Cincinnati: Robert Clarke, 1903.

"Important War Department Order." *Wisconsin State Journal*, April 7, 1864.

Lane, Ben. "Captain Posey's Narrative." *Mobile Register and Advertiser*, December 27, 1863.

LeDuc, William G. "The Little Steamboat That Opened the 'Cracker Line.'" In Johnson and Buel, *Battles and Leaders*, 3:676–78.

Madden, David. "Unionist Resistance to Confederate Occupation: The Bridge Burners of East Tennessee." *East Tennessee Historical Society Publications* 52–53 (1980–81): 22–40.

Raum, Green B. "With the Western Army: Sherman's March to Chattanooga." *National Tribune*, April 3, 1902.

———. "With the Western Army: Fight on Tunnel Hill." *National Tribune*, May 1, 1902.

"Rosecrans's Removal." *Indianapolis Times*, March 13, 1882.

Simpson, Brooks D. "What Happened on Orchard Knob? Ordering the Attack on Missionary Ridge." In *The Chattanooga Campaign*, edited by Steven E. Woodworth and Charles D. Grear, 84–105. Carbondale: Southern Illinois Press, 2012.

Smith, Tamara A. "A Matter of Trust: Grant and James B. McPherson." In *Grant's Lieutenants: From Cairo to Vicksburg*, edited by Steven E. Woodworth, 151–67. Lawrence: University Press of Kansas, 2001.

Smith, William F. "An Historical Sketch of the Military Operations around Chattanooga, Tennessee, September 22 to November 27, 1863." In *The Mississippi Valley Tennessee, Georgia, Alabama 1861–1864*, vol. 8 of *Papers of the Military Historical Society of Massachusetts*, 149–246. Boston: Military Historical Society of Massachusetts, 1910.

Smith, William Farrar, and Henry M. Cist. "Comments on General Grant's 'Chattanooga.'" In Johnson and Buel, *Battles and Leaders,* 3:714–18.

Smith, William Wrenshall. "Holocaust Holiday: The Journal of a Strange Vacation to the War-torn South and a Visit with U. S. Grant," *Civil War Times Illustrated* 18, no. 6 (October 1979): 28–40.

Stewart, Alexander P. "The Army of Tennessee: A Sketch." In *The Military Annals of Tennessee: Confederate,* edited by John Berrian Lindsley, 1:55–111. 1886. Reprint, Wilmington, NC: Broadfoot, 1995.

Walton J. E. "Mission Ridge." *National Tribune,* November 1, 1888.

Wood, Thomas J. "A Thrilling War Chapter: The Battle of Missionary Ridge." *New York Times,* July 15, 1876.

———. "The Battle of Missionary Ridge." In *Sketches of War History, 1861–1865,* edited by W. H. Chamberlin, 4:22–67. Cincinnati: Robert Clarke, 1896.

Books, Primary Sources

Aldrich, C. Knight, ed. *Quest for a Star: The Civil War Letters and Diaries of Colonel Francis T. Sherman of the 88th Illinois.* Knoxville: University of Tennessee Press, 1999.

Angle, Paul M., ed. *Three Years in the Army of the Cumberland: The Letters and Diary of Major James A. Connolly.* Bloomington: Indiana University Press, 1959.

Aten, Henry J. *History of the Eighty-Fifth Regiment, Illinois Volunteer Infantry.* Hiawatha, KS, 1901.

Bauer, K. Jack, ed. *Soldiering: The Civil War Diary of Rice C. Bull, 123rd New York Volunteer Infantry.* Novato, CA: Presidio, 1977.

Benefiel, W. H. H. *Souvenir the Seventeenth Indiana Regiment. A History from Its Organization to the End of the War, Giving Description of Battles, etc. Also, List of the Survivors; Their Names, Ages, Company, and P. O. Address; and Interesting Letters from Comrades Who Were Not Present at the Regimental Reunions.* Elwood, IN: Model Printing & Litho, 1913.

Brown, Alonzo L. *History of the Fourth Regiment of Minnesota Volunteers during the Great Rebellion, 1861–1865.* St. Paul, MN: Pioneer, 1892.

Buck, Irving A. *Cleburne and His Command.* With a foreword by Bell I. Wiley. Dayton, OH: Press of Morningside Bookshop, 1982.

Cadwallader, Sylvanus. *Three Years with Grant.* Lincoln: University of Nebraska Press, 1996.

Cathey, M. Todd, ed. *Captain A. T. Fielder's Civil War Diary, Company B, 12th Tennessee Infantry, C.S.A., July, 1861–June, 1865.* Nashville: Tennessee Historical Society, 2012.

Chancellor, Christopher, ed. *An Englishman in the American Civil War: The Diaries of Henry Yates Thompson, 1863.* London: Sidgwick & Jackson, 1971.

Collins, Robert M. *Chapters from the Unwritten History of the War between the States; or, The Incidents in the Life of a Confederate Soldier in Camp, on the March, in the Great Battles, and in Prison.* St. Louis: Nixon-Jones Printing, 1893.

Committee of the Regiment. *The Story of the Fifty-Fifth Regiment Illinois Volunteer Infantry in the Civil War, 1861–1865.* Clinton, MA: W. J. Coulter, 1887.

———. *Military History and Reminiscences of the Thirteenth Regiment of Illinois Volunteer Infantry in the Civil War of the United States, 1861–1865.* Chicago: Women's Temperance Publishing, 1892.

Cope, Alexis. *The 15th Ohio Volunteers and Its Campaigns, War of 1861–5.* Columbus, OH, 1916.

Crist, Lynda Lasswell, Kenneth H. Williams, and Peggy L. Dillard, eds. *The Papers of Jefferson Davis.* Rev. ed. Vol. 10, *October 1863–August 1864.* Baton Rouge: Louisiana State University Press, 1999.

Crow, Mattie Lou Teague, ed. *The Diary of a Confederate Soldier: John Washington Inzer, 1834–1928.* Huntsville, AL, 1977.

Dana, Charles A. *Recollections of the Civil War, with the Leaders at Washington and in the Field in the Sixties.* New York: D. Appleton, 1902.

Fitch, Michael H. *Echoes of the Civil War as I Hear Them.* New York: R. F. Fenno, 1905.

Gates, Arnold, ed. *The Rough Side of War: The Civil War Journal of Chelsey A. Mosman, 1st Lieutenant, Company D, 59th Illinois Infantry Regiment.* Garden City, NY: Basin, 1987.

Girardi, Robert I., and Nathaniel Cheairs Hughes Jr., eds. *The Memoirs of Brigadier General William Passmore Carlin, U.S.A.* Lincoln: University of Nebraska Press, 1999.

Grant, Ulysses S. *Personal Memoirs of U. S. Grant.* 2 vols. New York: Charles L. Webster, 1885.

Grant, Ulysses S. *The Personal Memoirs of Ulysses S. Grant: The Complete Annotated Edition.* Edited by John F. Marszalek, David S. Nolen, and Louie P. Gallo. Cambridge, MA: Harvard University Press, 2017.

Hay, John. *Lincoln and the Civil War: In the Diaries and Letters of John Hay.* Selected and with an introduction by Tyler Dennett. 1939. Reprint, Westport, CT: Negro Universities Press, 1972.

———. *Inside Lincoln's White House: The Complete Civil War Diary of John Hay.* Edited by Martin Burlingame and John R. Turner Ettlinger. Carbondale: Southern Illinois University Press, 1997.

Helm, Katherine. *The True Story of Mary, Wife of Lincoln, Containing the Recollections of Mary Lincoln's Sister Emilie (Mrs. Ben Hardin Helm), Extracts from Her War-Time Diary Numerous Letters and other Documents Now First Published.* New York: Harper & Brothers, 1928.

Hess, Earl J., ed. *A German in the Yankee Fatherland: The Civil War Letters of Henry A. Kircher.* Kent, OH: Kent State University Press, 1983.

Hewett, Janet B., Noah Andre Trudeau, and Bryce A. Suderow, eds. *Supplement to the Official Records of the Union and Confederate Armies.* 100 vols. Wilmington, NC: Broadfoot, 1994–2004.

High, Edwin W. *History of the Sixty-Eighth Regiment Indiana Volunteer Infantry, 1862–1865, with a Sketch of E. A. King's Brigade, Reynolds' Division, Thomas' Corps, in the Battle of Chickamauga.* Metamora, IN, 1902.

Hoffmann, John. *The Confederate Collapse at the Battle of Missionary Ridge: The Reports of James Patton Anderson and his Brigade Commanders.* Dayton, OH: Morningside House, 1985.

Howard, Oliver O. *Autobiography of Oliver Otis Howard, Major General United States Army.* 2 vols. New York: Baker & Taylor, 1907.

Hughes, Nathaniel Cheairs, Jr., ed. *Liddell's Record: St. John Richardson Liddell. Brigadier General, CSA. Staff Officer and Brigade Commander, Army of Tennessee.* Baton Rouge: Louisiana State University Press, 1985.

Johnson, Robert Underwood, and Clarence Clough Buel, eds. *Battles and Leaders of the Civil War.* 4 vols. Reprint, New York: Thomas Yoseloff, 1956.

Jordan, William C. *Some Events and Incidents during the Civil War.* Montgomery, AL: Paragon, 1909.

Kimberly, Robert L., and Ephraim S. Holloway. *The Forty-First Ohio Veteran Volunteer Infantry in the War of the Rebellion, 1861–1865.* Cleveland: W. R. Smellie, 1897.

LeDuc, William G. *Recollections of a Civil War Quartermaster: The Autobiography of William G. LeDuc.* St. Paul, MN: North Central, 1963.

McMurry, Richard M., ed. *An Uncompromising Secessionist: The Civil War of George Knox Miller, Eighth (Wade's) Confederate Cavalry.* Tuscaloosa: University of Alabama Press, 2007.

Noe, Kenneth W., ed. *A Southern Boy in Blue: The Memoir of Marcus Woodcock, 9th Kentucky Infantry (U.S.A.).* Knoxville: University of Tennessee Press, 1996.

Orendorff, H. H., et al. *Reminiscences of the Civil War from Diaries of Members of the 103rd Illinois Volunteer Infantry, 1904.* Chicago: Press of J. F. Leaming, 1904.

Osborn, Hartwell. *Trials and Triumphs: The Record of the Fifty-Fifth Ohio Volunteer Infantry.* Chicago: A. C. McClurg, 1904.

Partridge, Charles A. *History of the Ninety-Sixth Regiment Illinois Volunteer Infantry.* Chicago: Brown, Pettibone, 1887.

Porter, Horace. *Campaigning with Grant.* New York: Century, 1897.

Reddick, Henry W. *Seventy-Seven Years in Dixie: The Boys in Gray of 61–65.* Santa Rosa, FL, 1910.

Reinhardt, Joseph R., ed. *August Willich's Gallant Dutchmen: Civil War Letters from the 32nd Indiana Infantry.* Kent, OH: Kent State University Press, 2006.

Saunier, Joseph A., ed. *A History of the Forty-Seventh Regiment Ohio Veteran Volunteer Infantry, Second Brigade, Second Division, Fifteenth Army Corps, Army of the Tennessee.* Hillsboro, OH: Lyle Printing, 1903.

Schurz, Carl. *The Reminiscences of Carl Schurz.* 3 vols. New York: McClure, 1908.

Scott, Robert Garth, ed. *Forgotten Valor: The Memoirs, Journals, & Civil War Letters of Orlando B. Willcox.* Kent, OH: Kent State University Press, 1999.

Shanks, William F. G. *Personal Recollections of Distinguished Generals.* New York: Harper & Brothers, 1866.

Sheridan, Philip H. *Personal Memoirs of P. H. Sheridan, General United States Army, in Two Volumes.* 2 vols. New York: Charles L. Webster, 1888.

Sherlock, Eli J. *Memorabilia of the Marches and Battles in which the One Hundredth Regiment of Indiana Infantry Volunteers Took an Active Part, War of the Rebellion, 1861–1865.* Kansas City, MO: Gerald-Woody Printing, 1896.

Sherman, William T. *Memoirs of General William T. Sherman.* 2 vols. New York: D. Appleton, 1875.

Simon, John Y., and John F. Marszalek, eds. *The Papers of Ulysses S. Grant.* 32 vols. Carbondale: Southern Illinois University Press, 1967–2012.

Simpson, Brooks D., and Jean V. Berlin, eds. *Sherman's Civil War: Selected Correspondence of William T. Sherman, 1860–1865.* Chapel Hill: University of North Carolina Press, 1999.

Smith, William F. *Autobiography of Maj. Gen. William F. Smith, 1861–1864.* Edited by Herbert M. Schiller. Dayton, OH: Morningside House, 1990.

Sorrel, G. Moxley. *At the Right Hand of Longstreet: Recollections of a Confederate Staff Officer.* Lincoln: University of Nebraska Press, 1999.

Sprott, Samuel H. *Cush: A Civil War Memoir.* Edited by Louis R. Smith Jr. and Andrew Quist. Livingston, AL: Livingston Press at the University of West Alabama, 1999.

Styple, William B., ed. *Generals in Bronze: Interviewing the Commanders of the Civil War.* Kearny, NJ: Belle Grove, 2005.

Tower, R. Lockwood, ed. *A Carolinian Goes to War: The Civil War Narrative of Arthur Middleton Manigault, Brigadier General, C.S.A.* Columbia: University of South Carolina Press, 1983.

Tuttle, Russell M.. *The Civil War Journal of Lt. Russell M. Tuttle, New York Volunteer Infantry.* Edited by George H. Tappan. Jefferson, NC: McFarland, 2006.

Underwood, Adin B. *The Three Years' Service of the Thirty-Third Mass. Infantry Regiment, 1862–1865. And the Campaigns and Battles of Chancellorsville, Beverly's Ford, Gettysburg, Wauhatchie, Chattanooga, Atlanta, the March to the Sea and through the Carolinas in Which It Took Part.* Boston: A. Williams, 1881.

Villard, Henry. *Memoirs of Henry Villard, Journalist and Financier, 1835–1900.* 2 vols. Boston: Houghton, Mifflin, 1904.

Watkins, Sam R. *Co. "Aytch" Maury Grays, First Tennessee Regiment; or, A Side Show of the Big Show.* Edited by Ruth Hill Fulton McCallister. Franklin, TN: Providence House, 2007.

Welles, Gideon. *Diary of Gideon Welles, Secretary of the Navy under Lincoln and Johnson.* 2 vols. Boston: Houghton Mifflin, 1909.

White, William Lee, and Charles Denny Runion, eds. *Great Things Are Expected of Us: The Letters of Colonel C. Irvine Walker, 10th South Carolina Infantry, C.S.A.* Knoxville: University of Tennessee Press, 2009.

Wills, Charles W. *Army Life of an Illinois Soldier, Including a Day-by-Day Record of Sherman's March to the Sea: Letters and Diary of Charles W. Wills.* Carbondale: Southern Illinois University Press, 1996.

Wilson, James H. *Under the Old Flag: Recollections of Military Operations in the War for the Union, the Spanish War, the Boxer Rebellion, etc.* 2 vols. New York: D. Appleton, 1912.

Wright, T. J. *History of the Eighth Regiment Kentucky Vol. Inf. during Its Three Years Campaigns, embracing Organization, Marches, Skirmishes and Battles of the Command, with Much of the History of the Old Reliable Third Brigade, Commanded by Hon. Stanley Matthews, and Containing Many Interesting and Amusing Incidents of Army Life.* St. Joseph, MO: St. Joseph Steam Printing, 1880.

Books, Secondary Sources

Allendorf, Donald. *Long Road to Liberty: The Odyssey of a German Regiment in the Yankee Army, the 15th Missouri Volunteer Infantry.* Kent, OH: Kent State University Press, 2006.

Badeau, Adam. *Military History of Ulysses S. Grant, from April, 1861, to April, 1865.* 2 vols. New York: D. Appleton, 1885.

Bates, David Homer. *Lincoln in the Telegraph Office.* New York: Century, 1907.

Beaudot, William J. K. *The 24th Wisconsin Infantry in the Civil War: The Biography of a Regiment.* Mechanicsburg, PA: Stackpole, 2003.

Black, Robert C., III. *The Railroads of the Confederacy.* Chapel Hill: University of North Carolina Press, 1952.

Boedecker, Roger. *The Civil War Service of the 127th Illinois Volunteer Infantry.* N.p., 2007.

Catton, Bruce. *Grant Takes Command.* Boston: Little, Brown, 1968.

Chernow, Ron. *Grant.* New York: Penguin, 2017.

Coddington, Edwin B. *The Gettysburg Campaign: A Study in Command.* 1968. Reprint, in 2 vols. Norwalk, CT: Easton, 1997.

Connelly, Thomas L. *Autumn of Glory: The Army of Tennessee, 1862–1865.* Baton Rouge: Louisiana State University Press, 1971.

Conner, Robert C. *General Gordon Granger: The Savior of Chickamauga and the Man behind Juneteenth.* Philadelphia: Casemate, 2013.

Cozzens, Peter. *The Shipwreck of Their Hopes: The Battles for Chattanooga.* Urbana: University of Illinois Press, 1994.

Daniel, Larry J. *Cannoneers in Gray: The Field Artillery of the Army of Tennessee, 1861–1865.* Tuscaloosa: University of Alabama Press, 1989.

Davis, William C. *Breckinridge: Statesman, Soldier, Symbol.* Baton Rouge: Louisiana State University Press, 1974.

———. *The Orphan Brigade: The Kentucky Confederates Who Couldn't Go Home.* Garden City, NY: Doubleday, 1980.

Ecelbarger, Gary. *Black Jack Logan: An Extraordinary Life in Peace and War.* Guilford, CT: Lyons, 2005.

Garland, Hamlin. *Ulysses S. Grant, His Life and Character.* New York: Doubleday and McClure, 1898.

Goodwin, Doris Kerns. *Team of Rivals: The Political Genius of Abraham Lincoln.* New York: Simon and Schuster, 2005.

Hebert, Walter H. *Fighting Joe Hooker.* Indianapolis: Bobbs-Merrill, 1944.

Hess, Earl J. *The Knoxville Campaign: Burnside and Longstreet in East Tennessee.* Knoxville: University of Tennessee Press, 2012.

Hill, Jeffrey A. *The 26th Ohio Veteran Volunteer Infantry: The Groundhog Regiment.* Bloomington, IN: Authorhouse, 2010.

Hughes, Nathaniel Cheairs, Jr., and Gordon D. Whitney. *Jefferson Davis in Blue: The Life of Sherman's Relentless Warrior.* Baton Rouge: Louisiana State University Press, 2002.

Laine, J. Gary, and Morris M. Penny. *Law's Alabama Brigade in the War between the Union and the Confederacy.* Shippensburg, PA: White Mane, 1996.

Lamers, William M. *The Edge of Glory: A Biography of General William S. Rosecrans, U.S.A.* Baton Rouge: Louisiana State University Press, 1999.

Lewis, Lloyd. *Sherman, Fighting Prophet.* New York: Harcourt Brace, 1932.

Livingood, James W. *The Chattanooga Country: Gateway to History. The Nashville to Atlanta Rail Corridor of the 1860s.* Chattanooga, TN: Chattanooga Area Historical Association, 1995.

Lundberg, John R. *Granbury's Texas Brigade: Diehard Western Confederates.* Baton Rouge: Louisiana State University Press, 2012.

Marszalek, John F. *Sherman: A Soldier's Passion for Order.* New York: Free Press, 1993.

Marvel, William. *Burnside.* Chapel Hill: University of North Carolina Press, 1991.

McCray, Kevin B. *A Shouting of Orders: A History of the 99th Ohio Volunteer Infantry Regiment.* Xlibris, 2003.

McDonough, James Lee. *William Tecumseh Sherman: In the Service of My Country, a Life.* New York: W. W. Norton, 2016.

McKinney, Francis F. *Education in Violence: The Life of George H. Thomas and the History of the Army of the Cumberland.* Detroit: Wayne State University Press, 1961.

McMurtry, R. Gerald. *Confederate General Ben Hardin Helm: Kentucky Brother-in-Law of Abraham Lincoln.* Fort Wayne, IN: Lincoln National Life Foundation, 1959.

Melton, Brian C. *Sherman's Forgotten General: Henry W. Slocum.* Columbia: University of Missouri Press, 2007.

Mendoza, Alexander. *Confederate Struggle for Command: General James Longstreet and the First Corps at Chattanooga.* College Station: Texas A&M University Press, 2008.

Nicely, Mary. *Chattanooga Walking Tour & Historic Guide.* Chattanooga, 2002.

Nicolay, John G., and John Hay. *Abraham Lincoln: A History.* 10 vols. New York: Century, 1904.

Piatt, Donn, and Henry V. Boynton. *George H. Thomas: A Critical Biography.* Cincinnati: Robert Clarke, 1893.

Pickenpaugh, Roger. *Rescue by Rail: Troop Transfer and the Civil War in the West, 1863.* Lincoln: University of Nebraska Press, 1998.

Powell, David A. *Battle above the Clouds: Lifting the Siege of Chattanooga and the Battle of Lookout Mountain, October 16–November 24, 1863.* El Dorado Hills, CA: Savas Beatie, 2017.

Reyburn, Philip J. *Clear the Track: A History of the Eighty-Ninth Illinois Volunteer Infantry, the Railroad Regiment.* Bloomington, IN: Authorhouse, 2012.

Richardson, Albert D. *A Personal History of Ulysses S. Grant.* Hartford, CT: American Publishing, 1868.

Rose, Joseph A. *Grant under Fire: An Exposé of Generalship and Character in the American Civil War.* New York: Alderhanna, 2015.

Simpson, Brooks D. *Ulysses S. Grant: Triumph over Adversity, 1822–1865.* New York: Houghton Mifflin, 2000.

Skellie, Ron, ed. *Lest We Forget: The Immortal Seventh Mississippi.* Vol. 2: *A Regimental History Told by and for the Men of the 7th Mississippi Volunteers, Later the 7th Regiment Mississippi Infantry, and Their Comrades in Arms of the Mississippi "High Pressure Brigade" of the "Army of Tennessee."* Birmingham, AL, 2012.

Summers, Alexander. *Gone to Glory at Farmington: A Profile of Col. James Monroe of Mattoon, Hero of Two Regiments in the Civil War.* Mattoon, IL: Mattoon Historical Society, 1963.

Swan, James B. *Chicago's Irish Legion: The 90th Illinois Volunteers in the Civil War.* Carbondale: Southern Illinois University Press, 2009.

Sword, Wiley. *Mountains Touched with Fire: Chattanooga Besieged, 1863.* New York: St. Martin's, 1995.

Townsend, Mary Bobbitt. *Yankee Warhorse: A Biography of Major General Peter Osterhaus.* Colombia: University of Missouri Press, 2010.

Van Horne, Thomas B. *The Life of Major General George H. Thomas.* New York: Charles Scribner's Sons, 1882.

Varney, Frank P. *General Grant and the Rewriting of History: How the Destruction of General William S. Rosecrans Influenced Our Understanding of the Civil War.* El Dorado Hills, CA: Savas-Beatie, 2013.

Wills, Brian Steel. *George Henry Thomas: As True as Steel.* Lawrence: University Press of Kansas, 2012.

INDEX

Page numbers in italics indicate illustrations.

David A. Powell is the author of several books, including *The Maps of Chickamauga* (2009) and *The Chickamauga Campaign* trilogy (2014–16). His most recent works are *Tullahoma: The Forgotten Campaign That Changed the Course of the Civil War, June 23–July 4, 1863* (2020), coauthored with Eric W. Wittenberg; *Union Command Failure in the Shenandoah* (2019); and *All Hell Can't Stop Them: The Battles for Chattanooga—Missionary Ridge and Ringgold* (2018). He is vice president of Airsped, Inc., a specialized delivery firm.

THE WORLD OF  ULYSSES S. GRANT

Edited by John F. Marszalek & Timothy B. Smith

After the assassination of Abraham Lincoln, Ulysses S. Grant became the most popular American alive. He symbolized the Federal victory, the destruction of slavery, and the preservation of the Union. Grant remained a popular topic among historians who have written about those years, but over time scholars and the public removed Grant from his place in the pantheon of leading Americans. As the decades passed and attitudes toward the Civil War and war itself changed, the public's perception of Grant devolved: no longer a national idol, Grant was instead written off as a heartless general and corrupt president. In the early twenty-first century, however, Grant's place in history is being reinterpreted. Now he is increasingly seen as a success on the battlefield, a leading proponent of African American civil rights, and the first of the modern American presidents.

To further an understanding of Ulysses S. Grant through a close analysis of his life and work, this innovative book series provides a thorough examination of particular events and periods of Grant's life in order to present important insights into his generalship, presidency, influence, and reputation. Books in the series explore Grant's character as well as his role in American history. By delving into the deeper detail and context of what Grant did and saw, this series aims to break new ground and provide the historical profession and the general reading public with accurate, readable perspectives showing Grant's significant contributions to the world he lived in and to the years that followed.